EUROPEAN SECURITY, NUCLEAR WEAPONS AND PUBLIC CONFIDENCE

Both World Wars began as European wars. Today a global conflict seems more likely to result from events in the Middle East, Asia or Africa. In these circumstances the European nations' determination to avoid war is critical. This book examines European security and co-operation following the Helsinki and Belgrade conferences. Writers from Finland, the USSR, the USA, Canada, Britain, the two Germanies, Poland, Bulgaria and Scandinavia discuss the prospects. Scholarly analysis is set alongside political rhetoric. New weapons technologies and the problems of the Arctic and the Baltic areas receive special attention.

Most of the papers printed were originally given at symposia held at Helsinki, Finland and Zakopane in Poland under the auspices of the Pugwash Conferences on Science and World Affairs.

William Gutteridge, the editor, is Professor of International Studies and Head of the Political and Economics Studies Group, University of Aston in Birmingham. He was Director of Complementary Studies, also at the University of Aston. He has been Senior Lecturer in Commonwealth Government and History, Royal Military Academy, Sandhurst, and Head of the Department of Languages and Modern Studies, Lanchester Polytechnic, Coventry. He is Secretary of the British Pugwash Group, a member of the International Council of Pugwash Conferences for Scientists in World Affairs. He is assisted as editor by Marian Dobrosielski, Polish Vice Foreign Minister and Professor of International Relations at Warsaw University, and Jorma Miettinen, Professor of Radio Chemistry at the University of Helsinki, Finland.

Also by William Gutteridge

MILITARY REGIMES IN AFRICA

THE MILITARY IN AFRICAN POLITICS

MILITARY INSTITUTIONS AND POWER IN THE NEW STATES

ARMED FORCES IN NEW STATES

EUROPEAN SECURITY, NUCLEAR WEAPONS AND PUBLIC CONFIDENCE

Edited by
William Gutteridge

Assisted by
Marian Dobrosielski and Jorma Miettinen

St. Martin's Press   New York

ISBN 0–312–27085–2

Library of Congress Cataloging in Publication Data

Main entry under title:

European security, nuclear weapons, and public
    confidence.

   "Papers given at international Pugwash Symposia
in Zakopane, Poland (1978); Helsinki, Finland
(1979), and a Finnish Pugwash group meeting (1977).
   1. Europe – Defenses – Congresses.   2. Security,
International – Congresses.   I. Gutteridge, William
Frank, 1919–   .   II. Dobrosielski, Marian.
III. Miettinen, Jorma K.
D1053.E895   1981   355′.03304   81–1296
ISBN 0–312–27085–2   AACR2

Contents

Preface

The editing of a book of this character presents special problems of time and space as well as language. For one thing the papers were written at different times, over three years, for meetings at different places in Europe. The three editors, moreover, were unable to meet in the final critical stages, in the period January to April 1980, for the preparation of the publication. I hope my colleagues, Professor M. Dobrosielski and Professor J. K. Miettinen, are satisfied with what they now find in print. Without them the symposia from which the book derived would never have taken place in the first instance. Effectively their role as editors, though they did not know it at the time, began when they suggested contributors and subsequently guided the meetings and discussions. They played a large part both in preparing the original background papers and in writing the reports on the proceedings. The Pugwash conferences owe them a great debt as I know personally from having participated in the two official Pugwash symposia at Zakopane in Poland in April 1978 and at Helsinki, Finland, in April 1979 and assisted in the preparation of the reports on those occasions.

None of this effort would, however, have come to fruition had it not been for the enthusiasm and professional care of my secretary, Rhoda Finch, who not only retyped much of the manuscript but whose watchfulness has certainly greatly reduced the number of errors.

June 1980 WILLIAM GUTTERIDGE
The University of Aston in Birmingham
Editor on behalf of the Pugwash Council

Notes on the Contributors

NANSEN BEHAR is Head of the Economic Department of the Institute for Contemporary Social Theories at the Bulgarian Academy of Sciences and author of *Military-Industrial Complex*.

R. BOGDANOV is Deputy Director of the Soviet Institute for the Study of the United States and Canada and the author of books and articles on USA–USSR relationships.

RUDOLF BOTZIAN works with the government-sponsored Institute for International Politics and Security in the Federal German Republic.

HANS GUNTER BRAUCH is a Research Associate at the Institute for Political Science at Heidelberg University and Teaching Associate at the Institute for Political Science of Tübingen University.

DAVID CARLTON is Senior Lecturer in Diplomatic History at the Polytechnic of North London. He is author of *MacDonald versus Henderson: the Foreign Policy of the Second Labour Government* and *Anthony Eden: A Biography*.

MARIAN DOBROSIELSKI is Professor of International Relations at the University of Warsaw and has been Director of the Polish Institute of International Affairs since 1971. He was Polish Ambassador to London from 1969 to 1971. He is Vice-Foreign Minister at the Polish Ministry of Foreign Affairs and led his country's delegation at the Belgrade Conference.

BERNARD T. FELD is Professor of Physics and Head of the Division of Nuclear and High Energy Physics at the Massachusetts Institute of Technology and a member of the International Pugwash Council and has been Editor-in-Chief of the *Bulletin of the Atomic Scientists* since 1975.

WILLIAM GUTTERIDGE is Professor of International Studies and Head of the Political and Economics Studies Group at the University of Aston in Birmingham. He is also Secretary of the British Pugwash Group, a member of the International Pugwash Council and author of four books on the role of the military.

IVAR R. HESSLAND has been Professor in General and Historical Geology at Stockholm University and is an authority on sedimentology, paleontology and paleoenvironment, and economic and marine geology.

C. G. JACOBSEN holds the Visiting Chair of Strategic Studies at Acadia University, Nova Scotia, Canada, and is Adjunct Professor of the Institute of Soviet and East European Studies at Carleton University, Ottawa.

PAULI O. JÄRVENPÄÄ is a researcher at the Finnish Institute of Military Science and Research Associate at the International Institute for Strategic Studies, London.

MARTIN M. KAPLAN is Director-General of the Pugwash Conferences on Science and World Affairs and was a staff member of the World Health Organization, 1949–1976, holding a number of senior posts including Director, Research, Promotion and Development.

ANDRZEJ KARKOSZKA has been, since 1968, a Research Fellow in the Polish Institute of International Affairs and is currently Research Fellow at the Stockholm International Peace Research Institute (SIPRI).

JORMA K. MIETTINEN has been, since 1964, Professor and Head of the Department of Radiochemistry at the University of Helsinki, Finland. He is a member of the Pugwash Council and Chairman of the Finnish Pugwash Group.

WILLY ØSTRENG is Director of the Fridtjof Nansen Foundation and Lecturer in International Politics at the University of Oslo.

KALEVI RUHALA is Research Fellow at the Institute of Military Science, Helsinki, and a member of the Finnish Disarmament Board and of the Scientific Council of the Finnish Institute of International Relations.

MAX SCHMIDT is a member of the German Democratic Republic National Committees for Economics and Political Sciences and Director of the Institute of International Politics and Economics of the GDR.

JØRGEN TAAGHOLT has been, since 1967, the Danish Scientific Liaison Officer for Greenland, responsible for co-ordinating Danish scientific activities and those of other countries in Greenland.

Introduction

The papers in this collection derive from three related sources. The first of these in time was a meeting held in Helsinki in 1977 under the auspices of the Finnish Pugwash Group to discuss the regional problems of the Baltic and the Arctic. This was an important initiative and led not only to a privately circulated volume of proceedings but also to various publications in journals. Then in April 1978 the Polish Pugwash Group organised an international Pugwash symposium on European security and co-operation at Zakopane. This was intended to examine the evolution of the Helsinki agreement and its implementation in the period after the review conference at Belgrade. The senior Polish participant at this meeting was Professor Marian Dobrosielski, former Ambassador in London, and more recently Vice-Foreign Minister of Poland. He was also, significantly, the leader of his country's delegation at the Belgrade conference and is the author of Chapter 1 of this volume.

Following up the long-standing interest of the Pugwash Conferences in European security problems, the Finnish group sponsored another international symposium at Helsinki in April 1979. Their foreign minister, Paavo Vayrynen, opened the meeting, which considered the impact of current political developments and arms control efforts on European security. On this occasion, for the first time at such an event, much of the discussion centred on the notion of the indivisibility of *détente* and the repercussions of events outside Europe and the competition for raw materials on relationships between the West and the socialist countries within Europe. Professor Jorma K. Miettinen organised and chaired this meeting as well as contributing much of the essential background paper which is Chapter 2.

The papers now published represent between one-third and one-half of the total read and discussed on the three occasions. In one or two cases, as with that by Hans Gunter Brauch and those by Jorma Miettinen, there has obviously been substantial updating up to the end of January 1980. The revised versions which they have contributed are vital for an appreciation of developments in Europe relating to so-called military *détente*. Mostly, however, contributions are published as they stood at the time of the symposia with minor amendments and some editorial rewriting primarily to deal with language problems.

As the editor directly responsible, I have had, because of the variety of linguistic sources, to make a large number of decisions relating to the English usage. Where the intention of the author has been obvious I have used an often radical editorial discretion to bring the expressions in line with contemporary idiom and usage. In many cases, however, it seemed better to leave the text submitted on the grounds that quite often the choice of words and phrases even in a foreign language has an inimitable quality and deletion or amendment might distort the true meaning. Such decisions have, however, also, and more significantly, been influenced by the varied styles of contribution selected.

At symposia in which a wide range of ideological preconceptions are represented, inevitably the papers contributed are at a number of different levels. Some may be strictly academic and objective, while others, probably the majority from all quarters, contain an element of rhetoric. Rereading the papers which I had heard discussed, in particular, I was convinced that some of even the more blatant statements were vital to such a collection. More than the objective pieces they catch the atmosphere of the time. The passions aroused by the neuron bomb, for example, during 1977–78 deserve recording. This is particularly important in a volume which is concerned with public confidence, which in any case is more a matter of perceptions than objective truth. The inclusion of a variety of papers in this way may not only serve this purpose but implicitly reveal some truths about national standpoints and attitudes even as reflected in scholarly or scientific works.

Finally, and directly in line with what has been said above, there has been an attempt to achieve balance not just by weighing the geographical sources of contributions but more by taking into account the spectrum of viewpoints. There were unfortunately no Soviet participants at the symposium on the Arctic but this does not necessarily mean that their likely perspectives were neglected. All this may be perceived in some quarters as justifying a kind of editorial *carte blanche* to include whatever was arbitrarily preferred. In some ways the exercise has been much more like painting a picture than creating a logical and definitive structure. To have accepted exclusively academic criteria, would have been to preclude the kite-flying and the testing of propositions and means of reducing dangerous tensions which are essential if unofficial, subdiplomatic organisations like Pugwash are even to pretend to make a contribution to the improvement of international relationships.

W. G.

Part One
Introduction

1 Europe after Belgrade— Problems and Prospects

MARIAN DOBROSIELSKI

1. What role did the Belgrade Meeting play in the process of *détente*? What were its results? Did it affect the creation of a new situation in Europe? If so, then in which way?

While searching for answers to these and other questions concerning the future development of East–West relations, one should remember that the basic problems of security in Europe after Belgrade do not differ much from those which were to be solved before the Belgrade Meeting of representatives of the participating states of the Conference on Security and Co-operation in Europe (CSCE).

Most certainly, 'Belgrade 77' was not the only and the most important but was still one of the substantial elements of a complex process of *détente* initiated by the CSCE. It served its basic purposes: in Belgrade representatives of thirty-five countries reaffirmed the resolve of their governments to bring into effect the Final Act of Helsinki, and agreed some concrete steps in order to assure a continuous process of the CSCE on a multilateral level.

2. Many scientists, politicians and publicists usually connect formation of *a new co-relation of forces* with various congresses, conferences and summit meetings. This attitude is as common as it is little justified. Not to minimise the significance of such conferences and international meetings, it is true to state that they do not form a new reality, but merely reflect it. This was the case of the Vienna Congress (1815), the Paris Peace Conference (1919), the Conference at Yalta and Potsdam (1945), and the Conference on Security and Co-operation in Europe in Helsinki (1975).

Thus the evaluation of the Belgrade Meeting and its results also falls within this category. It was *a reflection of the current state of relations* between the East and the West, particularly between the United States and the Soviet Union. It was not 'Belgrade 77' that determined problems

3

and prospects of the development of the situation in Europe; it was a set of political, ideological, social, economic, diplomatic and military factors that had a vital effect on the shape of the Belgrade Meeting and its results.

3. In the West, various political circles manifest their *disappointment* with the results of the Belgrade Meeting. Though dramatisation of the situation is usually avoided, one can find in the newspapers opinions suggesting that the Meeting was an expression of a specific 'fatigue' of *détente*, or even regress of the very process of *détente*.

Disappointment is a function of expectation. It is obvious that hopes and expectations for the results of the Belgrade Meeting were undue, much exaggerated, and often only loosely related to the mandate defined in the Final Act of CSCE. This was partly a result of the tendency of the new American administration and some of the allies of the United States to use 'Belgrade 77' in order to give the process of *détente* a meaning differing from the aims and presumptions agreed in Helsinki.

The Mandate of the Belgrade Meeting, according to the Final Act of Helsinki, was limited to a thorough exchange of views on the implementation of the provisions of the Final Act as well as on the deepening of their mutual relations, the improvement of security and the development of co-operation, on the development of the process of *détente* in the future, and on terms of further meetings of Belgrade-type — all within the multilateral process initiated by the CSCE. These basic tasks were achieved in Belgrade: there was 'a thorough exchange of views', and the date of the next meeting in Madrid in 1980 was also appointed. I have no doubt that there could have been agreements on many many more points, but for an atmosphere of pressure and ideological confrontation as well as attempts to utilise the Meeting for goals differing from the spirit and the letter of CSCE provisions, that partially prevailed during the meeting. 'Belgrade 77' did not aim at the creation of a specific, shortened and selective version of the Final Act. The Belgrade Meeting could not change, complement or substitute the decisions of the CSCE.

4. *The standing of Helsinki* was basically incomparable with *that of Belgrade*. All provisions accepted in Helsinki constituted a far-reaching programme of development of the relations among all countries of Europe and North America — independently of their social and political systems.

Belgrade resolutions were of executive character. Their political significance depended on the fact that in spite of all the differences, obstacles and difficulties, all the countries expressed their common will to continue the multilateral process of strengthening security and co-operation in Europe. The participants at the Belgrade Meeting confirmed their governments' decision to implement fully all the provisions of the Final Act unilaterally, bilaterally and multilaterally. It was recognised that the exchange of views constitutes in itself a valuable contribution towards the achievement of the aims set by the CSCE.

5. 'Belgrade 77' was *an important lesson of political realism*. Its experiences undeniably indicate that any attempts to legalise interference into other countries' internal affairs, or any tendency to obtain unilateral advantages or reversion to force policy are doomed. It is worth remembering that in Belgrade the initial agreed proposals were much more far-reaching than those eventually included in the Concluding Document of the Meeting. The former concerned all spheres of security and co-operation regulated in the Final Act. Their acceptance would have meant both the fixation of the ten principles which should govern countries in their mutual relations, assent to the necessity of military *détente* and the strengthening of the observance of recommendations regarding economic, cultural and educational co-operation as well as information and contacts. NATO countries, however, made it impossible to include these provisions in the Concluding Document, making their incorporation dependent on the acceptance of some postulates which would have meant either a revision of the Final Act of CSCE or sanctioning of some countries' right to interfere in other countries' internal affairs.

Summing up, the Belgrade Meeting results, despite a limited range of conclusions, prove that all participants treat the problem of peace, *détente* and co-operation as of common and primary value. The main problem of contemporary Europe is still to make the process of *détente* dynamic, common and permanent, as well as to develop it. The best way to realise this aim is to utterly abide by all the principles and bring into effect all the provisions of the Final Act of the CSCE.

6. The analysis of the current situation in Europe indicates that *the main problem* and the gravest obstacle to imparting dynamism to the process of *détente* is the not only continuing but also increasing *arms race*. The plans to produce and equip the NATO army stationed in Western Europe with neutron bombs are particularly dangerous. To realise them would mean to initiate a new stage of the arms race, complicating and impeding the present disarmament negotiations; this would considerably contribute to military and political imbalance and destabilisation in Europe, and consequently in East–West relations as a whole. The neutron weapon is the epitome of the attitude of those people who

consider material goods as more important than the spiritual values. The neutron bomb stands for a philosophy regarding the right to have, much higher than the right to live.

In the light of these facts, the project of a convention on nuclear weapons prohibition presented to the UN Disarmament Committee in Geneva on 9 March 1978, is particularly worth mentioning. This proposal presented by socialist countries claimed not only the tendency to preserve the existing balance, to stop the arms race and eliminate the threat of a nuclear war. Poland and other socialist countries are strongly against nuclear weapons also because of a different scale of values, where 'to be' is prior to 'to possess'.

The programme of military *détente* contained in the Bucharest Declaration (October 1976), continues to be as timely as ever. This mainly concerns two significant suggestions, i.e. a project of a treaty providing that all countries in Europe and North America would decide not to use nuclear weapons against each other as first, and an agreement on non-expansion of the military and political groupings presently existing in Europe. Both suggestions were reiterated in the 'Platform of Acting on Behalf of Military *Détente* Consolidation in Europe', presented by the Soviet Delegation at the Belgrade Meeting. It stipulated special consultations to discuss the problem of military *détente* as a whole, to be organised after the Meeting. Unfortunately, opinions on this subject varied and a proper decision could not be taken.

The United States' attitude towards this idea was negative. They tended to strengthen military forces of their Western European allies. Frustrating all initiatives to intensify the feeling of security of nations living in this region of Europe, the United States motivated the necessity to realise the arms development programme by lack of progress in the sphere of military *détente*. During the negotiations (SALT, Vienna), the new American administration have undertaken an attempt to achieve unilateral advantages, which would change the present military balance in Europe to socialist countries' disadvantage. All actions aiming at the fixation of the existing divisions in Europe had an adverse influence upon the general state of East–West relations. This was illustrated by NATO countries' bloc attitude towards the most important matters of the Belgrade Meeting, although the CSCE process aims at overcoming the existing divisions, and the states formally participated in the meeting 'outside military alliances'.

Among other factors having an adverse impact on military *détente* are the widely spread opinions in neutral and non-aligned countries, suggesting that any progress in this sphere depends on the development of the so-called confidence-building measures, i.e. prior notification of military manoeuvres, invitation of observers, etc. The idea that restrained arms race, disarmament and reductions of arms could be substituted by limited notification on manoeuvres or by elaboration of a code of behaviour of observers, is a mere illusion. Although they play some psychological role, still it is a grave misunderstanding to limit military *détente* to these problems.

The main progress in this sphere is closely connected with the Soviet–American talks SALT, the Vienna negotiations, the resolutions passed by the Disarmament Committee in Geneva, and the results of a special disarmament session of the United Nations General Assembly.

7. In the course of the peaceful development of international relations and intensification of the process of *détente*, the range and significance of co-operation has been becoming more and more important. Apart from *security*, it developed to form an equally important factor in the creation of a new European system. In peaceful circumstances, a system based on military balance must be complemented with a balance of basic interests of co-operation in various spheres, such as policy and economy, science and technology, culture and education, information, tourism and other contacts. Creation of a new system of interdependence of all European and North American countries independently of their political systems should become an element of security as important as military balance. The basis for such a system should be a close observance of principles and provisions of the Final Act of CSCE, which specifies the forms, methods and scope of co-operation between countries of various political systems in the most comprehensive way. It is a fact that the East and the West countries continue to develop economic relations, cultural exchange, scientific and other contacts much more easily, which was also proved during the Belgrade debates.

8. In the sphere of *economic co-operation*, the problem of developing an all-Europe infrastructure for energy, transport and protection of the environment takes the lead. Implementation of the Soviet initiative to organise congresses and conferences at government level to take proper decisions would be a great step in this matter. Unfortunately, the West countries delay convocation of such conferences, putting forward various pretexts.

Apart from discriminative limitations persisting in some Western countries, a serious obstacle on the way to the development of economic co-operation between the East and the West is the lack of balance: socialist countries import more from the West countries than they export to them. A further dynamism could be imparted to the development of economic co-operation by the increase in the import of goods and services by the West countries from the socialist countries. This requires the abolition of import restrictions on the Western part, and the necessity of achieving a balanced trade turnover between the East and the West. In practice, one can observe a quite different phenomenon: the integration processes within the EEC, the increase of trade privileges in the EEC's relations with other highly developed European and non-European capitalist countries, and, last but not least, the import preferences for developing countries, put socialist countries in a position of the least preferential partner. Other difficulties are connected with the worsening of the market conditions in the capitalist world.

In effect, economic co-operation between the East and the West countries continues to remain in staggering disproportion to the industrial potential of socialist countries. Belgrade created possibilities for better understanding of the complexity of all problems to be solved in the course of further development of economic co-operation. This equally concerns the objections raised by the Western countries to all the impediments of bureaucratic character, to insufficient information on trade and on other aspects of economic activity in the East, as well as to the restrictions and protectionist tendencies which have increased in the West lately. A positive phenomenon is the recognition of the following facts:

(i) in the contemporary world co-operation is a necessary condition for optimum development of all states undergoing this process;

(ii) there exist sufficient formal and legal principles to stimulate co-operation between the East and the West (on a multilateral level — the Final Act of CSCE, in bilateral relations — the adequate agreements);

(iii) the Belgrade Meeting confirmed the argument that the process of mutual rapprochement and economic interdependence of countries representing various political systems is permanent.

9. Considerable development of *cultural and educational co-operation* between the Eastern and the Western countries, as well as a greater access to *information and greater contacts among people* are linked in relation and effect with the development and consolidation of *détente*. The experiences of the 1970s, especially the improvement of relations after Helsinki, testify to the truth of the thesis that increased *détente* involves greater co-operation, contacts and information.

There has been considerable progress in the solution of the humanitarian problems, e.g. reunification of families, marriages between the citizens of different states, wider contacts (tourism, professional, religious, youth and sports contacts, etc.). Improvement in this sphere is favourable to the creation of an atmosphere of mutual understanding and confidence among nations. Thus, there is a clear interdependence and dialectical relationship between the increase of contacts of co-operation in the field of culture, education, information, and the development and consolidation of *détente*.

Unfortunately, during the last few years there have been many attempts to misuse problems belonging to the so-called 'third basket' for objectives contrary to the assumptions of the Final Act and to the whole process initiated by the Conference in Helsinki. This mainly concerns the campaign on human rights unleashed by the new American administration. Various accusations, singling out of context separate provisions and one-sided interpretations do not prove favourable to mutual understanding and improvement of relations.

Various documents; i.e. covenants, treaties, declarations, and the Final Act of the CSCE contain a number of resolutions concerning human rights agreed by the states. There is no doubt that these obligations should be thoroughly observed and implemented. Simultaneously it must be remembered that the basic right of men and nations is the right to live in peace and security. This realisation is of utmost importance as it conditions the possibility to enjoy all other rights — civic and political, as well as economic, social, and cultural rights. Normalisation of the situation in Europe and the development of good relations between countries having different political systems prove that *détente* is favourable to an increased range of human rights and to their total observance; but instead of this a greater tension in international relations during the 'Cold War' caused reduction of freedom and liberties.

During the Meeting in Belgrade, the United States and other Western countries' way of treating the problems of human rights proved the ineffectiveness of all attempts to break the integrity of the Final Act of the CSCE, and to specifically legalise interference in the internal affairs of some countries on the one hand and it caused limited results of the Meeting on the other. One of the conclusions drawn from the debate in Belgrade is the thesis that human rights should not be used as a means of manipulation or a political instrument in propagandistic and ideological confrontation.

10. *Creation of a permanent system* of security and co-operation is a long-range process. There are three elements most important for the development of the situation in Europe:

(i) General acceptance of the basis of this system. Nowadays nobody calls in question the principles agreed in Helsinki: moreover they are confirmed by many bilateral and multilateral acts, among them the Concluding Document of the Belgrade Meeting. This does not imply, however, that there will be no attempts at tendentious reconstruction of the Helsinki provisions or of their misuse for aims not always compatible with the provisions agreed in the Final Act of the CSCE.

(ii) The will to continue the multilateral process in spite of various difficulties and tensions turns out to be most important. This is reflected not only in the agreement to hold the next meeting of representatives of thirty-five states in Madrid as well as three meetings of experts, but also in the tendency to take advantage of the already existing multilateral mechanisms: ECE, UNESCO, and, in the sphere of military *détente*: SALT, Vienna, the special disarmament session of the United Nations General Assembly;

(iii) The tendency to make the process of *détente* common, continuous and permanent, which was manifested in Belgrade. The proposals presented there will be consulted in bilateral talks and will intensify bilateral relations.

All those forming public opinion can and should play an important role in this process. Bringing up young people and whole societies in the spirit of better mutual understanding, growing confidence and rapprochement is indispensable to creating a new system of security and cooperation in Europe.

2 The Impact of Current Political and Arms Control Developments on Security in Europe

Background paper prepared by **Jorma Miettinen** assisted by Kalevi Ruhala and Pauli O. Järvenpää for the symposium held at Helsinki, Finland, 19–21 April 1979.

POLITICAL DEVELOPMENTS

For the first half of the decade, a growing sense of optimism pervaded analyses of European security. The sentiment was founded on the conviction, derived from the lessons of almost three decades of cold war, that security must rest upon the perfection of controls over the exercise of power. This conviction was reinforced by the success of US and Soviet efforts to establish limits on ballistic missile defences and offensive missiles in 1972. It was further strengthened by the convening in 1975 of the Conference on Security and Co-operation in Europe (CSCE) in Helsinki. In the minds of many Europeans, in the East as well in the West, the CSCE constituted a political framework for peaceful development and *détente* in Europe.

However, over the last couple of years, much of the earlier sense of optimism has dissipated. Co-operation in technological, economic and cultural fields in Europe has been satisfactory, in spite of the limited political results of the CSCE Review Conference in Belgrade. But it is in the area of 'military *détente*' where the fewest concrete results have been achieved, and the sorest disappointments have been felt. The instruments chosen to provide arms control — both SALT and the Vienna talks* — have been repeatedly called to task, and there is now a widespread concern that new approaches are needed to ensure European security.

Weakening of détente

Perhaps the most significant contribution to this sense of concern is the awareness that political relations between the United States and the Soviet Union are in decline. The points enumerated below do not pretend to offer an exhaustive list of destabilising factors in these relations. It should also be pointed out that the items in the list are not in a systematic order of importance. But it is felt that these points may reveal inter-connections between various strategic and political issues. They are presented here primarily as background for discussion.

Particularly in the West, some of the causes for this development have been seen as follows:

(i) a perceived shift in the overall military balance towards the Soviet Union during the 1970s;

(ii) a continuing build-up of the Soviet Navy's global capabilities;

(iii) modernisation of conventional and theatre nuclear forces in Europe by the Soviet Union and the WTO;

(iv) a relative decrease in the US military power during the 1970s;

(v) uncertainties caused by changes in the US executive/legis-lative relations in foreign policy issues during the last two administrations;

(vi) projection of military power to Africa by the Soviet Union and Cuba which has been perceived in the West as a challenge;

(vii) closer ties by the Soviet Union to countries in strategically sensitive areas (Angola, Ethiopia, South Yemen, Afganistan, Vietnam, the new government of Cambodia).

Particularly in the East concern has arisen about the balance of power politics, especially the use of the 'China card', by the United States and its striving for superiority in qualitative arms development. The following developments, among others, have seemed to cause suspicion in the Soviet Union:

(i) establishment of diplomatic relations between the United States and China, and the West's support of Chinese economic, industrial and military modernisation;

(ii) the US efforts to limit Soviet influence in the Middle East by unilateral diplomacy;

(iii) a 3 per cent real growth increase in Western defence budgets to finance long-range improvement programmes;

(iv) modernisation of the US tactical nuclear weapons in Europe (including procurement of enhanced radiation warheads);

(v) plans to introduce new intermediate range nuclear systems in Europe;

(vi) plans to upgrade civil defence in the United States;

(vii) decrease in Western interest in the Vienna negotiations.

Among further factors of uncertainty must be mentioned the Western European dependency on Middle East oil, the huge concentrations of armaments in the hands of governments in the Middle East, and the apparent eagerness of the great powers to use the sensitive changes in the area's balance of power to promote their own strategic interests.

Impact of Technological Developments

The political developments described have taken place during the critical stages of negotiations for the SALT II treaty. The negotiations have been complicated by advancing technology: not only the ICBMs but even the SLBMs of both sides can be expected to reach a high degree of accuracy during the early 1980s. Furthermore, technological breakthroughs in such varied fields as anti-submarine warfare, anti-satellite warfare and even chemical/biological warfare cannot be ruled out. A decisive breakthrough by one of the great powers in any of these military fields would certainly destabilise the strategic balance, and political advantages that might be perceived to be obtainable through a first-strike capability would be considerable.

For the first time in its history mankind may, therefore, be gliding towards a crisis between the two great nuclear powers as a result of technological developments unmanageable by the political leaders. Even if a SALT II treaty were to be achieved, the strategic balance would not remain stable, since offensive arms technologies will develop despite the treaty's stipulations.

Technological developments in conventional weaponry also begin to reach such levels that they have a direct impact on the sense of security in Europe.

Intra-European Problems

In addition to the great power political and strategic factors, one can discern some intra-European problems that might be of future concern to European security.

Political friction has been observed within alliances especially in connection with military budgets and at times there have been serious differences of opinion within both alliances over policies concerning areas outside the defence perimeters of the respective alliances. Do such developments affect the cohesion of the alliances and what kind of repercussions will this have for European security?

Social and economic problems undoubtedly affect foreign policies, and thus have a bearing on European security. What kind of links can be detected between the foreign and domestic policies? How gravely will such societal factors as unemployment, inflation, terrorism, economic stagnation and human rights test the fabric of the European societies?

Many observers are increasingly alarmed over the role of military technology in the conventional military build-up in Europe. To what extent does the looming technological arms race in conventional weaponry affect the structure and capabilities of armed forces in Europe? What are its consequences for the arms control prospects in Europe?

Sensitivity of the 'Flanks'

Europe has no unsolved border problems of such a severity that could provoke a war. Nevertheless, there are still areas with military tensions where a crisis may explode into an open conflict. The most sensitive areas are the maritime flanks: the Arctic Ocean, the Barents Sea, the Northern Atlantic, and the Mediterranean. In all of these cases, immutable geographic factors are the main causes for tension. In the north, Murmansk is the only ice-free naval base in the Soviet Union. The Soviet Northern Fleet is growing and this growth has caused counter-measures in Norway: improvements in the NATO forces earmarked for Norway. The situation in the North is complicated by the still open question as to the extent and delimitation of the continental shelf in the Barents Sea, and the dispute over the limits of Norwegian and Soviet rights in the demilitarised Svalbard.

In the Southern flank, geographic problems include the narrowness of the Marmara–Dardanelles strait which the Soviet Black Sea Fleet has to pass on the way to the Mediterranean, and the unsolved territorial dispute between Greece and Turkey. The situation in the south is further complicated by the internal instability of Turkey, the feud between Greece and Turkey over Cyprus, and the proximity of the Middle East, among others.

How unstable are the flanks politically and strategically? A question that deserves close attention from the point of view of arms control is the following: does the position of the flanks differ from that of Central Europe in such a way as to require a different kind of an arms control approach? If so, what are the specific arms control requirements in the Nordic and Southern flanks?

Non-European Crises

Finally, one has to consider the impact of non-European crises on Europe and European arms control efforts. Up to now these crises have had a limited impact on arms control negotiations, but the possibility of a critical intervention cannot be excluded. At least in one case — in the impact of Chinese foreign policy on the prospects of SALT — the linkage is inevitable sooner or later.

Non-European crises, such as the Sino-Soviet conflict, a possible crisis in the Persian Gulf area, an eventual escalation of a Far Eastern regional conflict (Vietnam/Cambodia, Korea, Taiwan) or clashes in Africa, all tend to increase tension in Europe and as such damage the prospects of European *détente*. But this observation leads to a series of more penetrating questions: What is the impact of increased international tension on arms control negotiations and arms control itself? Does it influence only the atmosphere in which the negotiations are conducted, or does it have a significant effect also on results? Do tension and crises merely rule out disarmament but make arms control ever more necessary and desirable?

ARMS CONTROL DEVELOPMENTS

SALT II and SALT III

During the early 1970s it was generally believed that the Strategic Arms Limitation Talks (SALT) between the Soviet Union and the United States could produce agreements that would contain the strategic arms race, reduce the risk of East–West nuclear war, and engage the negotiating parties in an overall process of *détente*. The optimism was based on the belief that in an emerging era of strategic parity:

   (i) the political utility of nuclear weapons had declined;
  (ii) efforts by either side to achieve a strategic superiority were counter-productive and exceedingly dangerous;

(iii) the SALT forum provided a conceptual framework for working out a stable strategic relationship between the two major nuclear powers.

Just as the optimism of the early 1970s was solidified into a dogmatic faith in arms control, now it is becoming a matter of conventional wisdom to maintain that the arms control approach has failed. The pessimism of today is based on the following assertions. It is maintained that the technological developments in missiles and their subsystems has outrun the practical importance of any restrictions possible in the negotiations. Furthermore, it has been pointed out that the quantitative approach to arms control has tended to make symmetry in military forces a central value, and the marked asymmetry of the strategic arsenals of the Soviet Union and the United States will defeat any agreement reached by negotiators. And finally, the assertion is often made that the scope of arms control has been far too wide, in that the negotiations have attempted to accomodate a diversity of weapons under the cover of the strategic arms limitations talks.

We start here from the premise that arms control matters and that the traditional arms control objectives — a reduction in the likelihood of war by increasing stability, an alleviation of the damage of war if the war does break out, and a reduction in the economic burdens of arms acquisition — are still valid, and that arms control remains an important instrument in the search for European security. The challenging question is now the following: how can the instrument be sharpened so that it will better serve the interests of security?

The following considerations might serve as starting points for discussion. First, what would be the advantages and disadvantages for European security of the current SALT approach (quantitative restrictions with some qualitative constraints)? Alternatively, what are the strengths and weaknesses of the mission approach advocated by Christoph Bertram in his recent writings?[1] Finally, the thrust of technological change has been toward weapons that blur the demarcation line between SALT and MFR. What opportunities and what obstacles does that technological development create for arms control, and, specifically, how will it affect arms control in Europe?

The 'Grey-area' Systems

In the past decade, arms control negotiations have been conducted under the aegis of two criteria: functional and geographic. In SALT the mutually agreed goal has been to set mainly quantitative restrictions on strategic capabilities, whereas the MFR negotiations have aimed at reducing the number of forces and weapons within a certain geographical area.

It is now widely recognised by arms control analysts that the nuclear weapons systems which do not readily conform to existing definitions of what is, and what is not, a strategic weapon, are acquiring increasing importance in SALT. It is also acknowledged that not only do these weapons systems spell troubles for SALT, but it is difficult to bring them under control through the geographic criterion chosen for the basis of the MFR negotiations.

In specific terms these systems, known as 'grey-area' systems include, for example, the following weapons:

The pair of Soviet ballistic missiles, the SS-16/SS-20 . . . an interchangeable combination of an ICBM and an IRBM, each with a mobile launcher-platform and a MIRV version; the non-ballistic aerodynamic cruise missiles; various kinds of RPV; attack air-craft with variable ranges and mission profiles, armed with cruise missiles with nuclear/or conventional warheads.[2]

The term 'grey-area' is a recent addition to the strategic lexicon, but it can be maintained that weapons systems like the ones described above have existed to blur the difference between district categories of weapons for a long time. Why are the grey-area weapons considered to be a problem for successful arms control just now; what is new?

Grey-area weapons reflect incompatibilities between technological possibilities and the formal categories of existing arms control negotiations. Advancing technologies are constantly creating new opportunities for weapons designers. The result has been the procurement of a wide range of multipurpose and multimission systems: weapons that cover a broad spectrum of operational characteristics, that can be armed with different types of warheads, and that, consequently, offer a large variety of military options. Therefore, special concern over the grey-area weapons systems is warranted for the following reasons:

(i) The attempt by the United States and the Soviet Union to decrease the number of strategic missile launchers within the SALT framework has made the European nuclear balance, the so-called Eurostrategic balance, appear more significant.

(ii) The SALT process has rechannelled weapons modernisation to areas not covered by strategic arms negotiations, and as a result, efforts to modernise nuclear weapons have concentrated in the grey-area (e.g. SS-20, Backfire, cruise missile and Pershing II).

(iii) New weapons systems are a distinct threat to the SALT process itself: these weapons do not conform to the current categories of weapons used in the arms control negotiations but most of them can be used interchangeably for both strategic and tactical purposes, equipped with either conventional or nuclear warheads.

(iv) New military equations are emerging: cruise missiles and the medium-range capabilities developed by the Soviet Union are changing the military balance in Europe.

(v) Several fundamental procurement decisions relating to medium-range nuclear forces appear to have been taken in the last few months, and they seem to both intensify the nuclear arms race in Europe and to contribute negatively to political *détente* in Europe.

Negotiations dealing with the grey-area weapons systems should, in one view, be able to deal with four sets of issues:

(i) quantitative constraints;
(ii) qualitative constraints;
(iii) geographical deployment restrictions;
(iv) associated and confidence-building measures.

The following considerations will be important in this context. Is it possible to devise a new arms control forum covering the whole spectrum of weapons from theatre to central strategic? What prospects are there for setting up special negotiating machinery somewhere between MFR and SALT to deal specifically with the grey-area systems? What are the political and technical obstacles in trying to include, within the framework of the two existing negotiations, those weapons systems on their periphery? If not included, to what extent would this devalue any agreement that might emerge?

In each of these alternatives, what would be the possible scope of participation of European states (and China)?

CBMs at the CSCE

The idea of confidence-building measures developed simultaneously with the preparatory process of the CSCE. In the course of preparations they became one of the most concrete issues to be negotiated within the first basket which dealt with questions relating to security in Europe. As promising newcomers to the arms control debate the CBMs were widely received with a sense of acceptance.

Prior to the Belgrade review conference hopes were high with regard to the further improvement of CBMs. In Belgrade various concrete proposals were tabled by the Western, neutrals and non-aligned as well as Socialist countries. These included:[3]

(a) notification of smaller-scale manoeuvres involving between 10 000 and 25 000 men;
(b) more specific information to be given as to the types of forces involved;
(c) an increase in the number of invitations to be extended to observers;
(d) a code of conduct for the treatment of the observers;
(e) compulsory notification of major military movements with specific parameters (Western proposals);
(f) notification of a set of individual smaller scale manoeuvres aggregating more than 25 000 troops;
(g) increasing the information provided in the notice (proposals of the NNA group);
(h) notification of air and naval manoeuvres;
(i) abstaining from multinational manoeuvres near the frontiers of other participating states (Romania);
(j) abstaining from manoeuvres above a certain level, say 50 000–60 000 men (the Soviet Union).

The participants suggesting improvements were, however, disappointed in their expectations. No changes in regard to the CBMs agreed upon in the Final Act of Helsinki were possible. On the basis of the Belgrade discussions it is in any case quite obvious that military matters will occupy a major role in the Madrid review conference in 1980. Still, the fate of CBMs in Madrid remains in question.

The record of CBMs so far gives justification to questions whether it is still relevant to link CBMs mainly with the CSCE. Arguments favouring the improvement of CBMs in context of the CSCE review process are based primarily on the partial success and adopted practice. On the other hand it may be argued that CBMs and associated measures might serve better the mutual force reduction talks. As applied in a limited area it is of course possible that CBMs could be made more mandatory and offer more promising results in other respects, too. Their possible inclusion in subregional arms control measures in Central Europe, however, by no means excludes the CSCE framework. The future of CBMs for the time being is thus in many respects an open question, but it certainly deserves a thorough exchange of ideas. Questions worth discussing might include, for instance, the following:

   (i) The role and significance of the CBMs in advancing arms control objectives: Are they real steps forward or merely cosmetic gestures without security implications?

  (ii) Forums and regional application of CBMs: Where should the main emphasis lie in improving CBMs, in CSCE or subregional arms control contexts like Central, Northern or Southern Europe, Balkans, Mediterranean, etc.?

 (iii) Which parameters should be set in each case as targets in order to attain a maximum confidence-building effect?

 (iv) The linkage of CBMs to other arms control measures, conventional and nuclear.

  (v) Should CBMs be conceived only as concerning the manoeuvres or troop movements or should they be widened to include other political and military measures?

The Vienna Negotiations

In the almost six years of the Vienna negotiations no concrete results have been achieved. Nevertheless, some progress has been made. Both sides have agreed on parity and balance, they are in agreement on a collective ceiling totalling 900 000 troops with a subceiling for ground forces of 700 000 troops. Furthermore, both sides have agreed that the reductions will have to take place in two phases and to begin with reductions of Soviet and American forces and armaments. For the first phase the Eastern side suggests the following American reductions: 29 000 troops, 1000 nuclear warheads, 36 Pershing missiles and 54 Phantom fighters. For the Soviet reductions the Eastern side proposes: 3 divisions, 1000 tanks and 250 armed personnel carriers, the Western proposal being 5 divisions and 1700 tanks. The main points of disagreement are still the following:

   (i) The East proposes that the Soviet Union and the United States should have one-sided cancellation rights if difficulties arise in the Phase 2 (a so-called 'blank-cheque clause').

(ii) The West does not agree upon the data given by the East on its own forces. The discrepancy is about 150 000 troops.

(iii) The East proposes that Canada and the European NATO countries should commit themselves to reductions of armaments in the second phase.

(iv) The East proposes that any single country can increase its forces only by a half of the reduction of any other country in the alliance.

(v) The West proposes associated measures of the type which were established in the Final Act of Helsinki, but obligatory instead of voluntary. The East has not been willing to discuss such measures in detail at this stage of the negotiations.

The Vienna negotiations have suffered from being only of secondary interest to the great powers who have paid their main attention to the SALT negotiations. With SALT unfinished there has not existed enough political will to accommodate in Vienna, where the negotiations have primarily dealt with technicalities.

If SALT II is to be completed no time should be lost but full attention focused on the Vienna negotiations. It would be unwise to put too great demands on these negotiations; even a modest agreement could alleviate the high economic burdens that the defence budgets mean for the European countries today. The best hope might lie in a relatively simple *status quo* agreement on manpower along the lines that have been already agreed upon. Since the most disturbing aspect to the West seems to be the Soviet troops in Eastern Europe and the greatest concern to the East the size of the Bundeswehr in NATO, an arrangement might be reached by which these two basic asymmetries could be offset and symmetrically stabilised. Since both the Soviet and the West German forces comprise approximately half of the manpower of their respective alliances in the guideline area it should not be impossible to agree upon such commitments.

CONCLUSIONS

Europe is undoubtedly a central element in the global security system. Yet, its security is highly dependent on international peace and security in other parts of the world. This dependency is reflected in the tendency of the great powers to stabilise their central balance by various military measures in Europe which comprise conventional as well as nuclear weapons. This being the case, prospects for isolating Europe from the negative consequences of the balancing efforts by means of regional arms control do not seem very promising.

But fortunately trends pointing to a more positive direction are also discernible. The two ongoing processes, the CSCE and MFR, offer a modest hope that perhaps some other arms control measures might be available for Europe.

One particular feature in these two processes should be kept in mind: each of them takes into consideration the great power interests in Europe. It seems that the precedent created in these negotiations is the only realistic starting point for discussions concerning arms control in Europe. An understanding of those interests affecting Europe, of the causes for arms development in general and of the obstacles to disarmament in particular, are further prerequisites for the establishment of meaningful arms control measures.

Thus it seems highly desirable to strive for the stabilisation of the situation in Europe in spite of the political and military competition of the great powers in various parts of the world, Europe itself included.

The symposium should attempt to elucidate the underlying causes of the destabilising trends and try to search for ideas for their elimination or at least their alleviation. Would it be possible to separate Europe from the global confrontation and make arms control a viable option for European security in a way that is likely to increase and not endanger the security of the countries concerned?

The activity of European countries in keeping *détente* alive and enhancing it by CSCE, CBMs and other policies, is only part of the answer. Still it would be useful to ponder what kind of a role the peoples in Europe could play in advancing the cause of security and arms control. Perhaps a thought could be given also to subregional arms control plans concerning areas such as the Balkans and Northern Europe. And what about the feasibility of unilateral restraints in restricting the size and quality of armed forces?

For obvious reasons it is at least as important to discuss the specific responsibilities of the great powers in the process of security and arms control in Europe. What can be done beyond SALT and other arms control negotiations like CTB and chemical disarmament? One is also tempted to ask whether the great powers could achieve positive results by showing restraint in other parts of the world. Such urgently needed agreements as nuclear arms control and verifiable reduction of forces and armaments seem to be minimum requirements for maintaining *détente* and managing Europe peacefully through the 1980s. In a world of expanding military build-up and shrinking resources where 150 nation states compete for political power and economic influence, the prospect of Europe drawn into a conflict originating in some other part of the world is far from satisfactory.

NOTES
*The official name of the Vienna negotiations is Mutual Reductions of Forces and Armaments and Associated Measures in Central Europe (MURFAAMCE). Also, abbreviations MFR and (in the West) MBFR are used.

REFERENCES
1. Christoph Bertram, 'Arms Control and Technological Change: Elements of a New Approach', *Adelphi Papers*, No. 146 (London: IISS 1978).
2. Lothar Ruehl, 'The "grey-area" Problem', in Christoph Bertram (ed), Beyond SALT II, *Adelphi Papers*, No. 141 (London: IISS 1978).
3. John D. Toogood, 'Military Aspects of the Belgrade Review Meeting', *Survival* (July/August 1978) pp. 155–8.

Part Two
Military Aspects

3 The 'Central Balance' in the 1980s—No Longer Central

C. G. JACOBSEN

The 'central balance', the East–West military confrontation in Europe, may be in the process of becoming less central. It is this author's judgement that the areas of prime concern for the 1980s lie beyond the traditional focus of attention.

Soviet forces in Europe were the beneficiaries of significant quantitative and qualitative up-grading efforts through the 70s. Greater mechanisation, of personnel transport and equipment (the new armoured personnel carriers, self-propelled artillery, etc.) improved mobility on the ground. An impressive array of helicopters, gunships and transporters, coupled with a theoretical and training exercise stress on the aeromobile potential of regular Motor Rifle Battalions, provided a new dimension of flexibility. The introduction of potent ground support and deep interdiction fighter-bombers added a formidable complement to the above. Yet the shifting correlation of forces was gradual, not precipitous; NATO superiority was eroded, not superseded. Both alliances were forced to rely on blatantly selective data manipulation in order to project the politically preferred image of embattled inferiority. NATO tank balance figures included Warsaw Pact reserves, but excluded own reserves, and excluded ground and helicopter-borne anti-tank means. Moscow highlighted the potency of US Forward-Based Systems, but downplayed 'Backfire' and SS-20 deployments. NATO equations ignored France; Moscow ignored the fact that France's stance of pro forma independence had (at least until recently) forced an overconcentration of Western communications and reserve facilities into more exposed forward areas.

The more arresting trends of the moment divide into three categories. One strikes at the core of the strategic balance, the concept of Mutual

Assured Destruction. Soviet predilection for an indigeneous defence capacity is long-standing, but technological inadequacies restricted immediate aspirations to 'ultimate' protection against third power (China) prospects. Today, however, new technologies — laser, neutron, particle-beam — have reinvigorated Ballistic Missile Defence advocates; BMD research is now attracting increased interest and funding in both Moscow and Washington. Still, although pivotal if attained, the prospect of comprehensive BMD remains distant and uncertain.

Categories two and three are more relevant to our concern, and the 1980s. The first relates to Moscow's development of interests and capabilities on the outerlying flanks of pan-Arctica and the southern hemisphere. In the north, the USSR pioneered many of the technologies that have revolutionised Arctic accessibility. As early as 1967 she was able to publish tectonic/metalogic maps of the ocean floors of the Polar regions, right up to Canada's Arctic islands, which have a discrimination ten times better than the best analagous Canadian maps of these islands' land structures. The USSR is perfecting the technologies to exploit Arctic wealth potentials. At the same time she has developed a route by which her attack submarines and older restricted-range SLBM vessels can circumvent the GIUK 'chokepoint' — although this may be of no more than marginal value, in view of her apparent confidence that NATO barrier designs are vulnerable. Of greater importance, then, is the degree to which Arctic familiarity and deployments extend the acreage and security of 'home waters' for her intercontinental-range SLBM strategic reserve. The success of Moscow's attempt to make these waters inviolable against US encroachment designs (as vice versa off Washington State's new Trident complex) will have a more profound impact on 'balance' calculations than any foreseeable shift on the central front. Pan-Arctika *is* a major theatre of confrontation.

On the southern flank events have equally burst the bonds of traditional perceptions. Until the early 70s the US/West could intervene in Africa or elsewhere with military impunity whenever economic, political or other interests were deemed to dictate action. The 70s have seen the development of distant Soviet state and economic interests of considerably greater consequence than is generally appreciated in the West — precisely the type of interests that have traditionally been thought to warrant and legitimise military projection capabilities. The decade also saw more assertive Soviet support for at least some 'liberation groups'. In the past vague if sometimes bombastic declarations of sympathy had mirrored inadequacy of means and hollow credibility. Now there was a pattern of definite commitment (at least within certain contexts), accompanied by a display of new and potent distant power projection capabilities, air and naval. The Soviet demonstration of the means *and* the will to intervene effectively in defence of distant state interests has revolutionised today's international environment. It has not negated US interventionary capabilities, which retain a definite, albeit shrinking advantage. But it has made credible a Soviet alliance alternative where such was not credible before. Similarly, the Soviet reliance on allies (Cuban, East German and others) in some situations is not novel — there are French troops in about as many African countries as there are Cuban — what is novel is that Moscow is acquiring options for action and reaction that were previously available only to her antagonist(s).

Meanwhile, Iranian events have spurred a dramatically new appreciation of energy and resource scarcities. As concerns energy, for example, the probably permanent 'loss' of much of Iran's production leaves developed economies tenuously stretched. Exploration, development, research, exploitation all take time. Even with decisions taken today, to explore for new oil and gas fields, to develop already known concentrations, such as the Canadian tarsands, to research and exploit the potentials of alternate energy sources, solar, tidal and others, and to expand nuclear generation, all these together could not promise energy sufficiency until about 1995. In the meantime there are those who say that our economies just could not accommodate the 'loss' of even one more energy producer. That perception appears to be prevalent in Washington. Now, there is scepticism in some quarters as to the long-term stability of Saudi Arabia, of Nigeria, of Venezuela, of Mexico, and perhaps of others. The point is: under normal circumstances the pros and cons of a particular interventionary prospect might have been open to debate; perceptions of vital necessity pre-empt debate. In conjunction with the Soviet emergence as a global rather than a regional superpower, the dictates of energy scarcity ensure that the potential flash-points to the South have also moved well beyond the geographical confines of yesteryear.

Finally, the third trend of concern. This relates to 'grey-area weapons', and the possibilities of meaningful arms control measures. There are two aspects to the question, each equally vexing. One concerns the superpowers' stated ambition to proceed beyond the bilateral SALT II negotiations, to a SALT III which will both bring in other affected parties and address weapon-systems peripheral to those hitherto subject to negotiations. Attention has revolved around the American 'Forward-Based Systems' and Soviet Intermediate-Range Ballistic Missiles, both of which fell between the stools of 'Strategic' Arms Limitation Talks and the

European theatre-centred Mutual (and Balanced?) Force Reduction negotiations. It was not that these weapon systems necessarily fell between
the two stools, rather that they represented problems so complex that
both powers agreed to exercise them *pro tem* for the sake of getting any
agreement(s) at all. But the problem has grown. Today Soviet IRBMs are
backed by a variety of attack craft with the range to strike London, while
US FBS are to be joined by Pershing II missiles capable of reaching
Soviet territory. In view of the problems their ancestors caused for early
SALT progress, the SALT III prospectus provides a field-day for those
of sceptical bent. And the situation is not helped by the advent of cruise
missile technologies. Suffice it to mention the 'private' German cruise
missile development in Zaire, or the very possible deployment of Soviet
cruise missiles on fishing vessels in the North Sea. The problem of verification alone appears beyond control. With the best of will on both
sides, it is difficult indeed to be optimistic about foreseeable arms control endeavours, especially as these pertain to Europe. Even with the
best of will a degree of continuing European tension or unease appears
inevitable.

4 Disarmament in Europe: Military *Détente* in Europe as an Aspect Of International *Détente*

R. BOGDANOV

The reorganisation of relations between states that has begun on the European continent was accompanied by the creation of a qualitatively new political atmosphere in the mutual contacts of countries belonging to different social systems. A radical improvement in the world political climate made it possible to place on the agenda the task of effecting a radical turn in the development of international relations towards co-operation and the construction of a system of genuine security and peace. It is common knowledge that these changes have been most pronounced in Europe. This is only natural, for it is on the European continent where the two military-political alliances with their powerful armed forces and big arsenals of nuclear weapons confront each other, that it is especially clear, due to purely physical conditions, that an outbreak of any armed conflict is fraught with the danger of its developing into a world thermo-nuclear holocaust.

It is quite natural, therefore, that the questions of lessening military confrontation and decreasing the level of the armed forces and arms in Europe are of paramount importance; on their solution hinges in many respects the further development of international relations both on the European continent and elsewhere in the world. The turn from the cold war and the policy of confrontation to peaceful coexistence, bolstered up by a whole series of treaties and agreements between states belonging to different social systems, has created real requisites for preserving and strengthening peace in Europe and making *détente* irreversible. The Conference on Security and Co-operation in Europe, whose Final Act bears the signatures of the leaders of thirty-five states in Europe and North

31

America, has opened up new possibilities for solving these tasks. The Soviet Union regards the Helsinki Conference not only as an outcome of the positive developments during the transition period from the cold war to *détente*, but also as the starting point for the subsequent progress of Europe along the road of peace and the elimination of war from the life of the peoples. The ultimate goal of *détente* is to check the threat of a new world war. Therefore, political *détente* cannot provide a full guarantee from a military threat, if it is not complemented by a *détente* in the military sphere. Military *détente* includes a whole range of components of the military and foreign-policy activities of states and bears on such vital problems as curtailing or freezing the military budgets, taking measures aimed at the elimination of danger of a sudden outbreak of an armed conflict, a limitation of and then a stop to the arms race and cuts in the armed forces and the stockpiles of weapons.

Without the implementation of measures of military *détente* and steps to curb the arms race there can be no successful progress of international *détente*.

Many tasks lie ahead. The curtailment of and then a stop to the arms race should be effected, some progress along the road leading to universal and complete disarmament achieved, military confrontation on the European soil lessened and the division of Europe into the opposing military blocs overcome.

Examining the problems of military *détente* we should take into account a whole number of objective difficulties standing in its way and connected with the complex character of the very process of *détente*, for the long period of the cold war has engendered a host of harmful traditions and ideas, and first and foremost, a lack of mutual trust, the elimination of which, naturally, requires no little time and effort. There is also a multitude of complex factors of a military-technical and political nature (the absence of criteria for comparing different types and systems of weapons, questions of inspection and control, etc), which also exert a negative influence on the process of disarmament and the limitation of the arms race.

Unfortunately, there are still forces in the world arena representing the interests of the military-industrial complex, the supporters of the cold war, who would like to push the European nations on to the dangerous road of further stepping up the arms race and creating the seeds of tension and conflict on the continent. Official NATO circles, it seems, are out to intensify the drive for new types of weapons of mass destruction. Plans of the production and deployment in Western Europe of neutron weapons hold a special place. It is quite evident that a decision to develop neutron weapons would initiate a new phase in the arms race, in the production of means of mass annihilation — with its negative consequences for the whole world, and especially for Europe. The neutron bomb, which is aimed primarily at living targets, must be regarded as an extremely dangerous weapon and resolutely condemned. This weapon, more than any other type, can cause nuclear escalation. The deployment of the neutron bomb on the European continent could only increase the danger of an outbreak of a nuclear conflict, raise the level of military confrontation, retard the process of military *détente* and put up fresh obstacles at the Vienna talks on the question of troops and arms cuts in Central Europe.

The prevailing conditions urgently demand that negotiations be started for a complete ban on the neutron weapon. As is known, the socialist countries have submitted to the Disarmament Committee in Geneva a draft convention on banning the production, stockpiling, deployment and use of the nuclear neutron weapon.

An agreement on banning the neutron weapon would, in the present situation, be a key factor in the strengthening of international security. This would contribute to a lessening of tension and the creation of a favourable atmosphere for a dialogue on disarmament, including the talks at the Hofburg Palace in Vienna on the reduction of armed forces and armaments in central Europe, which merit some more detailed consideration.

It is to be regretted that in almost four-and-a-half years since the start of the talks a mutually acceptable basis for concluding an agreement that would lead to the lessening of military confrontation in Central Europe has not yet been found.

Of course, the preparation of an agreement in Vienna is a complicated, and many would agree, delicate process, with a multitude of components of a political and military-technical nature. Yet the principal cause of the impasse at the talks seems to lie not in any insoluble technical difficulties but in the basic premises of the participating states in approaching the problems under discussion, in the objectives they set themselves.

The Soviet Union attaches great importance to the talks on mutual troop and arms cuts in Central Europe. She realises full well the great significance which the conclusion of an agreement in Vienna would have for the development of international relations on the European continent and throughout the world. For it is Central Europe that holds first place in the world in terms of troop and arms concentration. Here, in a comparatively small area of the globe, the powerful contingents of the armed forces of NATO and the Warsaw Pact Organisation, almost two million strong, are stationed, with thousands of aircraft and tanks and huge quantities of military equipment, tactical weapons and means of their delivery. All this goes to prove once again how urgent it is for states to take practical steps in order to lessen military confrontation in Europe, especially in the central region which is under discussion at the Vienna talks. These talks can be successful, provided only that all participants adhere to the underlying principles agreed upon by the participating countries in the course of preparatory consultations. These include such principles as non-infringement of the security of any party, mutual reductions of troops and arms, equal obligations assumed by sovereign states, precluding one-sided military advantage. It can be said that the essence of these principles boils down to reducing the high level of troop and arms concentration in the centre of Europe, without violating the balance of the forces of the parties to the talks that has already taken shape.

The delegations of the USSR and other socialist countries represented at the talks strictly adhere to these principles, striving for progress. Having set a concrete goal of reaching a mutually acceptable agreement in Vienna, the socialist countries proceed from the premise that there has for a long time been an approximate parity between the military forces of NATO and the Warsaw Treaty Organisation. This has guaranteed security and stability in the region, although the troop and arms concentration level was high.

But this general military parity in the centre of Europe does not mean that there are no disproportions between the two sides in particular categories of military units and equipment. Indeed, the existing correlation of forces in Central Europe has taken shape gradually, over a long historical period. Each side assessed its security requirements independently, with due account of all objective factors, and determined the ways and means for guaranteeing them on that basis. This process related to the heterogeneity of the military structures of the two military-political groupings in Europe and the existing disproportion between different armed forces and weapon systems. One side's superiority in one or more directions was compensated for by the other side's superiority in others. At the same time, despite certain difficulties in estimating the force ratios it is possible to say that there is no major disparity in size between the NATO and the Warsaw Pact forces in Central Europe. This fact is admitted by many Western statesmen and military experts. It is also confirmed by the official data exchanged by the two sides at the talks. It is to be hoped that an agreement reached at the recent round of the talks, on an exchange of some additional data, will remove outstanding issues and facilitate progress at Vienna.

Unfortunately, the Western powers' approach to the solution of the problem of troop and arms cuts cannot be regarded as realistic and constructive. The Western side seems to be trying to have the Warsaw Pact countries make bigger cuts with a view to obtaining one-sided military advantages, and refuses to assume concrete obligations concerning the second stage of troop and arms reduction. NATO countries attempt to belittle the military significance of the socialist countries' approach, while making it appear that it is the West alone that advances the proposals which can ensure military *détente* in Europe. It seems that Western countries are pursuing one objective at Vienna — to hamper progress at the talks and prevent the parties from reaching an agreement on troop and arms cuts in Central Europe.

NATO countries have rejected the concrete proposals of socialist states on keeping the numerical strength of the armed forces of the participants in the talks at the same level until agreement is reached on their reduction, and have proposed no alternative. Moreover, Western powers are increasing their armed forces, piling up in Europe and boosting military expenditures. The public is aware of US plans to expand its military presence on the continent by another 8000 men. Programmes are being elaborated to produce and deploy in Europe neutron weapons and other types of arms, including cruise missiles. Naturally, all these actions cannot but create additional difficulties at the Vienna talks and in the way of military *détente* in Europe.

However, despite this, progress at the Vienna talks is not only necessary, it is possible. If all the countries participating in the talks act in a constructive way and make proposals proceeding from the mutual, and not one-sided, interests of security and in strict accordance with the principles agreed earlier, agreement reached in Vienna will be a tangible contribution to military *détente*.

On a broader plane, the problem of military *détente* in Europe can be solved on the basis of combining regional and global measures to limit the arms race and stave off the danger of military conflicts. The development of *détente* in Europe is a major condition for ensuring universal peace and precluding possible use of force or a threat to use force in the international political climate. In turn, the implementation of measures to strengthen international security and steps to disarmament on a world scale, particularly agreement reached at the Soviet–America strategic arms limitation talks, would be an essential contribution to the consolidation of security of the European countries and a lessening of military confrontation on the continent.

The trend towards political and military *détente* in Europe is a continuing one. It is influenced by major, long-term factors, and this gives grounds for optimism in assessing the development prospects of the situation in Europe. However, a delay in solving the important issues of arms limitation and disarmament, the freezing of the process of military *détente* and marking time are fraught not only with the dangers of delay and the loss of precious days, but also with the emergence of new difficulties and sliding backwards. The time is ripe for concrete decisions. Political *détente* must be complemented by military *détente*.

NOTE
This paper was written early in 1978 before the US decision to suspend production of the neutron bomb.

5 Implications of New Conventional Technologies

ANDRZEJ KARKOSZKA

The most spectacular development of the last decade has been the introduction into military arsenals of weapons of great accuracy, the so-called precision-guided munitions. Their common feature is a high probability of hitting and destroying a target, independently of their range.

To this category belong all modern intercontinental and medium-range ballistic missiles, all modern strategic and tactical cruise missiles, different surface-to-surface, air-to-surface and surface-to-air tactical missiles, fin-steerable bombs guided by laser or optical systems, air-deliverable terminally guided submunitions, several types of mines and gun-projected rounds. All of these greatly extend the defensive and offensive efficiency of the forces possessing them. They put into question the battlefield usefulness of such hitherto powerful weapon systems as tanks, aircraft and large naval vessels, thus creating growing anxiety among military strategists as to future doctrines, tactics and the possible outcome of any future battle situation. Their enormous accuracy permits, even at very long distances, the attack of hard-point or area targets by conventional explosives, a feat that has hitherto been reserved exclusively for missiles with nuclear warheads. Morever, this capability, unlike nuclear weapon technology, will not be limited to a handful of countries, but will soon be within the reach of a number of countries, both medium and small powers. Such may be the outcome of introducing a new generation of Pershing missiles into West European armies, as is currently planned. One wonders whether this expanded capability will indeed enhance the security of these countries, or whether it will, in fact, undermine it.

Precision-action weapons require quick and accurate location of targets. This demand is currently satisfied by a great variety of optical, seismic and magnetic sensors, located either on the ground, under water or on aerial platforms. The most rapidly developing class of these platforms are pilotless vehicles remotely controlled, able to watch the battlefield and large areas behind it, to report the information thus gathered back to fire-control centres, to spot and designate the target with laser beams, to report the effects of the fire and to perform other reconnaissance functions. When armed, they are able to help in harassing and suppressing enemy forces, acting just like any other precision-guided weapon. In addition, progress in sensor technology has made it possible to design the first fully automated weapon systems, the true forerunners of the dehumanised automated battlefield. Examples of such weapons, although still at the development stage, are self-initiating anti-aircraft munitions and the CAPTOR encapsulated anti-submarine mine, both of them unmanned and waiting to be activated automatically by sophisticated sensors and control systems.

All of these weapon systems are connected to each other by extensive command and control networks, comprising all sensors and platforms, from the individual weapon, through sensor data fusion centres at army and division level, up to the highest commands. It is this command and control system which multiplies the effectiveness of modern weapons, although it is seldom viewed as a factor increasing the lethality of modern warfare.

Another dramatic development in conventional military technology is connected with advances in old and new munitions, such as hard-structure munitions, artillery, rocket- or air-delivered scatterable mines, rocket dispensers and fuel-air explosives. Fuel-air explosives (FAEs), or explosive gas mixtures, although considered as conventional weapons, have a destructive power which is many times greater than that of typical conventional high-energy explosives. It is said that one kilogram used in an FAE gives a yield two to five times greater than that of an equal amount of TNT. Thus a 500 kg FAE bomb may create a 'lethal envelope' of overpressure which is able to destroy a warship and everything on it within an area of several hundred metres. This is roughly the range of accuracy of current strategic ballistic missiles and much more than that of modern cruise missiles. These FAEs are currently planned for mine-clearing operations, but new generations of the weapon are soon expected to appear in anti-aircraft and anti-ship modes. It is not difficult to envisage their use against military targets that are currently the preserve of nuclear weapons. After all, they do not involve the latters' collateral physical damage. But what about the political consequences of this capability?

Similarly, modern controlled fragmentation cluster bombs, containing terminally guided submunitions, can cover large areas and destroy accurately a number of individual targets on the ground. An example of such a weapon is the MBB MWI STREBO multipurpose weapon which is able to destroy tanks, runways and aircraft shelters. In addition, new artillery systems such as SADARM (Sense and Destroy Armour) or STAFF (Smart Target-Activated Fire and Forget) can fire projectiles which can destroy several targets simultaneously by bursting submunitions from a single shell, all of them guided precisely by on-board sensors.

Technological developments do not only stress efficiency, however. One of the visible trends is towards the interchangeability of conventional and nuclear-capable-capable systems. More and more artillery and missile systems, for example, are being made dual-capable. Recently, the concept of an insertable nuclear component has been put forward, by which a conventional warhead could, within a short time, and in a simple operation, be changed into a nuclear device. Although this is not yet accepted as a practical possibility, it indicates a general technological trend, which will be of great military consequence.

Let us now turn to the military and political implications. The enormous human and technical resources placed at the disposal of the military have resulted in the creation of countless new modern weapon systems. The list grows every day. The main rationale behind this process is a desire to improve the performance characteristics of existing arsenals. However, one cannot help but notice that in many instances the process has become an end in itself. Several weapons being developed today are not necessitated by the requirements of current potential battlefields or by actual security considerations. The new systems are often only marginally better than those they replace, although they are always more costly. More importantly, they contribute to the well-known spiral of action–reaction in weapons acquisition processes between the opposing alliances.

It seems that, increasingly, the main military confrontation between the two alliances in Europe is that of the battle of technologies. In guarding against any military surprise, states maintain large research programmes, preserving a number of different options, taking expensive initiatives, and generally blurring the distinction between civilian and military research.

However, due to the fact that states of the opposing alliances have different policies regarding weapons acquisition, based on different doctrines and force organisations, they tend to acquire different weapon systems at different points in time. The other side, seeing a new weapon system appearing in the arsenals of its opponent, is compelled to match it, (a) by producing counter-measures to defend against it, and (b) often by producing the equivalent weapon for offensive use. The result is that, sooner or later, a general balance in offensive and defensive postures is restored, albeit at a higher level of sophistication and effective destructive power.

Technical improvements in the quality of weapons tend, in time, to have a bearing on states' perceptions of the balance of power, and of the threats to their security, and these perceptions are continually changing. States have the right and the obligation to respond to these threats. What is difficult, however, is an accurate assessment of the extent of the threat, where one has to know the enemy's number and types of forces, their geographical distribution, their structure and intentions, the value of their war reserves, the internal political situation and the inclinations of the enemy's allies. In fact, regrettably, countries tend to ignore most of the above, and to make their assessments of threats solely on the basis of numbers of weapons. And here, the continuous technological spiral makes the task of threat assessment a never-ending and thankless one. Moreover, the characteristics of the new weapons are not easily discernible from the outside, and very small, seemingly superficial outward modifications may dramatically affect a weapon's efficiency. To make things worse, the fact that one of the most dynamic and important elements in a new weapon is often its electronic components, of which new generations appear continuously, means that weapon characteristics accordingly change extremely rapidly. The real military threat posed by some weapons is thus never really completely understood. In addition, there is also the problem of the notion of threat being misused for political purposes.

One of the recurring arguments about the implications of new weapon technology that is often put forward in official Western statements and in the mass media, is that new technological developments tend to strengthen the defensive character of NATO's forces, to lower the nuclear threshold and to increase the credibility of the Western deterrence posture. Let us try to examine these claims objectively.

First, it should once again be stressed that the interaction of forces in land warfare is a matter of great complexity. Thus, to evaluate true offensive or defensive capabilities, one has to take into account a large matrix of factors, a matter far more complex than merely making simple static comparisons of weapon systems.

On the doctrinal level, NATO's strategy officially claims a defensive posture on the theatre level. However, this posture also envisages a dynamic, highly mobile defence, one which includes a variety of offensive operations. These operations are to be supported by penetrating air missions and ancillary amphibious manoeuvres. Enough about the doctrine. The other side can learn more from the weapons acquisitions made. New weapons are of greater and greater range and, because of their growing accuracy, can be directed against more valuable, protected military targets. All the new weapons systems are multipurpose. They can destroy tanks as well as they can attack airfields and strongholds of their opponent's defence positions. Weapons which are considered purely defensive, at least publicly, are in fact also classical offensive weapons. The range and accuracy of medium-range missiles operated by NATO countries, coupled with the great potential of different precision-guided tactical munitions located on fast-moving platforms, such as modern helicopters, aircraft and troop carriers, can easily launch a rapid offensive, especially 'against forces still wedded to tanks as a primary means of defence', to quote one of the prominent Western experts on the subject.[1] It is a common idea in the West that 'offensive' means a concentrated attack by armoured forces. In reality, however, an offensive can be equally carried out by missiles, PGMs and helicopters, all existing weapons. It is a corollary that the defensive intentions of those who acquire new weapons are usually completely misinterpreted by the adversary.

How does the 'nuclear threshold' relate to the new conventional weapons? The concept of nuclear threshold is apparently one of enormous political importance, yet its meaning is elusive. According to the former US Defense Secretary, nuclear weapons would be used 'in response to an overwhelming Warsaw Pact conventional attack where the consequences of conventional defeat are deemed more serious than nuclear escalation'. Thus 'nuclear threshold' is tantamount to a decision to 'go nuclear', which would be made by the leaders of nuclear powers according to their assessments of the outcome of early conventional hostilities. Such a decision is likely to be guided as much by psychological factors as by a subjective assessment of what constitutes 'defeat'. The definition of defeat is closely related to different and complex scenarios. The threshold is therefore dependent upon actual and unpredictable situations, and the decision to 'go nuclear' is affected both by military preferences and human temperaments. It is clear that the more sophisticated nuclear weapons become, the more closely they will meet specific military requirements. As they become more useful to the military forces so they will be in greater demand. On the other hand, the parallel sophistication of conventional weapons makes these as efficient as nuclear weapons against a growing number of targets. The crushing effect of an opponent's conventional weapons might force an antagonist to use nuclear weapons earlier than he might otherwise choose. In fact, for many military targets new conventional weapons are overtaking the gap between nuclear and conventional weapons in terms of their 'efficiency' or lethal effects. They therefore merit equal treatment from the point of view of their military usefulness. It is partly a geographical issue. Those strategic targets within the territory of a great nuclear power which could until now only be destroyed by nuclear and strategic means may now be successfully attacked by long-range conventional precision-guided missiles.

In closing the discussion of the 'nuclear threshold' it should be stressed that it is a purely academic concept. It seems almost irrelevant in view of the uncertainty surrounding the possibility of any hostilities involving Warsaw Treaty Organisation and NATO countries becoming immediately or even pre-emptively nuclear.

It is also argued that new conventional technologies expand the resources for successful defensive warfare and thereby expand the conventional element of the strategic deterrent in Europe. The moment at which it would be considered necessary to use nuclear weapons is thus delayed. Is it therefore necessary to increase the numbers and variety of small nuclear weapons? Those already in existence, plus new precision-guided missiles, should satisfy the desire for a deterrent. Every deterrence posture contains two parts, one intended to discourage a potential aggressor and the other for fighting a war, should the first part fail. When this latter part takes on proportions which the adversary sees as unwarranted, however, he reacts accordingly. Finding a compromise between what seems justified in one's eyes and unwarranted in those of the other, is the crux of the European problem. Nevertheless, armaments should not be built up and improved just in the interests of a stronger deterrent. The repercussions of such a move on international relations are equally, if not more, important. If it results in a similar move by the opponent group of states, then sooner or later the positive intentions become a much more serious military reality.

As indicated earlier, new technologies allow much scope for devious political manoeuvres and the creation of false impressions. Threats are interpreted in terms of subjectively perceived dangers, and new technologies inevitably add to the inaccuracy with which they are assessed since the increasing number of weapons makes for a more diffuse picture of the actual military balance. The problem is confounded by misconceptions which are created purposely in the interests of various domestic or economic policies or to suit allies following another policy. Successful arms control and arms limitation, and the more peaceful coexistence of nations in Europe and elsewhere are dependent upon the removal of these factors, which create distrust and accelerate the arms race.

The new conventional technologies may have a discernible negative political effect on the Mutual Force Reduction Talks in that they intensify the qualitative arms race in Europe. It is clearly more difficult for states to negotiate in the face of this intensification.

Moreover, the technological military progress has an important indirect effect in rendering the negotiations somewhat marginal for the actual military security of the states involved. Although the talks will maintain their political value, there will be less incentive to achieve any meaningful agreement.

As an effect of new military technologies many 'grey-area' weapons have resulted; that is, weapons outside known classifications as strategic (and thus belonging to SALT) or regional, European (and therefore belonging to the Mutual Force Reduction Talks). The disturbing effect of these military advances is even broader, as the existing distinctions between weapons become redundant. The multipurpose and modular character of new weapons means that they cannot be categorised as tactical or strategic, conventional or nuclear, offensive or defensive. The language of future arms limitation agreements will therefore have to be radically modified. All the basic characteristics of weaponry, such as range, yield and accuracy will become meaningless since they may be changed at will without notifying other parties to the agreement.

Furthermore, there will be a reluctance to enter into long-term agreements since it will be impossible to foresee future security requirements created by as yet unknown sophistications of old weapons and the development of completely new technologies. It is increasingly likely that new weapons will soon render existing arms limitation measures, modest as they are, valueless. It could be asked, for example, whether future SM-2 tactical missiles armed with nuclear warheads and directed by the modern Aegis-type fire control system might not be better than any ABM system forbidden today. In addition, the new technologies tend towards more mobile, smaller, modular and multipurpose weapons whose real capabilities are obscure to any known sensor. It all comes down to the fact that monitoring compliance with treaties concerning such weapons would be completely ineffective. This would obviously hamper negotiations on arms control. On the one hand, it would create understandable political, technical and legal difficulties, and on the other hand there would be ample excuse for those not interested in arms limitation.

Finally, the intensified technological sophistication of weapons is accompanied by a growing overlap between military and civilian research and development. 'Good' and 'bad' technologies are developed side by side, such as satellites which are used both for the strategic targeting of ICBMs and for the monitoring of climatic changes. To impose a ban on military uses of modern technology is difficult when they are increasingly inseparable from civilian uses of radar, communication and navigation networks.

There seems to be only one way out of the deadlock created by the intricacies of the technological arms race: it is to try to ensure security by co-operation from all sides and to restrain our unilateral efforts to enhance our security by resort to military force.

NOTE
1. R. Burt, *Adelphi Paper*, 126, p. 13 (1976).

6 Grey-area Systems and European Security

HANS GUNTER BRAUCH

(This paper was rewritten in January/February 1980)

INTRODUCTION: A NEW COLD WAR OR MILITARY *DÉTENTE* IN EUROPE

For several years the state of East–West *détente* and especially of the central American–Soviet relationship has never been more uncertain than in early 1980. Two events highlighted the gradual return to competitive and confrontative patterns of the cold war:

(i) the decision by NATO countries of 12 December 1979, both to modernise its theatre nuclear forces ('grey-area systems') in Europe and to enter into parallel arms control negotiations;

(ii) the Soviet intervention into Afghanistan a fortnight later.

Has the decade of *détente*, of strategic arms control (SALT) and the multilateral phase of East–West negotiations on European security (M(B)FR, CSCE) come to an abrupt standstill? Will Europe return to a new period of remilitarisation and of ideological demarcation? Will the concern for domestic reform and global economic readjustment (new international economic order) be replaced by a period of intense political and military confrontation for scarce commodities, raw materials and markets? Will Europe provide the scene for a new Euro-nuclear arms race that will enhance the decoupling from the American nuclear umbrella and that will increase the probability of a local Euro-nuclear war? Or will Europe gradually return — after an icy intermission — to a new era of military *détente* marked by real arms reductions and limitations of offensive military options?

Basing our argument on the optimistic assumption that both the USA and the USSR will return to the joint task of lowering the risk of nuclear confrontation and of reducing their nuclear armaments once the respective leadership problems have been solved we suggest that the 'icy intermission' should be used to re-evaluate the traditional arms control theory and practice and especially the bargaining chip technique. Lessons should be drawn from the failure of arms control efforts to restrain technological change, a major determinant of armaments dynamics. In an attempt to contribute to this inevitable reassessment we shall concentrate on the following aspects: (1) the definition of major terms and criteria relating to 'theatre nuclear forces', 'tactical nuclear weapons' or 'grey-area systems;' (2) the evaluation of major changes, the comparison of sources and the discussion of possible developments relating to TNF of long-, medium- or short-range; (3) criticism of the traditional arms control approach; (4) and on conclusions and suggestions for arms restraint in the Euro-nuclear area.

DEFINITION OF 'GREY-AREA SYSTEMS' AND OF TNW/TNF: A PRE-CONDITION FOR THE MILITARY BALANCE OF NUCLEAR WEAPONS IN AND FOR EUROPE

Those nuclear weapons systems not covered by SALT II and by Vienna talks on mutual force reductions M(B)FR have been referred to as 'grey-area systems' by Western and as 'grey-zone forces' by Soviet writers.[1] Others preferred to use the term 'tactical nuclear weapon' (TNW) defined by exclusion from the category of 'strategic nuclear weapons'.[2] The former American Secretary of Defense, James R. Schlesinger, introduced the term TNF in his report to Congress of April 1975 on *The Theater Nuclear Force Posture in Europe*.[3] Jeffrey Record admitted in his study: *US Nuclear Weapons in Europe* as a major problem in any discussion of tactical nuclear weapons 'the lack of a precise definition of the term itself'.[4] The Soviet general and military writer, M. Milshtein, rejected the term 'tactical nuclear weapons' as a very conditional and vague term that 'does not really reflect either the potential of these weapons or their specifications'. He suggested as a more correct term for these weapons: 'Theatre nuclear weapons' (as applicable to the Central European Theatre).[5] More recently the German Defence White Paper 1979 transcribed TNF (theatre nuclear forces) as 'nuclear weapons in and for Europe'.[6] In this study we shall use both terms: 'theatre nuclear forces' in describing those launchers and nuclear warheads presently deployed within the geographic boundaries of Europe, assigned to the European nuclear strike plan (NOP)[7] and targeted against European military and civilian objects and 'grey-area systems' for those Euro-nuclear weapons that are presently not being part of arms control negotiations. The 40–8 Poseidon C3 SLBMs (submarine-launched ballistic missiles), with their 400–80 warheads respectively, that have been assigned to SACEUR will be counted as TNF; however, being limited under SALT they cannot be treated as 'grey-area systems'. Soviet sources introduced the term 'forward-based systems' (FBS) during the SALT I negotiations in pointing out the 'US aircraft capable of reaching Soviet territory from carriers at sea and from bases in the United Kingdom.'[8]

Though no agreement exists on the scope of the 'grey area', at least two different definitions influenced the debate. According to the majority view among strategists and arms controllers 'grey-area systems' may be defined

as noncentral systems that are strategically significant; theater systems that fill theater-strategic, rather than theater-tactical roles; systems that have utility in both strategic and theater warfare; and those not included in SALT, but whose proliferation effectively would undermine SALT.[9]

This definition, in combining both the armament and the arms control aspect, focuses only on the long-range theatre nuclear forces (LRTNF) but it comprises the special features of the cruise missiles that may be used for short, medium, long and intercontinental missions with both nuclear and conventional warheads. This very 'multifunctional capability' endangers the verifiability of future arms control agreements.

Some politicians, like Willy Brandt, suggested that arms control negotiations should be extended to those nuclear systems not covered by SALT and MBFR. In this context he referred to the neutron weapon (ERW), a warhead for both short-range nuclear launchers (SRTNF), such as 155 mm and 8 in nuclear artillery howitzers, and for medium-range ballistic missiles (MRTNF) such as Lance.[10]

Lothar Ruehl, a West German military writer, cited the following examples for the 'grey-area' problem:

The pair of Soviet ballistic missiles, the SS-16/SS-20, present an interchangeable combination of an ICM and an IRBM, each with a mobile launcher platform and a MIRV version; the non-ballistic aerodynamic cruise missiles; various kinds of RPV; attack aircraft with variable ranges and mission profiles, armed with Cruise Missiles with nuclear and/or conventional warheads; all of these are typical of the systems that produce the 'grey area problem'.[11]

While the first problem of SS-16/SS-20 has been solved by the SALT II treaty (Art IV, 8) which prohibits 'dual-capable' launchers the second problem of the Cruise Missile will remain a major negotiation item for the years ahead.

For heuristic purposes we have distinguished in previous papers among three definitions of the 'grey area':

   (i)   *a narrow definition* that covers only American and Soviet LRTNF with a range beyond *1000 km*, especially the Soviet SS-20, the Backfire and American SLBMs, Forward-Based Systems and future ground-launched cruise missiles (GLCM);
  (ii)   a *medium definition* that includes the TNF of third countries (France, Great Britain);
 (iii)   *a wide definition* that comprises all substrategic systems presently deployed in the geographic boundaries of Europe or targeted against Europe.

NATO foreign and defence ministers in the communique of their special session on TNF modernisation and arms control on 12 December 1979, subscribed to the narrow definition suggesting that arms control negotiations should be limited to American and Soviet land-based LRTNF within the framework of SALT II.[12] For both theoretical and political reasons we shall argue for comprehensive negotiations on arms restraint within the framework of a wide definition of the grey area.

American nuclear weapons were deployed in the 1950s 'both as an adjunct of the US strategic capability and as a "substitute" for NATO conventional forces, since conventional parity with the Warsaw Pact was then judged politically and economically unattainable'.[13] The Soviet development of continental strategic nuclear systems (IRBM/MRBM) spurred the national nuclear programmes of Britain and France and it stimulated discussion on a NATO MRBM and the creation of a Multilaterial Force (MLF). Upon dropping the MLF proposal the United States proposed an improved consultation mechanism which evolved into the NATO's Nuclear Planning Group.[14] After the withdrawal of US MRBMs from Italy and Turkey in the aftermath of the Cuban Missile crisis the United States maintained a number of Polaris submarines in the Mediterranean, and later allocated a substantial number of Poseidon SLBM RVs to SACEUR for targeting purposes in order to tighten the coupling between 'tactical' and 'strategic' systems. In 1967, when NATO approved the new doctrine of flexible response (MC-14/3), TNW or TNF respectively, 'became the central leg of a "NATO Triad" which tied together NATO's conventional and strategic forces, while leaving deliberately vague the circumstances under which nuclear weapons, either theater or strategic might be employed'.[15] According to the Schlesinger Report of April 1975: 'Theater nuclear forces deter and defend against theater nuclear attacks; help deter, and, if necessary, defend against conventional attack; and help deter conflict escalation'.[16]

Referring to their military functions, Halperin defined TNW/TNW simply as 'nuclear weapons designed to support land forces',[17] while Newhouse believes them to be those weapons 'designed to influence the land or air defense battle directly, rather than indirectly (for example, by interdicting an enemy's lines of communication or by carrying a threat to his homeland'.[18] TNWs have also been defined by Lawrence as 'nuclear weapons for limited tactical military purposes'.[19] According to the Field Manual of the American Army these 'nuclear weapons are limited to the defeat of opposing forces in a theater of operations. Implicit in this definition is the condition that a strategic nuclear exchange on the belligerents' homeland does not occur'.[20] This definition ignores the fact that even the tactical use of TNW on German soil would be of strategic significance for Central Europe.

No agreement exists between American writers on the one side and Soviet and West European analysts on the other side on the definition of 'tactical' and 'strategic' systems and modes of employment. For Milshtein TNWs 'are tactical only with respect to the USA. As for the countries on whose territory these weapons may be used, they are essentially strategic weapons because their use would lead to disastrous consequences'.[21] In the European view all those theatre nuclear systems that can target either one of the nuclear powers in Europe are being defined as strategic systems. Both the French and the British conceive of their national deterrent as a strategic force. For the West German military nuclear weapons with a range beyond 1000 km (e.g. 621 statute miles), the distance between West German and Soviet territory, are being defined as strategic, Euro-nuclear or continental strategic nuclear systems. In the Soviet view any nuclear system targeted against the Soviet Union is being considered as a strategic system.

Milshtein prefers the term 'theatre nuclear weapons' in full agreement with the more recent American literature: 'This term covers nuclear weapons that are deployed, could be deployed, or are intended for use in the theatre of hostilities. It does not qualify the weapons' nature, yield range or destruction potential. The term covers all nuclear weapons in all armed forces in the theatre'.[22]

Theatre nuclear weapons or forces may be distinguished against the upper end of the Triad consisting of ICBMs (Intercontinental Ballistic Missiles), SLBMs (Submarine-Launched Ballistic Missiles), long-range heavy bombers, fractional orbital space-borne systems, and probably ABMs (Anti-Ballistic Missiles).[23] Towards the lower end of the Triad, with the increased miniaturisation and accuracy, some authors have suggested that Mininukes may be used in a 'para-conventional' way.[24]

According to the Schlesinger Report NATO theatre nuclear forces in Europe consist of SSMs (surface-to-surface missiles), artillery, tactical aircraft, SAMs (surface-to-air missiles), ADMs (Atomic demolition munitions), and SLBMs. Leitenberg lists the following non-strategic categories of nuclear weapons: air-dropped, free-fall bombs and glide bombs, air-to-surface missiles and air-to-surface stand-off missiles, air-breathing cruise missiles, surface-to-air missiles, shorter range surface-to-surface missiles, air-to-air missiles, artillery, depth charges, torpedoes and rocket torpedoes, atomic demolition munitions, or nuclear land mines, and Ocean mines.[26] Milshtein distinguishes among three major groups: land-based tactical (theatre) nuclear weapons (ADMs, nuclear artillery, SSMs, SAMs), nuclear-capable tactical aircraft (nuclear planes carrying nuclear bombs, air-to-air missiles, air-to-surface missiles) and sea-based tactical (theatre) nuclear weapons (nuclear-capable aircraft-carrier planes carrying nuclear bombs, AAMs, ship-to-air missiles).[27] Jeffrey Record suggested two basic approaches for defining TNW according to yield and range.

Given the general confusion associated with TNW/TNF we examine 'theatre nuclear forces/weapons' (TNF/W) by applying the following criteria:

(1) theatre of operations that comprises both the location of the target and of the delivery system;
(2) weapon range;
(3) military purpose and performance;
(4) weapon yield;
(5) quantitative and qualitative criteria;
(6) associated criteria.

1 The Theatre of Operations

All nuclear systems assigned to the nuclear strike plan of NATO (NOP), all nuclear RVs located in the theatre and all targets that can be destroyed by non-central systems from outside the theatre are to be included. The term of the German Defence White Paper 1979: nuclear weapons in and for Europe, provides a fair definition. The European theatre may either be defined as the area for the application of CBMs according to the CSCE (narrow definition) or as the geographical Europe from the Atlantic to the Urals (wide definition) that includes eleven of sixteen Soviet military districts. Both the Soviet SS-20 IRBM deployed east of the Urals that can cover targets in Western Europe (NATO) and the 400–80 Poseidon SLBMs that have been assigned to SACEUR have to be included in our balance of Euro- or continental strategic (LRTNF) systems.

2 Weapon Range as a Major Definition Criterium

Jeffrey Record separates the American TNW into three categories: *battlefield* or *short-range theatre nuclear weapons* designed to influence directly the outcome of combat with a generally low yield (0.1 to 2 kilotons) and a limited range; *long-range theatre nuclear weapons* designed to influence indirectly the outcome of combat by interdicting the movement of enemy troops and supplies with a higher yield (3 to 400 kilotons) and longer ranges (up to 400 miles); and *semi-strategic nuclear weapons* that could reach and return from targets inside the Soviet Union from present locations.[28]

The International Institute for Strategic Studies differentiates among three categories for land-based missiles using the following range criteria:

(i)   *IRBM* ('intermediate'-range systems): 1500–4000 miles (2413.5–6436 km);

(ii) *MRBM* ('medium'-range systems): 500–1500 miles (804.5–2413.5 km);

(iii) *SRBM* (short-range systems: below 500 miles (804.5 km).[29]

Some American arms control experts used different range criteria for the IRBM: 1050–2950 nautical miles (1950–5500 km), the *MRBM*: 160–1050 nm (300–1950 km) and the *SRBM*: below 150 nm (300 km).

The German Defence White Paper 1979 subdivides the nuclear forces in and for Europe in three groups:

(i)   *SRTNF* (short-range theatre nuclear forces): systems with a range
      below 100 km: nuclear ADM, artillery, howitzers, SRBM;
(ii) *MRTNF* (medium-range TNF): systems with a range of 100–1000
      km: nuclear-capable land- and sea-based tactical aircraft, missiles;
(iii) *LRTNF* (long-range TNF): systems with a range beyond 1000 km:
      medium-range bombers, heavy fighters, MRBM/IRBM and
      SLBMs.

Depending on the range criteria used one will obtain different balances
that cannot be compared among each other. Different range criteria for
fighters (maximum range vs range under fighting conditions) lead to a
certain overlap among fighters assigned to MRTNF or LRTNF. Some
Soviet SRBMs may be categorised both as SRTNF and as MRTNF. An
isolated segmentalised analysis of TNF according to range and systems
criteria, e.g. land-based LRTNF, and the demand for segmentalised
balances both by armament and by arms control efforts may both spur
a Euro-nuclear arms race in Europe and thereby further the nuclear
decoupling of Western Europe.

3 Military Purpose and Performance of TNF

According to the Healey syndrome TNF perform a double function both
to deter the Soviet Union and the Warsaw Treaty Organisation (WTO)
against aggression and to reassure the West Europeans about the credibility of the American nuclear commitment in Europe. Though inse-
curities about American foreign policy actions and motives may have
weakened the American credibility in the perception of some Europeans,
various constants fortify European confidence in coupling: the presence
of some 300 000 American soldiers in Europe, US business investments
in Europe, a large number of American citizens permanently resident in
Europe and the understanding that American interests would be damaged should Soviet influence extend to Western Europe.[30] It appears to
be highly questionable whether psychological reassurance questions can
be solved by hardware solutions. An enhanced nuclear visibility by the
deployment of the US LRTNF at the same time increases the vulnerability of Western Europe against potential intimidation and pre-emptive
strikes.

Within the framework of NATO's doctrine of flexible response the
theory of escalation and linkage requires a range of NATO options in
order to (i) maximise Soviet uncertainty about the nature of NATO's response to attack; (ii) minimise the political burden on West European

governments of a rigid employment plan which might imply an automatic recourse to nuclear weapons; and (iii) enable NATO to attempt to control escalation in the event of war.[31] Various options are provided by the overall coupling of US strategic forces by recent US planning for Limited Nuclear Options, under which US strategic forces could be used selectively in direct support of Alliance objectives. Western advantage both in the number of TNF warheads (USA in Europe: about 7000 warheads for TNF launchers) and in strategic warheads (in 1979: USA: about 11 000 warheads, USSR: 5000 warheads) still provides a clear advantage in overall target coverage by NATO.

According to the Schlesinger report's overall concept of use of TNF two levels are discussed: (a) response to a theatre-wide, pre-emptive nuclear attack and (b) response to an overwhelming conventional attack. From these two purposes several general characteristics for NATO forces are drawn:

First, the theater nuclear forces and their essential support (e.g. warheads, delivery systems, intelligence, command, control and communications (C3), and logistics) must be sufficiently survivable to have credible rataliatory capability. . . . Second, NATO conventional forces should be able to operate satisfactorily in a nuclear environment. . . . Third, the level, mix and characteristics of NATO theater nuclear forces should provide capabilities . . . to destroy targets such as front line and second echelon WP armored units and their immediate support. . . . Fourth, while theater nuclear forces for deep interdiction have less immediately decisive effects on the tactical situation, such forces are needed in the event that nuclear attacks on WP forward armored units and their support are not sufficient.[32]

This general rationale provided the basis for the discussion within the Nuclear Planning Group of NATO on TNF-modernisation since 1975.

4 Weapon Yield

The weapon yield is the least satisfactory criterion for the evaluation of TNF. The yield of TNF-warheads includes both subkiloton mininukes and warheads in the megaton range for IRBM/MRBM. The assignment of the same system for theatre and strategic functions, e.g. the Poseidon C-3 warheads, and the targeting both within the framework of the SIOP (Single Integrated Operational Plan) and NOP (Nuclear Operations Plan of Allied Command Europe) further reduces the definitional value of the yield criterion. General Giller in Congressional testimony frankly admitted: 'The target system describes the purpose of the bomb perhaps better than the yield'.[33]

5 Quantitative and Qualitative Criteria

Important quantitative criteria for the military balance of TNF are the number of launchers, re-entry vehicles (RVs) or delivery systems, and the number of warheads available for use in the European theatre. Estimates of US TNW have ranged from 50 000 in 1966 to 22 000 in 1975 with an approximate breakdown as follows: Europe: 7000, Atlantic Fleet: 1000, Asia: 1700 Pacific Fleet: 1500 and United States: 10 800. In 1974 Secretary of Defense Schlesinger testified: 'There are approximately 7000 US nuclear weapons in Europe, including naval weapons. All of these US weapons are available for NATO missions; none is a SAC weapon. . . . The mix of weapons within that total has changed to provide for modernisation. . . . Our stockpile has been reduced, in overall totals, from over 7000 to less than 7000 since the mid-1960s.'[34] No numbers have been published on the warheads of the French and British TNW. The number of the Soviet warheads for theatre nuclear use is unknown. Most publications refer to an estimated 3500 Soviet warheads, a figure that is not based on direct evidence. While in 1974 Record uses the number of 3500, in 1975 he wrote that '. . . an estimate 2250 Soviet TNW confront a NATO deployment of some 7000'.[35] Other writers maintained that the USSR had already obtained parity in the number of TNF warheads.[36]

In the 1979–80 issue of the *Military Balance*, IISS introduced various qualitative criteria to evaluate the 'Balance of Theatre Nuclear Forces in Europe' such as: *serviceability* (i.e. the number of systems actually ready for use at any moment), the *system utilisation*, *survivability* (i.e. the ability of a system to withstand conventional and nuclear attack: its hardness and concealment), *penetration* (i.e. the ability of a missile or aircraft to penetrate missile and air defence systems), and *flexibility* (i.e. the responsiveness to retargeting and the range of targets, and the accuracy). These five factors and indices were summarised in a *system utility figure*. Additional qualitative parameters for the comparison and evaluation of TNF launchers are their *accuracy* over long distances, the *mobility* of the delivery systems, the *vulnerability* of nuclear storage sites, the *reload capability*, *yield*, *throw-weight* and the capability to carry more than one warhead (*MRV, MIRV*) and the *payload* (capability to carry a certain number of nuclear bombs) of nuclear-capable aircraft. Difficulties exist in the counting of the number of nuclear-capable aircraft that may perform both theatre nuclear and conventional roles and of dual-capable SRBM and artillery shells that may use both nuclear and conventional warheads.

6 Associated Criteria of Relevance to an Assessment of the TNF Balance

The authoritative Schlesinger Report in its evaluation of the TNF Posture in Europe included the *command, control and communications* (C^3) support as essential to both deterrence and flexible employment of theatre nuclear forces by a continuing upgrading of NATO Integrated Communications System (NICS): the *target acquisition* by reconnaissance and data processing systems; the enhancement of system *survivability* by an improvement of air defences and the reduction of *collateral damage* for civilians and the containment of uncontrolled escalation. In our military balance of theatre nuclear forces in Europe we use as the theatre of operations Europe in its geographical boundaries, we employ the range criteria of the German Defence White Paper and the qualitative criteria of the IISS analysis for two sources on LRTNF.

MILITARY BALANCE OF THEATRE NUCLEAR FORCES IN AND FOR EUROPE

All data on TNF rely nearly exclusively on Western sources, both official releases and unofficial political estimates. The Soviet Union and the Warsaw Treaty Organisation (WTO) do not publish any information on their nuclear launchers and warheads. Given these informational constraints, scientific analysis is limited to the methodological criticism of individual sources and to the comparison of publicly available evidence.

1 The Euro-strategic Balance of Long-Range Theatre Nuclear Forces (LRTNF)

In the Euro- or continental-strategic balance we include all LRTNF with a range between 1000 and 5500 km, that are deployed within the geographical boundaries of Europe, assigned to SACEUR's nuclear operations plan (NOP) and which are targeted from outside by SLBM forces in the Atlantic and the Mediterranean and by IRBM deployed east of the Urals.

In 1979, F. Zimmermann, an influential member of the conservative CSU in the West German Parliament, maintained that ten years ago NATO had a clear advantage (in LRTNF) over the USSR. In the meantime, the argument goes, the USSR has achieved a 6:1 superiority over NATO's land-based missiles in Europe.[37] On the other hand, Leonid Breshnev stated in East Berlin on 6 October 1979: 'As Chairman of the defence council of the USSR I declare with all determination: During the past ten years the number of launchers for nuclear weapons of medium range (LRTNF) deployed on the territory of the European part of the Soviet Union has not been increased by a single missile, by no single aircraft. On the contrary, the number of launch platforms for LRTNF missiles as well as the yield of these missiles have even been slightly decreased.' Which of these two controversial statements provides a more correct assessment of the changes in the LRTNF balance?[38]

According to *Military Balance* (IISS) the number of Soviet IRBM/MRBM was reduced from 750 in 1969 to 600 in 1972 and it slightly increased again to 710 in 1979. The number of Soviet medium-range bombers were reduced from 1050 in 1969 to 693 in 1979.

In Table 6.1, we have summarised the available IISS data for four subcategories of LRTNF systems: SLBMs, IRBM/MRBMs, medium-range bombers and for fighters for eight years between 1970 and 1979. We have listed separately the number of launchers of the United States, of the European NATO (France, Britain), of the Soviet Union and of the People's Republic of China.

While the US and the NATO countries had a slight advantage in LRTNF in 1970 over the USSR of 2959 to 2720 systems, or 1.09:1 respectively, this Western advantage was even increased to 1.23:1 in 1974. Between 1974 and 1975 (the year of the Schlesinger Report) occurred an increase in the number of Soviet nuclear launchers in Europe from 2910 in 1974 to 4081 in 1979. In 1975 and 1976 IISS reports a slight Soviet advantage of 1.09:1 or 1.07:1 respectively that shifted in 1977 (after the discussion on TNF modernisation had started in NATO's nuclear planning group) to 1.57:1 in 1978 to 1.35:1 and in 1979 (the year NATO decided on TNF-modernisation) to 2.96:1 in favour of the Soviet Union. However, if one compares for 1977 the IISS data for the Soviet Union on one side and for the US, European NATO and China on the other side one finds an approximate equality that shifted even to a slight Soviet inferiority in 1978 (1:1.06)

The following tentative conclusions may be drawn based on IISS

TABLE 6.1 Changes in the LRTNF Launchers and Delivery Systems of the USA, NATO, China and the Soviet Union from 1970–9[39]

Category	Country/Alliance	Number of systems deployed in July							
		1970	1972	1974	1975	1976	1977	1978	1979
SLBM	USA	?	?	?	?	?	?	40–8	40–8
(A)	F,GB(NATO)	48	80	112	112	128	128	128	128
	USA + NATO	?	?	?	?	?	?	168–76	168–76
	China	?	?	?	?	?	?	?	?
	Soviet Union	120	66	60	51	60	60	60	78
IRBM/	USA	—	—	—	—	—	—	—	—
MRBM	F,GB(NATO)	—	18	18	18	18	18	18	18
(B)	China	—	20–30	70–80	70–80	50–80	60–80	60–80	92–122
	NATO + China	—	38–48	88–98	88–98	68–98	78–98	78–98	10–140
	Soviet Union	700	600	600	600	600	620	690	710
Medium-	USA	35	76	66	66	66	68	66	66
range	F,GB(NATO)	110	80	50	50	50	50	48	50
bombers	USA + NATO	145	156	116	116	116	118	114	116
(C)	China	—	100	100	60	65	80	80	80–90
	NATO + China	145	256	216	176	181	198	194	196–206
	Soviet Union	550	800	800	780	810	805	665	693
Fighter	USA	1200	??	1600	1500	1400[a]	350[a]	556[a]	390[a]
aircraft		900	??	1000	1200	1400[a]	200[a]	100[a]	100[a]
(D)	F,GB(NATO)	666	688	743	792	787	862	928	940
	USA + NATO	2766	??	3343	3492	3587[a]	1412[a]	1584[a]	1430
	China	150	500	600	700	700	800	700	700
	NATO + China	2916	??	3943	4192	4287[a]	2212	2284	2130

(continued)

(*Table 6.1 continued*)

Category	Country/Alliance	1970	1972	Number of systems deployed in July 1974	1975	1976	1977	1978	1979
	Soviet Union	1000	1300	1300	2500	2500	1000[a]	1000[a]	3500
	+ WTO	350	150	150	150	150	150	146	150
TOTAL (A)–(D)	USA	2135	??	2666	2766	2866	618	762–70	596–604
	F,GB(NATO)	824	866	923	972	983	1058	1122	1136
	USA + NATO	2959	??	3589	3738	3843	1676	1884–92	1732–40
	China	150	620–30	770–80	830–40	915–45	940–60	840–60	890–930
	NATO + China	3109	??	4359–69	4568–78	4758–88	2616–36	2724–52	2622–70
	Soviet Union	2720	2916	2910	4081	4120	2635	2561	5131

[a] Only those systems deployed in Europe are included according to IISS.

LRTNF data for the decade of *détente*: The number of American systems deployed in Europe increased from 2135 in 1970 to about 2866 in 1976, then jumped to 618 in 1977 and were stabilised around 600 in 1979. This sudden reduction of American LRTNF systems, however, is the result of the change in the reporting on American fighters from 2800 in 1976 to about 550 in 1977. The number of Soviet systems were decreased from 2720 in 1970 to 2561 in 1978 and then doubled to 5131 in 1979. This sudden increase is also the result of a change in the reporting: while in the 1978 issue of *Military Balance* IISS counted about 1000 Soviet nuclear-capable aircraft stationed in Europe, the 1979 issue reported 3500 Soviet nuclear-capable aircraft. The number of European LRTNF gradually increased during the 1970s from 824 to 1136 nuclear-capable launchers, and the number of the respective Chinese systems also increased from about 620 in 1972 to 890–930 in 1979. Based on these IISS data the Zimmermann hypothesis cannot be substantiated. If we compare the trend in Soviet IRBM/MRBM development between 1969 and 1979 a slight decrease of forty launchers can be observed; if we compare the figures for Soviet fighters for 1972 and 1979 a further decrease from about 800 to 693 systems can be found: and if we compare the trend for the Soviet fighter aircraft from 1972 to 1979 a slight reduction from 1300 to 1000 systems can be noted. The reality appears to be somewhat closer to the Breshnev statement of 6 October 1979. The hypothesis by many *détente* critics that the LRTNF balance shifted from a slight Western advantage in 1970 to a substantial Soviet advantage in 1979 cannot be supported from IISS data.[40]

In a second step we compare six Western sources by using as a joint sample those nuclear systems contained in a table (Table 6.2) of the Biden Report that was released in October 1979 after a declassification by the American Defense Department.[41] In Table 6.2 we have summarised the subtotals for SLBMs, IRBM/MRBMs, all aircraft for both NATO and WTO countries contained in four German, one American and one international source.[42] Furthermore we have presented the data for launchers (L), warheads (W) and system utility figures (SUF) and the ratios for launchers and warheads in favour or disfavour of the NATO countries. Although this broad comparison permits us to detect the difference in the evaluation of subcategories, however, it does not indicate the difference in individual systems.[43]

The comparison of system totals of five sources resulted in the following ratios in favour of the Soviet Union: *Forster* 3.32:1; *German Defence White Paper of 1979* 3.16:1; *Metzger/Doty* 2.35:1; *IISS Analysis* 2.21:1 and *D. S. Lutz* 1.81:1. By using the same sample the extreme assessments

TABLE 6.2 Comparison of Subtotals of LRTNF Systems and Warheads for Six Sources According to the Criteria of the Biden Report for 1978/79[44]

Category	L/W SUF	NATO/WTO	Hoffman/Steinr.	Weißbuch 1979	M. Forster SPD	Metzger/Doty	IISS 1979-80	D. S. Lutz
					Sources			
SLBM	L	NATO	144 +	128	160–78	176	168	168
		WTO	43	20	39	33	54	12
	W	NATO	272 +	—	528	736	456	656
		WTO	?	—	39	33	33	18
	SUF	NATO	—	—	—	—	336	467
		WTO	—	—	—	—	21	12
	R/L		3.35:1	6.4:1	4.1(.6):1	5.3:1	3.1:1	9.3:1
	R/W		?	—	13.5:1	22.3:1	13.8:1	38.9:1
IRBM/MRBM	L	NATO	18	18	18	18	18	18
		WTO	960–1080	600	900	640	710	520
	W	NATO	18	—	18	18	14	18
		WTO	1680–2040	—	1320	740	640	760
	SUF	NATO	—	—	—	—	9	12
		WTO	—	—	—	—	447	549
	R/L		1:53.5(60)	1:33.3	1:50	1:35.6	1:39.4	1:28.9
	R/W		1:93(113)	—	1:76.1	1:41.1	1:45.7	1:42.9
Aircraft	L	NATO	976(?)	240	237	313	387	387
		WTO	840	600	440	521	503	503
	W	NATO	(ca.2200)	—	389	545	682	682
		WTO	—	—	780	1202	567	567
	SUF	NATO	—	—	—	—	423	423

(continued)

(Table 6.2 continued)

Category	L/W SUF	NATO/WTO	Hoffman/ Steinr.	Weißbuch 1979	M. Forster SPD	Metzger/ Doty	IISS 1979-80	D. S. Lutz
		WTO	—	—	—		300	300
	R/L		?	1:2.5	1:1.85	1:1.67	1:1.3	1:1.3
	R/W		?	—	1:2.0	1:2.2	1.2:1	1.2:1
TOTAL	L	NATO	?	386	415–33	507	573	573
		WTO	1883–963	1220	1379	1194	1267	1041
	W	NATO	?	—	935	1299	1152	1356
		WTO	?	—	2139	1975	1240	1345
	SUF	NATO	—	—	—	—	768	902
		WTO	—	—	—	—	768	861
	R/L		?	1:3.16	1:3.32	1:2.35	1:2.21	1:1.81
	R/W		?	—	1:2.28	1:1.52	1:1.07	1.005:1
	SUF			—			1:1	1.05:1

Sources

NOTES

SLBM : submarine-launched ballistic missiles
IRBM : intermediate-range ballistic missiles
MRBM: medium-range ballistic missiles
L : nuclear launcher, or delivery system

W : warhead
SUF : system utility figure
R/W : ratio for launchers
R/W : ratio for warheads

by the German Defence White Paper (3.54:1 in favour of the USSR) and by Lutz (1.15:1 in favour of the USSR for LRTNF missiles only) are somewhat modified.

If we compare the data on warheads for four sources the differences increase as a result of different assumptions about the number of warheads per delivery system. Michael Forster, a defence adviser of the SPD faction in the Bundestag, maintains a Soviet superiority of 2.26:1, Metzger and Doty, two America Harvard-based arms control analysts, report a ratio of 1.52:1 and the IISS analysis a slight advantage of 1.07:1 in favour of the USSR/WTO while Lutz states a slight NATO advantage in warheads of 1.008:1.

If the qualitative criteria of the IISS analysis are included for the Biden sample we receive an exact parity for the IISS data and a slight Western advantage of 1.05:1 for NATO for the Lutz data. In our longer and more detailed analysis of the LRTNF data we concluded that the 'worst-case assumptions' of Hoffman/Steinrücke[45] of the German Defence White Paper[46] and of M. Forster[47] are methodologically as doubtful as the 'best-case assumptions' by D. S. Lutz.[48] Although we have several reservations against both Metzger/Doty[49] and the IISS Analysis[50] we agree with the results of the analysis: 'that something very close to parity now exists between the Theatre Nuclear Forces of NATO and the Warsaw Pact, although it is moving in favour of the Warsaw Pact'.[51] Helmut Schmidt, the West German Chancellor, stated on 6 February 1979 in a speech to the SPD faction in the Bundestage:

> If the Soviet side adds 30–40 new SS-20 missiles every year, each with at least three warheads, and if the Soviet Union would deploy 30–50 new Backfire bombers every year, one can foresee that a shift of power may occur during the 1980s — I am not talking of 1979, 1980, 1981 and 1982 — that may enable future leaderships in the Soviet Union, theoretically, to use these potential military threats for political ends[52]

If we assume that the USSR adds one SS-20 missile weekly and 25–30 Backfire bombers annually from 1980–3 and that it does not retire any old systems for bargaining purposes it may add 208 SS-20 missiles and 624 SS-20 warheads, and 100–20 Backfire bombers with 500–600 additional warheads if we assume that each bomber will carry five nuclear bombs. Under these 'worst-case assumptions' the number of Soviet LRTNF launchers — according to IISS data — would increase from 1267 in 1979 to 1575–95 in 1983 and the number of Soviet LRTNF warheads would increase from 1240 by an additional 1124–224 to a new total of 2364–464. If we assume that these Western projections are correct then it appears doubtful why the 572 new LRTNF systems to be deployed by NATO after 1983 should be an incentive for the USSR either to stop arming or to achieve a LRTNF balance. On the Western side Metzger/Doty projected till 1985 the introduction of 530 Tornados and of 248 F-16 nuclear-capable fighters as a replacement for the ageing F-104 NATO fighters. If we include in our projections the pessimistic assumptions of Metzger/Doty for 1985 — the Western advantage in strategic warheads of 1.95:1 in 1978 will decrease to 1.07:1 in 1985 under the constraints of SALT II — the number of surplus central strategic warheads available for SACEUR's NOP may decrease. Helmut Schmidt, in his 1977 Alastair Buchan Memorial Lecture, stressed the necessity to extend arms control negotiations to the nuclear grey area in Europe. He referred to the 'close proximity between the hazardous arms race, on the one hand, and a successful control of arms, on the other'. In the West German Chancellor's view: 'Changed strategic conditions confront us with new problems. SALT codifies the nuclear strategic balance between the Soviet Union and the United States. To put it another way: SALT neutralises their strategic nuclear capabilities. In Europe this magnifies the significance of the disparities between East and West in nuclear tactical and conventional weapons.' Schmidt warned that 'strategic arms limitations confined to the United States and the Soviet Union will inevitably impair the security of the West European members of the Alliance vis-à-vis Soviet military superiority in Europe if we do not succeed in removing the disparities of military power in Europe parallel to the SALT negotiations'.[53]

If a new Euro-nuclear arms race is to be avoided in the 1980s efforts at arms restraint must focus increasingly on the nuclear grey area in Europe. Will a primary concern with LRTNF and especially its IRBM/MRBM component be sufficient? Will an extension of the SALT process and the inclusion of these land-based LRTNF in SALT III, as suggested in NATO's arms control offer of 12 December 1980, prevent a new Euro-nuclear arms race? Before a discussion of the arms control strategy and options a detailed analysis of the sub-Euro-strategic balance for MRTNF and SRTNF is necessary.

2 The Balance of Medium-Range Theatre Nuclear Forces (MRTNF)

The medium-range theatre nuclear forces with a range of 100–1000 km

include on the NATO side the four Short-Range Ballistic Missiles
(SRBM): Pershing Ia, Lance, Sergeant and the French Pluton and the
fighter aircraft: Buccaneer, F-104, F-4 Phantom, Mirage III and Jaguar.
On the WTO side we include the three Soviet SRBMs: Scaleboard, and
SCUD A and SCUD B, the Soviet SLBM SS-N4 Sark, the longer range
Soviet cruise missile Shaddock SS-N-3 and the Soviet fighters: Fencer
SU-24, Foxbat Mig 25, Fitter A(SU-7) and C/D (SU-17/20), the Flogger
B/D/F, the Brewer B/C, Fishbed Mig 21.

In our comparison of IISS data for MRTNF systems we detected
a high level of stability in Western MRTNF system totals. An analysis of its two major components, SRBM and aircraft, indicates a
decrease of NATO SRBM from 875 in 1970 to about 302 and an increase in NATO aircraft from 630 in 1970 to 1198 in 1979. On the
part of the USSR and its WTO allies, given the lack of data and the
special categorisation that links LRTNF and MRTNF fighter aircraft and often MRTNF and SRTNF SRBMs, no clear trend can be
detected.

Table 6.3 compares MRTNF data from five different sources.[54] According to IISS the Western superiority in MRTNF in 1970 (3.01:1) has
been changed to a slight WTO advantage of 1.02:1 in 1979. SIPRI
detected a slight WTO advantage of 1.23:1 supported by Lutz' ration of
1.25:1. The American arms control expert J. E. Coffey argued in 1977
that in mid-1976 NATO had a clear MRTNF advantage of 2.8:1; an advantage he decreased in a later version to 1.55:1. However, the similarity
of the SIPRI and of the Lutz data is superficial because Lutz excludes aircraft while SIPRI includes MRTNF aircraft. If one combines for
heuristic purposes the SRBM-data from Lutz and the aircraft data from
SIPRI the balance shifts further in favour of the USSR (1.60:1). Based on
IISS data for 1970 and Coffey's 1976 assessment we may conclude that
the NATO advantage in MRTNF systems gradually shifted during the
1970s to a parity (as IISS maintains) or even to a slight WTO advantage as
Lutz and SIPRI state.

Because MRTNF systems will most likely not be included in arms control negotiations within the SALT III framework it may be assumed that
if LRTNF arms control talks should be successful, rechannelling effects
will focus on sub-Euro-strategic MRTNF and on short-range battlefield
systems. The Soviet development and probable deployment of the SS-22
missile and the modernisation of the NATO MRTNF systems (e.g.
neutron warheads for the Lance) may lead to a new segmentalised
MRTNF arms competition during the 1980s.

TABLE 6.3 Comparison of Subtotals of MRTNF Systems and Warheads for Five Sources[55]

| Category | L/W | NATO/WTO | Sources | | | | | J. Record | | |
			1970	IISS 1979	SIPRI Year book 1978	J.I. Coffey 1977	J.I. Coffey o.J.	Buch (1974)	ACT (1975)	D.S. Lutz 1979
Short-range missiles	L	NATO	875	302	700	266	266	180	108	303
		WTO	300	532	226	168	232	—	—	378
	W	NATO			(2233)				324	
		WTO								
	R/L		2.9:1	1:1.76	3.1:1 / 9.9:1	1.6:1	1.15:1			1:1.24
Aircraft	L	NATO	630	1198	1370	1519	1519	684	612	not included in our comparison
		WTO	(200)	1000	2320	470	921	—	—	
	W	NATO		(3740–4040)					1224	
		WTO								
	R/L		3.15:1	1.2:1 (1:3.7–1:4.4)	1:1.69	3.2:1	1.64:1			
Cruise Missiles	L	NATO		(1420)?		?	?			108 (?)
		WTO		(1224)?		?	?			
Total	L	NATO	1505	1500	2070	1785	1785	864	720	303
		WTO	500	1532	2546	638	1153	—	—	378
	W	NATO		(4272–572)	(3603)	?	?		1548	
		WTO			2546					
	R/L		3.01:1	1:1.02 (1:2.85–1:3.05)	1:1.23 (1.42:1)	2.8:1	1.55:1			1:1.25

3 The Balance of Short-Range Theatre
Nuclear Forces (SRTNF)

It is even more difficult to obtain data on the nuclear battlefield systems (SRTNF) with a range of up to 100 km. In this separate balance (Table 6.4) we distinguish among four subgroups: atomic demolition munitions (ADMs), nuclear artillery, surface-to-surface missiles (SSM) and nuclear-capable surface-to-air missiles (SAMs). No reliable data exist as to whether the USSR possesses ADMs, nuclear artillery and nuclear-capable SAMs. They number 515 for IISS, 786 for the Biden Report, 880 for Coffey up to 2340 for Lutz, while Hoffman/Steinrück assume a Western advantage in nuclear artillery of 3.33:1. Lutz maintains a Western advantage of 15.6:1. Though a general agreement exists relating to the SSMs of the WTO countries, the figures for NATO SSMs range from 91 for IISS, 128 for Coffey, 320 for Lutz and 328 for SIPRI. Only SIPRI, Record and Lutz refer to nuclear-capable NATO SAMs (Nike-Herules). Other sources, like Jane's, Collins and the handbook *The Soviet War Machine*[57] stress that the USSR also possess up to 1800 nuclear-capable SA-5 Gammon.

All five sources[58] presenting data on the nuclear battlefield systems of both alliances agree that the West maintains a clear advantage in the field of SRTNF ranging from 1.25:1 for IISS and 7.91:1 for Lutz.

One component of the SRTN modernisation, the introduction of the neutron or enhanced radiation warhead for the 155 mm and the 8 in nuclear artillery, aroused global public awareness in 1977.[59] With the increased miniaturisation of nuclear warheads (mininukes) nuclear wars may appear to be more fightable and winnable and may lower the nuclear threshold. The doctrinal consequences of these developments require detailed analysis.[60]

4 The sub-Euro-strategic Balance of MRTNF
and SRTNF Launchers

If we add the totals of MRTNF and SRTNF for IISS, SIPRI, Coffey and Lutz we obtain a sub-Euro-strategic balance (see Table 6.5) that identifies the scope of the *new grey area* that will most likely be excluded from future TNF-arms control negotiations. According to the 'worst-case' data of IISS a Soviet/WTO superiority of 2.38:1 already exists while according to the 'best-case' analysis of Lutz NATO still maintains a 5.21:1 advantage. If we compare the 'best-case' data of IISS and the 'worst-case' data of Lutz we obtain a Western advantage of 1.2:1 for IISS and of

TABLE 6.4 Comparison of Subtotals of SRTNF Systems and Warheads for Six Sources[56]

Category	L/W	NATO/WTO	IISS 1979–80	SIPRI 1978	J. Record	J. Coffey 1977	Hoffmann Steinrücke 1979	D. S. Lutz 1979	Other Sources
Atomic Demolition Munitions (ADM)	L/W	NATO	—	300	300	—	Überlegen	300	Biden: —
		WTO	—					—	
Nuclear artillery	L	NATO	515	880	1010	1799	500	2340	Biden: 786
		WTO	?			16–270	150	(150)	Res.USA: 200
	W	NATO		3000	3030		3000		
		WTO							
	R/L					111.9:1–6.66:1	3.33:1	15.6:1	
Surface-to-Surface Missiles (SSM)	L	NATO	91	328	175	128	140	320	
		WTO	206–450	303	—	255–327	?	311(650)	Biden: (—)
	W	NATO	—		175				
		WTO							
	R/L		1:2.26 1:4.95			1:1.99 1:2.55		1.03:1	
Surface-to-Air	L	NATO	—	535	720		?	709	Collins: 126 (continued)

(Table 6.4 continued)

Category	L/W	NATO / WTO	IISS 1979–80	SIPRI 1978	J. Record	J. Coffey 1977	Sources Hoffmann Steinrücke 1979	D. S. Lutz 1979	Other Sources
Missiles (SAM)		WTO							bis 1800
	W	NATO			720		—	—	
		WTO		—					
	R/L								
Total	L	NATO	606	2043	2205			3669	
		WTO	206(450)–	303	4225			461–800	
	W	NATO				1927	640		
		WTO				271–597	150+(?)		
	R/L		2.9:1 (1.25:1)	6.74:1		7.11:1– (3.23:1)	4.3:1	7.96:1 4.59:1	

3.37:1 for Lutz. SIPRI offers a Western advantage of 1.44:1 and Coffey's data indicate a Western advantage that ranges from 2.12:1 to 4.08:1.

According to our own detailed analysis both D. S. Lutz and to a certain extent J. I. Coffey portray a too optimistic assessment of Western superiority in the sub- Euro-strategic balance. Besides NATO's option 3 at MBFR that included the reduction of Western Phantoms, Pershings and of both MR and SRTNF warheads, MRTNF and SRTNF systems have not become a negotiation item of nuclear arms control talks and most likely they will be excluded from SALT III negotiations. This *new Euro-nuclear grey area* requires much political attention in order to avoid a further lowering of the nuclear threshold.

5 Summing Up the Results of the TNF Military Balances

On the level of continental strategic (LRTNF) launchers the Soviet Union presently has a clear 2:1 advantage, and a slight advantage in LRTNF warheads. If one includes qualitative criteria parity exists. If present Western projections of an annual production rate of 52 SS-20 warheads and of 25-30 Backfire bombers with 125–50 warheads are correct, the Soviet Union will achieve a clear LRTNF advantage in the 1980s that cannot be balanced by the 108 Pershing IIXR missiles and the 464 ground-launched cruise missiles, that are to be introduced in Western Europe after 1983.

For the medium-range theatre nuclear forces (MRTNF) we could observe a trend towards parity with a slight Soviet advantage. For the nuclear battlefield systems (SRTNF) we found a clear Western advantage (three to eightfold). Under worst-case assumptions even in this category we can already assume an approximate parity. If we combine MRTNF and SRTNF launchers to a *subcontinental strategic balance* we still obtain a clear overall Western advantage (ranging from 1.2:1 to 5.2:1). Because NATO still maintains a clear advantage in these two categories for the present there was never any inclination to include this *new grey area* in prospective arms control deliberations.

THE FAILURE OF THE TRADITIONAL ARMS CONTROL APPROACH

Arms control has essentially failed. Three decades of US-Soviet negotiations to limit arms competition have done little more than

TABLE 6.5 The Sub-Euro-strategic Balance of MRTNF and SRTNF Launchers[61]

	L R/L	NATO WTO	IISS	Sources SIPRI	Coffey	Lutz
SRTNF	L	NATO	606	2043	1927	3669
		WTO	206 (450)–	303	271–597	461–800
	R/L		2.9:1	6.74:1	7.11:1	7.96:1
			(1.25:1)		(3.23:1)	4.59:1
MRTNF	L	NATO	1500	2070	1785	303
		WTO	1532	2546	(638–1153)	378
			(4272–572)			
	R/L		1:1.02	1:1.23	2.8:1	1:1.25
			(1:2.85–3.05)		(155:1)	
SRTNF + MRTNF	L	NATO	2106	4113	3712	3972
		WTO	1738 (1982)	2849	(909–1424)	764–1178
			(4478–778)		1235–5022)	
			(4722–5022)			
	R/L		1.2:1 (1.06:1)	1.44:1	4.08:1	*5.2:1*
			1:2.13 (1:2.38)		3.0:1–2.12:1	3.37:1

codify the arms race. . . . In this stage of Soviet-American relations, it may be wise to think of arms control negotiations essentially as confidence- and stability-building exercises.[62] (Leslie H. Gelb, former director of the State Department Bureau of Political-Military Affairs, 1977–79.)

With this sceptical remark one of NATO's leading arms control experts recently started a critical reassessment of the traditional arms control practice. After two years' of practical experience, Gelb confirmed many of the criticisms raised earlier by both peace researchers and liberal arms controllers[63] who had concluded that the piecemeal approach to arms control did not lead to any disarmament, with the sole exception of the Convention on Biological Weapons.[64] The American debate on the ratification of SALT II in 1979 emphasised the negative impact of three mechanisms, identified by Rathjans, Chayes and Ruina, by which arms control efforts can provide an impetus to weapons programmes: the tendency to achieve a symmetry at a high level ('levelling up'), the impact of intragovernmental negotiations (buying off the military, rechannelling effect) and the effect of intergovernmental negotiations (bargaining chips).[65]

The traditional causative theory of armaments dynamics (action-reaction theorem)[66] has been increasingly challenged by many empirical studies focusing on various domestic and societal determinants of armaments dynamics, such as economic, technological, bureaucratic, psychological and ideological factors.[67] Allison and Morris in their exploration of the determinants of American strategic forces in the 1960s concluded: 'that the weapons in the American and Soviet force posture are predominantly the result of factors internal to each nation'. What conclusions may be drawn from these studies on the failure of the traditional arms control approach and on the causes of armaments dynamics?

A new approach to arms restraint and reductions should avoid many of the fallacies of the traditional arms control approach. This new approach should pay more attention to the various domestic determinants of the weapons acquisition process and to the problems of military innovation ('qualitative aspects'). Arms limitation efforts for 'grey-area systems' should address besides the hard data of the military balance also the domestic roots of the expressed concern ('perception of the Soviet threat', 'credibility of the American nuclear umbrella', legitimation techniques for TNF modernisation). The potential political implications of hardware decisions should be attributed as much weight as the projections of potential Soviet TNF arms production during the 1980s. The new consultation mechanism, established by NATO in December 1979, may provide a forum for a longer term politico-military assessment for the implications of the introduction of new non-verifiable weapons systems on arms control and *détente* in Europe.

CONCLUSIONS AND GENERAL SUGGESTIONS FOR ARMS RESTRAINT IN THE GREY AREA

The double decision by NATO's foreign and defence ministers both to produce and to deploy 108 Pershing IIXR missiles and 464 ground-launched cruise missiles, linked with the unilateral withdrawal offer of 1000 American nuclear warheads from Europe and the proposal to include certain portions of the LRTNF potential in future bilateral SALT III negotiations, has been rejected by the Soviet Union in 1980. After the American decision to postpone the SALT II ratification till after the 1980 Presidential election, as a direct response to the Soviet intervention into Afghanistan, most probably no arms control negotiations dealing with the Euro-nuclear grey area will start during 1980 in the framework of SALT III. This 'icy intermission' caused by the increase in tensions between the two superpowers and their respective military alliances, NATO and WTO, should be used for a fundamental reconsideration of NATO's decision of December 1979. If the Soviet Union shoul be ready to offer an immediate halt in the production and deployment of its SS-20 missiles, NATO should be ready to offer a non-deployment moratorium for its 464 GLCMs in Europe.

However, decisive for the discussion of potential future developments and for new initiatives for arms restraint will be the state of US–Soviet relations, the domestic politics within both superpowers and their implications for the foreign policy leverage for European countries and on the relationship between developed and developing countries. At least two alternative trends for East–West relations during the early 1980s appear to be plausible:[68]

(1) A further worsening of Soviet–American relations with a fallback to a new cold war and a halt in the co-operation in the fields of arms control, trade, functional co-operation and with a more limited crisis management will lead to a basic change in international relations.

(2) After a short deterioration in US–Soviet relations, once the

Presidential election is over and the succession problems in the Soviet Union have been solved, a new period of co-operation will recommence.

Under the first set of assumptions both the ratification of SALT II and the start of grey-area arms control negotiations appear to be doubtful. If the worsening is only temporary, then SALT II ratification may be likely. A policy of mutual restraint abiding to the SALT II restrictions may create pre-conditions for a conceptual reassessment of the overall arms control policy. Given these alternative foreign policy frameworks potential consequences on TNF modernisation and 'grey-area arms control' will be discussed within the framework of three scenarios.

Scenario A: If the political worst-case assumptions (new cold war) should become reality, two alternative consequences for TNF appear to be possible:

(a) A new cold-war mentality will eliminate the domestic opposition to the introduction of new TNF in Europe. Most probably more than 1000 modern and highly accurate ground- sea- and air-launched cruise missiles (GLCM, SLCM, ALCM) will be produced and deployed in Western Europe. A new Euro-nuclear arms race in all three TNF groups (LRTNF, MRTNF, SRTNF) will be conceivable.

(b) Even if a return to a cold-war framework should occur, with an intensified competition of alternative ideologies and social systems, new global conditions (scarcity of resources, North–South conflict formation) will nevertheless persuade both alliances to continue their co-operation in a limited scale and to prevent an uncontrolled Euro-nuclear arms race, if only for economic reasons.

Scenario B: If we assume that the competition of the alternative social systems and military alliances, especially among the two superpowers, will focus on the ideological, economic and humanitarian issue area, a policy of limited co-operation in the area of crisis management and arms control will most likely continue:

(a) Under political worst-case assumptions SALT II will not be ratified in 1981, in order to prevent a defeat in the US Senate. However, both governments declare unilaterally or jointly that they will apply the SALT II agreement in their weapons procurement

policies. One rechannelling effect might be an increased emphasis to be given by both blocs to their Euro-strategic systems. One consequence might be a Euro-centred nuclear arms race leading to a decoupling from the American nuclear umbrella.
(b) SALT II will be ratified by the US Senate with various amendments relating to continental strategic systems in Europe. SALT III negotiations will start dealing in two tiers with central strategic systems and with selected LRTNF based on the traditional arms control approach. This approach may cause rechannelling effects into the new grey area (MRTNF/SRTNF) in Europe.

Scenario C: Starting from optimistic assumptions that after a short period of worsened East–West relations a new era of co-operation in all major issue areas of *détente* will resume, at least two options appear to be plausible:

(a) Salt II will be ratified by the US Senate with amendments and SALT III negotiations will resume immediately within the traditional framework (B, b).
(b) After SALT II ratification in 1981, SALT III negotiations will resume focusing on central strategic systems. SALT III will deal with the most likely strategic war options and scenarios (mission approach) and with the control of the rapid change in military technology (qualitative restraints). 'Grey-area systems' will be discussed in a separate forum on Theatre Arms Limitation Talks (TALT) under active European participation. TALT will follow a new arms control approach that includes geographical (Europe), mission (war options and military doctrines) and weapons systems components. TALT will address nuclear weapons in Europe of long, medium and short range (LRTNF, MRTNF, SRTNF).

Our suggestions for arms control in the grey area are orientated at the latter option (Scenario C, option b).

Arms control efforts dealing with the grey area should start out from a wide definition comprising all substrategic systems at present deployed within the geographical boundaries or targeted against the European territory by non-central systems (LR, MR, SRTNF). At least four arms control fora may be considered: *a two-tier SALT III* with the first tier dealing with central systems and the second focusing on all European-based TNF under active participation of European countries in the preparatory consultation and in the negotiation process. Alternatively, separate *Theatre Arms Limitation Talks* (TALT) may be started, irrespective of the fate of SALT II in the US Senate, as a *new bilateral TALT forum* of the two superpowers, as a *multilateral forum* of all four European nuclear powers, adding France and Great Britain, or as a *multilateral TALT forum* representing besides the four nuclear powers those countries deploying nuclear weapons or four countries each of the NATO, the WTO and the neutral and non-aligned countries. We would recommend a multilateral TALT forum of the four nuclear powers or of those European countries who own or deploy a significant number of nuclear weapons.

A new aproach to grey-area arms control should combine the negotiated treaty approach with reciprocated unilateral restraints (RUR) or with gradual and reciprocated initiatives in tension-reduction (GRIT).[69] A policy of mutual example and restraint — as practised in 1964[70] — may provide the general political atmosphere for more successful arms control negotiations, avoiding the high price of the traditional approach as a result of rechannelling effects, of levelling up and of bargaining chips.[71] For Christoph Bertram both the RUR and GRIT concepts are of a limited utility as a supplement to the treaty solution. 'To replace arms-control accords by a web of unilateral undertakings is, therefore, no realistic way out of the arms-control dilemma posed by technological change.'[72]

An alternative approach to grey-area arms control should draw conclusions from the empirical studies on the domestic societal and international determinants of armaments dynamics.[73] On the national level, the development of new procedures such as the introduction of arms control impact statements[74] and the institutional upgrading of arms control in the foreign and military decision-making process[75] as well as conversion strategies may contribute to more favourable domestic conditions for successful arms control negotiations.

As far as the international systems level of negotiations on grey-area systems is concerned, we suggest three elements of a new approach:

  (i) a new regional and geographical component;
 (ii) a mission component that deals with military options and doctrines;
(iii) a system component.

Grey-area arms control negotiations should deal with the European theatre within its geographical boundaries. Geographical elements of the regional component may comprise nuclear-free buffer zones close to the forward edge of any potential battlefield and limited nuclear-free zones in Europe, e.g. in the Balkans and in Scandinavia.

The mission component of grey-area arms control should concentrate on the different theories and military doctrines relating to deterrence and the potential use of nuclear weapons in Europe. It should make nuclear surprise attack options, pre-emptive nuclear strikes and forced nuclear escalation as a result of forward deployment of nuclear battlefield systems and of atomic demolition munitions less likely. The mission component would have to take into account geographical, technological and doctrinal asymmetries. Restrictions on the deployment and the use of theatre nuclear weapons, as suggested in the draft of the Pugwash movement for a non-use of nuclear weapons agreement[76] as well as restraints on the introduction of new ADMs and nuclear artillery shells or of mobile land-based LRTNF may enhance the warning time against a nuclear surprise attack or, by removing relatively vulnerable land-based TNF, reduce the incentives for a nuclear pre-emptive strike.

The system component should concentrate on those theatre nuclear weapons that tend to lower the nuclear threshold, e.g. more usable battlefield systems such as mininukes with enhanced radiation warheads. Alternative defence and security structures that stress small, highly mobile troops armed with sophisticated anti-tank weapons (precision-guided munitions)[77] may permit a gradual downgrading of SRTNF and of land-based systems in general.

A new approach to grey-area arms control could deal with quantitative and qualitative constraints and with confidence-building measures. The following quantitative constraints could be considered: limitation or freeze of the number of delivery systems, reduction of the number of nuclear warheads, moratorium for the introduction of additional theatre nuclear mobile systems (e.g. for SS-20), moratorium for the production and deployment of long-range cruise missiles, reduction and eventual elimination of dual-capable systems, production and deployment freezes for new Euro-strategic launchers and for battlefield systems. One goal might be the achievement or maintenance of an overall parity relating to TNF.

Qualitative constraints may include the following measures: restraint of modernisation and growth beyond current levels, introduction of procedures that require a 'pausing' before new nuclear weapons are being deployed, agreements on non-development, non-production, non-deployment of new grey-area systems, prohibition of testing of new TNF-launchers and warheads.

Confidence-building measures for TNF may include the prohibition of any exercises for war-fighting under nuclear conditions, the multi-lateralisation of the existing crisis management agreements and the establishment of a permanent crisis management structure along the lines of the Standing Consultative Commission of SALT, efforts to increase openness and transparency and an improved verification system, e.g. by the creation of a European satellite monitoring and verification authority organised along the lines of the UN peacekeeping forces that may be dominated by the European neutral and non-aligned states.[78]

The icy intermission in East–West arms control negotiations should be used for a conceptual reassessment of the traditional arms control approach to grey-area systems in Europe. Any failure to enter into an arms control dialogue on nuclear weapons in and for Europe may spur the technological competition and the introduction of additional TNF in Europe, thereby contributing to an intensified Euro-nuclear arms race.

In order to get grey-area arms control negotiations started more than 130 scientists, former government officials and members of parliament urged those governments concerned in an 'Appeal for a nuclear weapons moratorium':[79]

— to halt production and deployment immediately of the missiles known as SS-20 (production and deployment freeze);
— not to decide in December 1979 or later for the production and deployment of any new long-range theatre nuclear missiles in Europe as long as the production freeze is being observed (production and deployment moratorium);
— to enter into immediate negotiations with the aim not to enhance the existing nuclear potentials and progressively reduce the overall number of nuclear weapons in Europe.

Even after the NATO decisions of December 1979 and after the events in Afghanistan the message of the Amsterdam appeal remains unchanged.

NOTES
This contribution has been written in the context of a research project on 'United States policy of détente (1969–1980)' that is being funded by the German Association on Peace and Conflict Research in Bonn, FRG. Previous versions of this paper have been presented to various international conferences, e.g.: 'Gray Area Systems — Heuristic Arms Control Considerations' in *Proceedings of the Twenty-Eighth Pugwash Conference on Science and World Affairs*, Varna, Bulgaria, 1–5 September 1978; 'Global Aspects of Disarmament and Security'

(London), pp. 91–8; 'Gray Area Systems and Problems of European Security — Suggestions for policy-oriented Peace Research Efforts', paper for 8th Nordic Conference on Peace Research, Turku, Finland, 11–13 January, 1979 (62 pp., unpublished); 'Gray Area Systems and Problems of European Security — A West German Perspective on the Arms Control Potential', paper for the 20th International Studies Association Convention in Toronto, Canada, 21–24 March, 1979 (57 pp., unpublished); 'Nuclear Weapons of the "Gray Area" Between SALT and M(B)FR and Problems of European Security', Paper for the Pugwash Symposium on Impact of Current Political Developments and Arms Control Efforts on European Security, Helsinki, Finland, 19–21 April 1979, to be published in Jorma K. Miettinen (ed.), Helsinki 1980; 'The Arms Race Potential of Gray Area Systems: Possible Worst Case Scenarios and Political Suggestions', paper distributed and discussed at the 29th Pugwash Conference, Mexico City, Mexico, 18–23 July 1979; 'Mittelstreckenraketen und Rüstungskontrolloptionen' in *Die Neue Gesellschaft*, October 1979, pp. 910–14; with Jørgen Dragsdahl and Paul Rusman, 'Kernkoppen: balans of wedloop' in *de Volkskrant*, 8 December, 1979; Brauch/Rusman/Dragsdahl, 'Forvirrende og vildledende grundlag for NATO raketter' in *Information* (Copenhagen), 27 November 1979. The results of these various studies will be contained in a monograph, 'Euronuklearer Rüstungswettlauf oder militärische Entspannung, Frankfurt (Haag & Herchen)1980.

1. Lothar Ruehl, 'The Gray Area Problem' in Christoph Bertram (ed.), *The Future of Arms Control, Part I, Beyond SALT II*, *Adelphi Papers*, No. 141, Spring 1978, pp. 25–34; Jack H. Harris and William D. Bajusz, 'Arms control and Gray-Area Systems' in *Air Force Magazine*, February 1978, pp. 36–9; Robert Metzger and Paul Doty, 'Arms Control Enters the Gray Area' in *International Security*, Winter 1978/1979, Vol 3, No. 3, pp. 17–52: Robert S. Metzger, 'Strategic Arms Control and West European Interests', Report on a Conference Co-sponsored by Aspen Institute Berlin, The International Institute for Strategic Studies, The Aspen Arms Control Consortium, 13–16 June, 1978, Aspen Institute for Humanistic Studies 78/3; M. Milshtein, 'Tactical nuclear weapons: problems of definition and application' in Frank Barnaby (ed.), *Tactical Nuclear Weapons: European Perspectives* (SIPRI, London 1978), pp. 169–74.

2. M. Leitenberg, 'Background information on tactical nuclear weapons (primarily in the European context)' in Barnaby (ed.), op. cit., pp. 3–136.

3. James R. Schlesinger, *The Theatre Nuclear Force Posture in Europe*, A Report to the United States Congress in compliance with Public Law 93-365, Washington, April 1975.

4. Jeffrey Record, *U.S. Nuclear Weapons in Europe, Issues and Alternatives* (The Brookings Institution, Washington, 1974), p. 3.

5. M. Milshtein (*see* note 1), p. 173.

6. *Der Bundesminister der Verteidigung, Weißbuch 1979, Zur Sicherheit der Bundesrepublik Deutschland und zur Entwicklung der Bundesweshr* (Bonn 1979), pp. 105–9.

7. Uwe Nerlich, 'Zwischen Verteidigungs- und Verhandlungspolitik: Zur Auseinander-setzung über die sogenannten "Neutronenwaffen" in *Stiftung Wissenschaft und Politik* (ed.), Polarität und Interdependenz. (Beiträge zu Fragen der Internationationalen Politik, Baden-Baden 1978), pp. 187–202.

8. John B. Ritch, III. and Alfred Friendly, Jr., *SALT and the Allies*, A Staff

Report to the Subcommittee on European Affairs of the Committee on Foreign Relations, United States Senate, Washington October 1979 (Biden-Report), p. 1.

9. Harris, Bajusz (*see* note 1), pp. 36–9.
10. Willy Brandt, 'Dokumentation: Thesen zur Abrüstung' in *Die Neue Gesellschaft*, December 1977, pp. 999–1001.
11. L. Ruehl (*see* note 1), p. 25.
12. For text *see*: 'Kommuniqué über eine Sondersitzung der Außen-und Verteidigungs-minister der an der integrierten Verteidigungsstruktur beteiligten Mitgliedstaaten des Nordatlantikpakts in Brüssel am 12. Dezember 1979' in Europa-Archiv, 2/1980, January 25, 1980, pp. D 35–D 37; *see also NATO-Review 6/1979.*
13. Biden-Report (*see* note 8), p. 1.
14. Catherine McArdle Kelleher, *Germany and the Politics of Nuclear Weapons* (New York, London, 1975); Dieter Mahncke, *Nukleare Mitwirkung: Die Bundesrepublik Deutschland in der atlantischen Allianz 1954–1970* (Berlin, New York, 1972); John D. Steinbruner, *The Cybernetic Theory of Decision, New Dimensions of Political Decision* (Princeton 1974).
15. Biden Report (*see* note 8), p. 3.
16. Schlensinger Report (*see* note 3), p. 1.
17. Morton H. Halperin, *Defense Strategies for the Seventies* (Boston, 1971), p. 5.
18. John Newhouse and others, *U.S. Troops in Europe: Issues, Costs, and Choices*, Brookings Institution, Washington 1971, p. 45.
19. Robert M. Lawrence, 'On Tactical War; Part I, *Revue Militaire Générale*, January 1971, p. 46.
20. Department of the Army, Field Manual 100-30 (Test), Tactical Nuclear Operations, Headquarters, Department of the Army, August 1971, pp. 2–1.
21. Milshtein (*see* note 1), p. 173.
22. Milshtein (*see* note 1), p. 173.
23. M. Leitenberg (*see* note 2), p. 3.
24. Johann Graf von Kielmannsegg, 'A German View of Western Defence' in *RUSI Journal*, March 1974, republished in *Strategic Review*, 1974 and in *Military Review*, November 1974.
25. Schlesinger Report (*see* note 3), pp. 16–18.
26. Leitenberg (*see* note 2), p. 4.
27. Milshtein (*see* note 1), p. 170.
28. Record (*see* note 4), p. 7.
29. The International Institute for Strategic Studies (IISS), *The Military Balance 1979–1980*, p. 90.
30. Biden Report (*see* note 8), p. 4.
31. Biden Report (*see* note 8), p. 4.
32. Schlesinger Report (*see* note 3), pp. 14–15.
33. M. Leitenberg (*see* note 2), p. 5; Military Applications of Nuclear Technology, Joint Committee on Atomic Energy, Congress of the United States, 93rd Congress.
34. M. Leitenberg (*see* note 2), p. 17.
35. M. Leitenberg (*see* note 2), p. 78; IISS, *The Military Balance 1970–1971*, p. 95; J. Record, *Sizing Up the Soviet Army* (Washington 1975), p. 40.

36. J. Erickson, 'Soviet military capabilities in Europe' in *Journal of the Royal United Services Institute for Defense Studies*, Vol. 120, No.3, March 1975.

37. Friedrich Zimmermann, 'Verschoben zugunsten Moskaus — Tatsachen und Schlußfolgerungen' in *Bayernkurier*, October 27, 1979.

38. For a detailed analysis see my study 'Euronuklearer Rüstungswettlauf oder militärische Entspannung' (Frankfurt, 1980).

39. The figures have been taken from eight issues of IISS' annual publication, *The Military Balance*, from 1970–71 to 1979–80.

40. For details see my study 'Euronuklearer Rüstungswettlauf' (note 1).

41. Biden Report (*see* note 8), pp. 38–9.

42. Hubertus Hoffmann und Rolf Steinrücke, *Rüstung und Abrüstung im euronuklearen Bereich — Die Mitwirkungsmöglichkeiten der europäischen Staaten an den SALT III — Verhandlungen —* Eine Kurzstudie im Auftrage der Bundestagsabgeordneten (Peter Kurt Würzbach und Markus Berger, Washington/Bonn, April–May 1979); *Weißbuch* 1979 (*see* note 6); Michael Forster, 'Zur Datendiskussion des Kräfteverhältnisses bei den Nuklearwaffen großer Reichweite in Europa (LRTNF)', distributed by Paul Neumann, Chairman of the working group on security questions, SPD-faction in the Bundestag, 26 November, 1979; Metzger/Doty (*see* note 1); IISS, *The Military Balance* 1979–80, pp. 114–19; Dieter S. Lutz, *Das militärische Kräfteverhältnis im Bereich euronuklearer Waffensysteme. Ein Forschungsbericht, ISFH-Forschungsberichte*, Heft 12, October 1979.

43. For details see my study 'Euronuklearer Rüstungswettlauf' (note 1).

44. For sources see note 42. Table 6.2 summarises the results of a detailed system-by-system comparison of data contained in my study on the Euronuclear arms race.

45. Hoffmann and Steinrücke (*see* note 42) based their analysis on worst-case assumptions offering lower figures for NATO and higher figures for WTO counties. See my study 'Euronuklearer Rüstungswettlauf' for detailed criticisms.

46. The German Defence White Paper (*see* note 6) does not include the 400–80 SLBM warheads on 40–8 Poseidon C3 SLBM assigned to SACEUR. The White Paper does not count the sea-based US fighters stationed on US carriers in the Mediterranean. However, it does include 150 Soviet Fencer fighter bombers without mentioning equivalent fighters of NATO (F-104, F-4).

47. M. Forster (*see* note 42) does include 400 Poseidon C-3 warheads but he neglects American sea-based fighters. Assuming a reload capability for the SS-4 and the SS-20 Forster concludes that the WTO countries possess 50 times as many IRBM MRBM than NATO countries. Forster's study comes close to the worst-case analysis of Hoffman/Steinrücke.

48. Lutz assumes the highest Western advantage in SLBM launchers and warheads and the lowest Western inferiority in IRBM/MRBM. Lutz 'best-case' assumptions are somewhat modified by the Biden sample. In his original sample Lutz had assumed a NATO superiority in LRTNF launchers (except aircraft). LRTNF warheads and a qualitative edge in favour of the West as well.

49. While Metzger/Doty's data on SLBM and IRBM/MRBM warheads indicate only a slight Soviet advantage, they assume a higher Soviet advantage in nuclear warheads carried by aircraft. In general, Metzger and Doty's analysis

indicates a better knowledge of publicly available sources and a higher level of sophistication in the interpretation of the data.

50. As the only study the IISS analysis developed a methodology for the assessment of the qualitative features of LRTNF and MRTNF systems. Western criticism of the IISS methodology seems to be highly political in nature. The main thrust of the IISS results remained unchanged for the smaller IISS-sample for LRTNF.

51. IISS, *The Military Balance* 1970–71, p. 117.

52. Chancellor Helmut Schmidt, Talk to the Social Democratic Parliamentary Group in the Bundestag, 6 February, 1979.

53. Helmut Schmidt, 'The 1977 Alastair Buchan Memorial Lecture' in *Survival*, Vol *XX*, No.1, January/February 1978, pp. 3-4.

54. IISS, *The Military Balance* 1970–71 and 1979–80 (London 1970 and 1979); SIPRI *Yearbook 1978*, Appendix 14B, NATO and WTO nuclear weapons and delivery vehicles deployed in Europe, 1977 pp. 423–9; J. Coffey, 'Arms Control and Tactical Nuclear Forces and European Security' in Frank Barnaby (ed.) (*see* note 1), pp. 178–80; J. I. Coffey, 'Arms Control, Tactical Nuclear Forces and European Security, Occasional Papers, Center for Arms Control and International Security Studies, Pittsburgh, without year: J. Record for his book (*see* note 4); J. Record, 'U.S. tactical nuclear weapons in Europe: 7000 warheads in search of a rationale ', in *Arms Control Today*, Vol. 4, No. 4, April 1974, pp. 3–13; D. S. Lutz (*see* note 42).

55. J. I. Coffey, *Arms Control and European Security — A Guide to East-West Negotiations* (London 1977), pp. 248–9.

56. IISS, *The Military Balance*, 1979–80 (London, 1979); SIPRI *Yearbook 1978* (London, 1978); J. Record, 'U.S. tactical nuclear weapons in Europe: 7000 warheads in search for a rationale' in *Arms Control Today*, Vol. 4, No. 4, April 1974, pp. 3–13; Coffey (*see* 2 sources in note 54); Hoffmann/Steinrücke (*see* note 42); D. S. Lutz (*see* note 42); Biden Report (*see* note 8).

57. Jane's Pocket Book 10, *Missiles*, New Edition, ed Ronald Pretty (London, 1978), p. 100; John M. Collins, *American and Soviet Military Trends Since the Cuban Missile Crisis* (Washington, 1978), pp. 143–5; John M. Collins, *Imbalance of Power — Shifting U.S.-Soviet Military Strengths* (San Rafael, London, 1978), pp. 98–9; Ray Bonds (ed.), *The Soviet War Machine* (Secaucus London, 1976), p. 214.

58. *See* note 56.

59. See Hans Günter Brauch, 'Enhanced Radiation Warhead — A West German Perspective', in *Arms Control Today*, June 1978, pp. 1–4; Brauch, 'Neutron Weapons — Potential Arms Control Linkages and Breakthroughs' in *Bulletin of Peace Proposals*, Vol. 9, 3/1978, pp. 227–33.

60. F. Barnaby, 'The irrationality of current doctrines', in F. Barnaby (ed.), *Tactical Nuclear Weapons: European Perspectives* (SIPRI, London 1978) pp. 213–22; J. Miettinen, ' ''Mini-nukes'' and enhanced radiation weapons' in F. Barnaby, op.cit., pp. 223–46; J. Prawitz, 'Mini-nukes and non-aligned defence. The case of Sweden' in Barnaby, op. cit., pp. 247–61.

61. *See* notes 55 and 56 for sources.

62. Leslie H. Gelb, 'The Future of Arms Control, A Glass Half Full. . .' in *Foreign Policy*, No. 36, Fall 1979, pp. 21–32 (p. 21).

63. Dieter Senghass, *Aufrüstung durch Rüstungskontrolle — Uber symbolischen Gebrauch von Politik*, (Stuttgart — Berlin — Köln — Mainz, 1972); G. W. Rathjens, Abram Chayes and J. P. Ruina, *Nuclear Arms Control Agreements: Process and Impact* (Washington, 1974); Graham T. Allison and Frederic A. Morris, 'Agreement and Arms Control: Exploring the Determinants of Military Weapons' in Franklin Long, George Rathjens (eds.), *Arms, Defense Policy, and Arms Control* (New York, 1976), pp. 99–129; Christoph Bertram, *The Future of Arms Control: Part II — Arms Control and Technological Change: Elements of a New Approach* in *Adelphi Papers*, No. 146 (London, 1978); Hans Günter Brauch, *Entwicklungen und Ergebnisse der Friedensforschung (1969–1978). Eine Zwischenbilanz und konkrete Vorschläge für das zweite Jahrzehnt* (Frankfurt am Main, 1979).

64. Rathjens, Chayes, Ruina (*see* note 63); Jane M. O. Sharp, 'MBFR as Arms Control' in *Arms Control Today*, Vol. 6, No. 4, April 1976, pp. 1–3.

65. Rathjens, Chayes, Ruina (*see* note 63); B. James Woolsey, 'Chipping Away at the Bargains' in Franklin B. Long and George W. Rathjens (*see* note 63), pp. 175–196; Robert G. Gray and Robert J. Bressler, 'Why Weapons Make Poor Bargaining Chips' in *The Bulletin of the Atomic Scientists*, September 1977.

66. Lewis Fry Richardson, *Arms and Insecurity: A Mathematical Study of the Causes and Origins of War* (London, 1960).

67. Dieter Senghass, *Rüstung und Militarismus* (Frankfurt, 1972); Hans Günter Brauch, *Struktureller Wandel und Rüstungspolitik der USA (1940–1950). Zur Weltführungsrolle und ihren innenpolitischen Bedingungen* (Ann Arbor; London, 1977).

68. Hans Günter Brauch, Euronuklearer Rüstungswettlauf oder militärische Entspannung (*see* introductory note 2).

69. Herbert Scoville, Jr., 'A Different Approach to Arms Control — Reciprocal Unilateral Restraint' in David Carlton and Carlo Schaerf (eds.), *Arms Control and Technological Innovation* (London, 1977), pp. 170–5; Charles Osgood, *An Alternative to War and Surrender* (Urbana, 1962); Charles Osgood, 'GRIT for MBFR: A Proposal for Unfreezing Force-Levels Postures in Europe' in *Proceedings of the Twenty-Seventh Pugwash Conference on Science and World Affairs*, Munich, 24–29 August 1977 (London, 1978), pp. 385–9; Amitai Etzioni, *The Hard Way to Peace* (New York, 1962); Donald Granberg, 'GRIT in the Final Quarter: Reversing the Arms Race through Unilateral Initiatives' in *Bulletin of Peace Proposals*, Vol. 9, No. 3, 1978, pp. 210–21; Ernst-Otto Czempiel, 'Peace as a Strategy for Systemic Change' in *Bulletin of Peace Proposals*, Vol. 10, No. 1, 1979.

70. Abraham S. Becker, 'Appendix B: The U.S.-USSR "Mutual Example Episode", 1963–1964' in Becker, *Military Expenditure Limitation for Arms Control, Problems and Prospects, With a Documentary History of Recent Proposals* (Cambridge, 1977).

71. Hans Günter Brauch, Chapter 9: 'Rüstungsdynamik und Rüstungskontrolle — Rüstungskontrollansätze und Rüstungskontrollaussichten in Europe' in Brauch, *Entwicklungen und Ergebnisse der Friedensforschung* (*see* note 63), pp. 260–311.

72. Christoph Bertram (*see* note 63), p. 17.

73. Hans Günter Brauch, 'Confidence Building Measures and Disarmament Strategy', paper presented to the 11th International Political Science Association World Congress, Moscow, 12–18 August, 1979 and to the 8th IPRA Congress in Königstein (FRG), 19–22 August, 1979. An abridged version is being published in *Current Research on Peace and Violence* (Tampere, 1980).
74. Duncan Clarke, *Politics of Arms Control, The Role and Effectiveness of the U.S. Arms Control and Disarmament Agency* (New York, London, 1979).
75. Volker Rittberger (ed.), *Abrüstungsplanung in der Bundesrepublik, Aufgabe, Probleme, Perspektiven. Studien zur Abrüstungsplanung*, Vol. 1 (Baden-Baden, 1979), pp. 103–14.
76. 'Submissions by the Pugwash Executive Committee to the UN Special Session on Disarmament: (a) Outline of a Convention for the Renunciation of Nuclear Weapons' in *Pugwash Newsletter*, Vol. 15, No. 4, May 1978, pp. 106–8.
77. H. Afheldt, 'Tactical nuclear weapons and European security' in F. Barnaby (*see* note 1), pp. 262–95.
78. IPRA Disarmament Study Group, Building Confidence in Europe in *Bulletin of Peace Proposals*, 1/1980.
79. 'Appeal for a Nuclear Weapons Moratorium', in: *Militärpolitik Dokumentation Frankfurt* (Haag & Herchen), 1980.

7 The Neutron Bomb and Nuclear Disarmament in Europe

JORMA K. MIETTINEN

(This paper was rewritten in January 1980)

For a long time after their introduction to Europe a quarter-century ago, tactical nuclear weapons were a 'taboo' subject, too sensitive to be publicly discussed. In Western Europe few people questioned in public the proclaimed deterrent value and possible use of these dubious weapons until the summer of 1977, when an emotional debate on the neutron bomb exploded. In Eastern Europe the justification for tactical nuclear weapons on the part of the Warsaw Pact has never been publicly questioned; all criticism there has been directed at Western weaponry alone.

In the West the neutron bomb was debated not only by peace researchers and disarmament lobbyists, but by political factions, parliaments, governments, the press and the general public as well. The East, for its part, carried out a specific propaganda campaign against the neutron bomb. The reason for such interest in one particular tactical weapon probably goes back to the early, emotional releases in the American press (June 1977) where it was held up as an unprecedented evil. Then, some NATO officials, European politicians and American columnists further fuelled the debate by defending it naïvely, as if it were an omnipotent superweapon. In such a charged atmosphere the forest tends to be overlooked for the trees.

It also turned out that NATO, as a loose alliance of democratic states, was unable to handle this political issue coherently. President Carter demanded that the Federal Republic of Germany, a nuclear-free state, which has a strong anti-nuclear lobby and a sensitive, special relationship with the East, should openly support the production and deployment of this contradictory new weapon in Europe. When Chancellor

Schmidt had — at considerable political cost — acquired such support, President Carter postponed the decision. But this effectively blurred the issue; the new warheads would be produced with the structural features providing for conversion to neutron warheads simply by inserting a separate hydrogen container. Thus new dual-capable warheads are being produced and only an 'insertion' decision by the US President is needed to convert them to neutron warheads. The time needed for the conversion is not known, but is probably very short and may be only a matter of days.

The main reason why the neutron warhead should not be deployed remains in the view of the author the fact that it is, as are all nuclear weapons, illegal. Its development, like that of the new mobile Soviet IRBM 'SS-20', is against the commitment the nuclear weapon powers made in the Nonproliferation Treaty (NPT), 'to progress towards nuclear disarmament'. The development of this new weapon not only contravenes the NPT, but also is at variance with the recent proposals for a ban on radiological weapons, made by the USA and USSR. To ban weapons containing fission products (beta- and gamma-emitters) while simultaneously deploying a new type of nuclear weapon, which is based on the vastly more toxic neutron radiation, is at the least hypocritical.

Neutrons are slow killers. A lethal dose of fast neutrons — say 5 Gray (500 rads) — kills in a few weeks, after a painful radiation illness. For a faster effect upon the enemy, doses of 80–180 Gy are 'recommended'. To generate such doses against soldiers inside tanks, doses up to two to five times greater outside the tanks are necessary, i.e. 160–900 Gy. When used against tanks in cities, neutron warheads are thus likely to submit large numbers of the civilian population to the deleterious effects of fast neutrons. The survivors would suffer the delayed effects of neutron radiation, e.g. different forms of cancer and accelerated ageing. The carcinogenic effects of fast neutrons are up to twenty times higher than those of gamma radiation. Probably serious, though not yet well known, are the genetic effects of fast neutrons upon man. Submitting large numbers of young people to even a fraction of one Gy could be disastrous for future generations of Europeans. Quite large numbers of people would be subjected to such doses in areas where neutron weapons were used in densely populated cities.

The protagonists of the neutron bomb say that it will not be used against tanks in urban areas, only against tank formation in the open. Such noble intentions are not going to hold in war. When nations are fighting for their existence, they try to defeat the enemy forces wherever they can be reached. If cities were to be regarded as sanctuaries, then the enemy would inevitably direct his major offensive through urban areas.

The fact that effectiveness of the neutron bomb depends upon fast neutrons makes it a dubious weapon on legal grounds when compared even with other nuclear weapons. Over a period of many years the majority of member states in the United Nations have been attempting to have nuclear weapons banned as illegal under international law. The nuclear weapon states have opposed such resolutions, claiming that the weapon effects of nuclear explosives are qualitatively similar to those of conventional high explosives: overpressure and thermal radiation. In the case of 'classical' nuclear weapons the lethal radius of those effects is indeed wider than that of the initial nuclear radiation.

But the neutron bomb is not protected by such an argument. On this basis it becomes a dubious weapon because its effect is based on highly toxic neutron radiation which is characterised by its delayed effects and its potential to cause 'unnecessary suffering'.

The neutron warheads themselves do not constitute a dramatic change in the sense that quantitatively their weapon effects are not significantly worse than those of the earlier and many times bigger fission warheads. More dangerous is the shift of military doctrine which they symbolise. Both sides are changing their military doctrines towards more effective use of theatre nuclear weapons in war-fighting as contrasted with deterrence. The USA is modernising all of its theatre nuclear weapons and improving their accuracy, mobility, invulnerability, controllability, command, target identification and selection of yield, even 'tailoring' the weapon effect (the 'full-fusing option bomb') to the target.

The Soviet Union, too, is modernising its battlefield nuclear weapons by the development of a new, accurate short-range ballistic missile SS-21 (one kiloton with maximum range of 120 km) as replacement for its FROG series of artillery rockets, and a new longer range missile SS-22 as replacement for its 'Scaleboard' missile (20–500 kt; maximum range 900 km). It is deploying nuclear artillery (based on the M-55 203 mm howitzer) which gives it great flexibility on the battlefield.

The long-range SS-20, of which sixty triple warhead mobile missiles are said to be deployed against Western Europe, is said to have a high accuracy which makes it particularly effective against fixed military targets.

Nuclear weapons are now being assimilated into military doctrines as if they were normal instruments of warfare. This 'conventionalisation' of nuclear weapons seems to me the greatest danger of all. Military writers on both sides now expound nuclear battlefield doctrines as if the use of nuclear weapons would be a normal part of warfare. But on the battlefield itself, being a target of nuclear weapons may be far from 'normal'. Let us think of the case of a battlefield commander who has the responsibility for defending a certain strongpoint which comes under nuclear threat from the enemy. Soldiers are human beings and attitudes change when the chances of survival are reduced to zero. Such a change of attitude may be facilitated by the fact that none of the younger officers up to the level of battalion commander will have had war experience except a few possibly in Vietnam. In such circumstances military discipline and organisation might well collapse under the threat of nuclear salvos because of the unbearable psychological burden placed on the surviving units and troops.

A main argument used in justification of the neutron bomb is that it increases the deterrent effect by improving defence. But it is not at all sure that the advantages the neutron bomb might bring in battle would increase deterrence, i.e. prevent the outbreak of war. Neither of the superpowers would be fighting on their own soil and, as matters stand now, would both certainly presume the use of tactical nuclear weapons were war to break out.

The neutron bomb is said to be a purely defensive weapon, specifically designed against armoured columns spearheading an offensive. It is justified by the alleged three-to-one supremacy of Soviet tanks in Central Europe. The neutron bomb is said to be an ideal weapon to blunt armoured Soviet attacks and thus to neutralise this Soviet superiority. Unfortunately, this line of argument is simplistic.

The Soviet Army will surely find effective counter-measures against a neutron bomb used as an anti-tank weapon. It can modify its tactics by delaying massed tank assaults until the adversary's nuclear launchers within range of the offensive corridor have been destroyed. The tanks can be improved by providing them with extra neutron-absorbing shielding. Airborne troops can be used along the offensive corridor to disrupt the defender's firepower so that tanks can advance in dispersed formations, unsuitable for nuclear 'anti-tank' weapons. All in all, the neutron bomb is hardly an ideal anti-tank weapon. As an ordinary nuclear weapon it is politically so sensitive that it probably would not be released during the initial phase of the war when it would be most useful. Yet its assumed battlefield advantages would probably encourage the dangerous temptation to use it before other theatre nuclear weapons were employed. Thus it could lower the nuclear threshold without bringing the advantages for which it was designed. Being a typical battlefield weapon it would also weaken the linkage with the American strategic deterrent.

The Soviet Union, too, seems to be moving towards greater accuracy, mobility and flexibility as well as improved command and control of its theatre nuclear forces. The accuracy of its SS-20 is said to be vastly improved compared with the obsolete SS-4 and SS-5. Half of the SS-20s to be deployed in Europe according to the information published by US sources will be mobile. The new swing-wing fighter bomber Su-19 (Fencer A) and the heavy bomber Tu-2M (called in the West Backfire) have longer ranges and improved electronics. Clearly, the Soviet Union has achieved a capability for 'selective nuclear strikes' in Europe.

NATO has long suspected that the Soviet 203 mm howitzer M-55 has a dual capability and during the Bari meeting of its Nuclear Planning Group NATO advised that the Soviet 152 mm self-propelled howitzer M-1975[1] and a 240 mm howitzer also have similar flexibility.

Combined with an offensive doctrine, nuclear artillery implies warfighting rather than deterrence. Neutron warheads would be even more advantageous for offensive than defensive purposes because they would produce less destruction in cities and fewer logjams in forests than the standard fission warheads. Since they would create no fallout they would not hamper the advance of the offensive. The Soviet Union has announced that it will also develop neutron warheads if the USA is going to deploy them. There is no doubt that it can, if it so decides, because the Soviet Union is just as far advanced in fusion research as the USA and in any case the enhanced radiation effect has been there for implementation for some time.

Thus it seems that the neutron warhead is a prime catalyst of the nuclear arms race and fuels it at the worst possible level and place — the low tactical level in central Europe.

On 9 March 1978 the Soviet Union along with a number of other socialist states proposed at the CCD an international treaty prohibiting the production, stockpiling, deployment and use of neutron bombs (CCD/559). The United States and the United Kingdom considered this to be a demand for a unilateral measure, since the enhanced radiation warheads were an important part of the modernisation of the US tactical nuclear weapons, while the Soviet Union had not yet developed the weapon.

It is true that, because of the asymmetry of the arsenals, it is probably impossible to ban this specific feature of modernisation in isolation. A similar, symmetric asset is the Soviet modernisation of their IRBMs with the fixed and mobile versions of the SS-20. At the request of the Federal Republic of Germany the USA within NATO started in 1977 to plan medium-range nuclear missiles for NATO to counter the SS-20 in arms control negotiations and, if these fail, on the field. This planning led to a decision by NATO on 12 December 1979 to deploy 108 Pershing II missiles (range 1800 km) as replacement for the Pershing I and 464 ground-launched cruise missiles with US forces in several NATO countries, beginning in 1983 if arms control negotiations with the USSR do not in the meantime result in a mutually agreed reduction. This is a particularly sad development, because the risk of nuclear war in Europe increases and everybody's security decreases.

The Soviet Union has refused to start negotiating control of theatre nuclear arms unless the USA and NATO cancel their 12 December 1979 decision, that is freeze the decision to produce and deploy in Europe the planned NATO 'Euromissiles'. Presumably the USSR is ready to freeze its own production and deployment of theatre nuclear weapons at the same time.

It ought to be possible to return to the negotiating table on the basis of such mutual 'freeze'. Both East and West are against nuclear war and a new spiral in the nuclear arms race. To avoid these, there is no alternative but to return to the negotiating table. In these negotiations the reduction of theatre nuclear weapons in Europe should be treated in a comprehensive way. All nuclear weapons having a role in the European military balance should be considered and the neutron warheads would naturally be included in these negotiations.

The Vienna negotiations have shown that it is difficult for the superpowers to agree on reductions of military forces in Europe if they cannot agree on their global relations and particularly on SALT II. Recent developments in the global strategic situation make it unlikely that the US Congress will ratify SALT II as it has been negotiated. In January 1976 the US Congress denied weapons aid to FNLA in Angola, countering the combined Soviet/Cuban operation instead by increasing the strategic budget for 1977. Feelings in the US Senate seem to be even stronger now, after the events in Ethiopia, South Yemen, Vietnam and Afghanistan. Deployment of Soviet military forces overseas for ideological reasons is seen by the USA as a challenge it can best answer by maintaining its technological lead. In the USA the opinion seems to be growing that a new spiral in the strategic arms race will be more damaging to the Soviet Union than the USA. The USA will speed up its Trident and cruise missile programmes and the giant mobile MX. The fixed land-based missiles will become obsolete by the middle of the 1980s. The USA is also reinforcing NATO, developing closer relations with China, supporting upgrading of the military forces of South Korea, encouraging rearmament of Japan and speeding up the modernisation of its own naval and intervention forces including strategic air-lift and naval transports. It is regrettable that the global confrontation of the superpowers outside Europe has to result in the upgrading of their nuclear arsenals and military machines in Europe. There are now no border problems in Europe which could become causes of war, and mutual exchange and co-operation between the countries of Eastern and Western Europe are steadily increasing.

The present wave of rearmament and of active modernisation of weapons systems even in Europe is mainly due to the deterioration in superpower relations. The nations of Europe ought to work more efficiently toward complete removal of nuclear forces from Europe and attempt to balance their military forces on a purely conventional base, at a lower level and in a more symmetrical way. Such a development would increase general security. Alternatively, there is the grim prospect of modernised nuclear artillery, eventually with neutron warheads, and modern mobile IRBMs and CMs deployed in Europe by both superpowers.

NOTE
1. Also called M 1973 in NATO circles, *Atlantic News*, No. 970, 26 October 1977.

8 A Splendid Opportunity[1]

B. T. FELD

The decision by President Carter — that the United States will not now produce the neutron bomb for deployment in Europe — will be welcomed by all those who have been striving to avert further escalation of the nuclear arms race. However, it would be a mistake to think that this decision is entirely, or even mainly a result of public opposition to the neutron bomb organised by the various peace groups.

On the contrary, this decision — which is by no means a popular one in the United States, and may not be very popular in West Europe as well — which is arousing strong opposition in the US Congress, resulted from the President's strong personal conviction that what is now needed is motion in the direction of ending the arms race, rather than escalating it. His decision was made in spite of the growing impression that the Warsaw Pact forces are being strengthened and improved at a pace in excess of what is required to counteract any possible military threat from West Europe. The President's decision was a firm and unequivocal endorsement of the principles of *détente*.

In this respect, there now exists a splendid opportunity for application of the concept of disarmament by mutual example. If the Warsaw Pact nations, the Soviet Union in particular, would quickly grasp this opportunity for a comparable and parallel gesture of restraint, this might start a process of mutual, reciprocated arms control and disarmament measures of unprecedented and incalculable importance.

Clearly, the particular measure by the Soviet Union would have to be chosen by Soviet authorities taking into account East European security needs as well as the pressures of the various internal forces that determine Soviet military policy. This is a matter on which an outsider can only speak with the greatest degree of diffidence. Nevertheless, merely for purposes of illustration, and entirely in a friendly spirit of promoting a constructive discussion, I hope I may be permitted to outline a possible (only one of many possible) scenario for a constructive series of unilateral steps that might put us once again squarely on the road to nuclear disarmament.

Suppose that the Soviet Union were to announce a decision to postpone indefinitely the deployment of its new mobile missile, the SS-20, in the hope and expectation that a new emphasis would be placed on nuclear weapons reduction rather than weapons improvement. Such a move would relieve the fears of Western military analysts that a new generation of concealable (and therefore non-verifiable) missiles was about to be introduced into the Soviet strategic arsenal. The American response could easily be the cancellation of the new, hidden MX-missile and/or the abandonment of the testing and deployment of a new generation of highly accurate ICBMs (weapons capable of executing a first strike against Soviet missile silos). This move, in turn, could convince the Soviet Union that further build-up of its powerful SS-18 and SS-19 rocket forces has become unnecessary, and thus make possible a SALT III agreement at greatly reduced levels of large, MIRV'ed ICBMs.

I believe that my point is an obvious one: each step of restraint, starting with the recent Carter rejection of the neutron bomb, if it is followed by a freely chosen measure of roughly comparable restraint by the other side, can lead naturally to the next measure — all in the direction of unwinding that deadly nuclear spiral that has, until now, moved only in the direction towards disaster.

This is the sense in which President Carter's wise decision represents a splendid opportunity. It would be a tragedy if this opportunity were missed.[1]

NOTE
1. This paper was written soon after the American decision in 1978 to suspend production of the so-called neutron bomb and is published primarily to demonstrate how quickly and radically the perspective in these matters changes.

9 Theatre Nuclear Weapons in Europe

JORMA K. MIETTINEN

(This paper was written in January 1980)

INTRODUCTION

The question of modernising NATO's theatre nuclear weaponry (TNWs) by acquiring and locating in Europe new American medium-range missiles to counter the Soviet M/IRBMs, particularly the new SS-20s, came to a head in the autumn of 1979, concurrent with the approaching ratification of the SALT II Treaty. Although the problem of the credibility of the American nuclear deterrence when extended to the protection of its Allies has existed since the beginning of the 1960s it has intensified with the SALT negotiations and treaties. It was brought to public attention by Chancellor Helmut Schmidt in 1977[1] and by Henry Kissinger in September 1979.[2] While SALT II codifies nuclear parity on the strategic level, there exists no such agreement on the theatre level.

Throughout the SALT process the Soviet Union is reported to have taken the position that SALT must also reckon with the American 'Forward Based Systems' but the US has refused to discuss the FBSs because they would also involve the security interests of its NATO Allies. The strategic talks would have become enormously complicated and the negotiations could have become militarily and politically destructive to the Alliance. The deterrence/defence doctrine of NATO is based on defence capability on three levels: strategic nuclear, theatre nuclear and conventional. The easily accessible terrain and lack of depth in the defences of Western Europe demand a forward defensive system. A 'stalwart' conventional defence is needed to ensure time for reinforcements to arrive, to delay recourse to nuclear defence and to allow diplomatic negotiations within NATO regarding escalation and with the opponent to try to terminate the hostilities. NATO justifies the TNWs as a hedge against conventional breakthrough, as a counter to the Soviet TNWs, and as a linkage with the strategic nuclear weapons. Thus, the US FBSs have a central and sensitive position in the Western nuclear doctrine and posture.

The Western European NATO members welcomed the US assurances that FBSs were not discussed in SALT. But they became worried regarding the non-circumvention clause in the SALT II agreement on cruise missile technology, which forbids either party to circumvent the SALT treaty 'either directly or through third parties'. The Soviets insisted on a 'non-transfer' clause but the Americans only accepted a 'non-circumvention' clause. Secretary Vance assured the European NATO allies that transfer is possible in so far as it does not mean circumvention. The USA has traditionally transferred multipurpose technology to its allies and evidently feels free to do so even regarding cruise missile technology in the limits of habitual arrangements. Western Germany is interested to have Pershing II in its territory and some other European allies are interested in ground-launched cruise missiles (GLCM), as will be described below.

In the earlier phases of the nuclear arms race the USA has already taken various measures to counter the growing Soviet strategic power. At the beginning of the 1960s it changed its strategic doctrine from 'massive retaliation' to 'mutual assured destruction' and in 1967 NATO adopted its 'flexible response' doctrine. In 1970 President Nixon[3] initiated another doctorinal change which was made public by the US Secretary of Defense James R. Schlesinger in 1974.[4] This 'Schlesinger strategy' puts the stress on flexibility, i.e. the possibility of executing limited strategic options. At the beginning of the 1970s President Nixon also initiated a long-range programme to modernise the whole US tactical nuclear arsenal.[5] This was made public to some extent in May 1972.[6] This modernisation is now being stepped up with new emphasis on the medium-range systems capable of reaching the Soviet homeland from the Western Europe. This is primarily justified as a counter-measure to SS-20s but serves perhaps even more as a strategic counter-measure to the Soviets' global projection of military power.

THE SOVIET M/IRBMS SS-4 AND SS-5 AND THEIR REPLACEMENT BY SS-20s

Why is the new SS-20 causing more worries than the more massive SS-4s and SS-5s ever did?

The Soviet Union started to deploy its first MRBM, SS-4, in 1959 and its IRBM, SS-5, in 1961 with the intent of countering the overwhelming superiority of the American theatre nuclear arsenal which had grown up in Europe during the 1950s. These two missiles were logical deterrents for the Soviet Union at that time. It was then several years ahead of the USA in heavy missile technology but behind it in miniaturisation of nuclear weapons for front-line use. Also, its doctrine did not pre-suppose any short-range nuclear weapons because all of its nuclear weapons had to remain under strictly centralised control, being designed only for major strategic tasks.

In the West the SS-4s and SS-5s have always been considered to be pure deterrents: massive, inaccurate block-busters with over 2 kilometres' probable error, having a high yield (1 Mt), being slow to fill with liquid fuel (requiring several hours) and therefore rather vulnerable in their fixed silos. Over 500 SS-4s and 100 SS-5s were deployed during the 1960s and remained operational until recent years.[7] Through this deterrent the Soviet Union got Western Europe as hostage at a time it was unable to match the American strategic forces.

In 1977 the SS-4s and SS-5s began to be replaced by SS-20s at a rate of about 25 to 50 missiles per year. Presently there are reportedly only 530 SS-4s and SS-5s left. Horrendous though these missiles are, they have never raised particular fears in the West because they were considered deterrable (and perhaps even destroyable before launch) by the American strategic forces. They have been considered obsolete since the beginning of the 1970s and their modernisation has been foreseeable.

SS-20 comes in two varieties, fixed and mobile. It can be provided either with one 1–2 Mt warhead or with three 350 kt MIRV warheads. It has a range of 4800–5400 km, and — according to the Americans — a very high accuracy, its CEP being smaller than 400 m. Such high accuracy would make feasible even much smaller yields than 350 kt — one-tenth of that — against soft targets (and most military targets are soft). This has aroused suspicions in the West that the Soviets have gone over to selective targeting in an attempt to minimise collateral damage.[8] There are other reasons, too, for believing that the Soviet doctrine has shifted in recent years from one of deterrence towards one of war-fighting, just like the American doctrine; for example, they have acquired nuclear artillery and a new short-range missile, the SS-21, which has a 1 kt warhead. Evidently, they now also have a kind of flexible retaliation doctrine. However, it is an exaggeration to ascribe to the SS-20 any first strike capability, at least for the time being. There exist only 100 operational SS-20s, 60 targeted to Western Europe,

40 to China and NATO provides well over 1000 targets in peacetime location.

Some Western strategists suspect that the Soviet Union has acquired the SS-20 because it has specific nuclear aims regarding Western Europe. I do not really see any clear evidence to back up such suspicions. The SS-20 was originally developed as a three-stage ICBM missile, the SS-16, but the Americans resisted it violently in the SALT negotiations because it would have been indistinguishable from its two-stage sister and unverifiable because of its mobility. Also, the Americans say privately that its third stage did not work very well. What was more natural then than to use it as a replacement for the obsolete SS-4s and SS-5s? I also doubt the accuracy ascribed to the SS-20, CEP<400 m. If it is so accurate, why such big warheads? The Soviets have always been many years behind the Americans in missile guidance. How could they now suddenly meet or surpass the Americans in missile accuracy?

The Soviet Union maintains that SS-20 is not a new system. Maybe it is not, but realistically, compared with SS-4 and SS-5, it is so much improved being mobile, many times more accurate than the earlier ones, and MIRVed, that a Western reaction was to be expected. The Soviet Union also says that it is not against Western Europe but the American FBSs. Although not necessarily intended against Western Europe as mentioned above, it can be best used against fixed targets, being not usable against the most important American FBSs, the carrier-based nuclear aircraft and the SLBMs submitted to NATO.

It is nonetheless important that the number of SS-20s remains as low as possible. Maybe a low number can be negotiated, since many of them are said to be located in the Urals, from where they can reach both all of Western Europe and Western China. They are presently a major challenge to arms control in Europe and must be dealt with in SALT III.

The Soviet Union has been modernising its other theatre nuclear weapons, too, during the 1970s. By replacing older tactical aircraft with modern dual-capable fighters and fighter bombers such as the swing-wing varieties Su-17, Su-19 and Mig-23, it has greatly increased range, accuracy and payload. The medium-range bomber Tu-22M (Backfire) was limited by SALT II exclusively to theatre roles. A short-range missile SS-21 (120 km, 1 kt) has been introduced and another one (SS-22) is under advanced development. And the nuclear artillery (estimated 300 tubes today[9]), a true battlefield weapon, guarantees flexibility in nuclear fighting. The number of delivery systems has increased and their theatre-wide command, control and communication system improved.[10]

AMERICAN AND NATO RESPONSES TO
THE SOVIET IRBMS

The SALT II Treaty designates two primarily strategic Soviet systems — the Backfire and SS-16 — to the European theatre by putting limitations to their range (refuelling and the third stage, respectively). The European NATO members have reacted strongly to this: the Soviet Union introduces two new semi-strategic systems to the European theatre at a time it has reached strategic parity with the USA and ought not need any more to keep the Western Europeans as hostages, particularly if it has any confidence on *détente*. It is therefore understandable that the US offer of Pershing II and GLCMs as counter to these Soviet systems has been accepted by the West European members, although only reluctantly by the smaller ones which would not like to participate in the global power game of the superpowers.

Pershing II was originally part of the US's TNW-modernisation programme which aims at increased accuracy, flexibility and safety and reduced yields and radioactive residues. This programme has included artillery shells, missile warheads and glide bombs. Advanced development of Pershing II started in 1975 and still in the FY1978 Arms Control Impact Statement[11] it was announced that 'its range would remain at 400 nautical miles . . .'. But when the Soviet Union introduced the SS-20 and Chancellor Schmidt requested a European balance, the goal of the Pershing II modernisation changed. It is now presented as one of several medium-range nuclear systems with an extended range (1800 kms) to engage high-priority, fixed or semi-fixed land-based military targets.[12] Its warhead will be terminally guided by an all-weather radar, which correlates the target terrain with a reference map stored in a small computer in the warhead. This system will provide an improvement in accuracy of one order of magnitude, the Circular Error of 50 per cent Probability (CEP) being estimated at a few dozen metres. Because of such an ultra-high accuracy it can feasibly be provided with very small warheads, down to 1 kt. Pershing II is now in engineering development. A production decision is scheduled for July 1983.

The Ground-Launched Cruise Missile (GLCM) is another novelty, a version of the US Navy's Tomahawk CM adapted for launch from a vehicle mounted launcher rack.[13] There will be four missiles per launcher. Its range will probably be 2500 to 3000 kms. Its warhead can be anything from 1 kt to over 100 kts depending on the hardness of the target. Its accuracy will be about 30 m with the terminal guidance system. Production is also scheduled to start in 1983.

THE MILITARY BALANCE IN EUROPE

Let us now turn to the European military balance, because this is a central issue in the Euro-missile debate. It is mentioned as a truism in the West that the Warsaw Pact has a conventional superiority and a superiority regarding longer range, and perhaps even all, theatre nuclear weapons. The matter is extremely complicated, with the situation highly asymmetric. To speak of a purely Euro-strategic balance is therefore really misleading because Europe is only one theatre in which almost all strategic weapons can be used. I shall simplify the matter by looking briefly at three key aspects which doubtlessly will feature prominently in the Euro-missile debate:

    (1) the conventional balance;
    (2) the theatre nuclear weapons; and
    (3) the nuclear doctrines.

1 The Conventional Balance

First, the troop levels in Central Europe. These have been studied in microscopic detail in Vienna during the past six years; and although NATO continues to maintain that there is a discrepancy of 150 000 troops, as it chanced to state in 1973, both sides know that in reality the discrepancy is considerably smaller. The official figures for 1.1.1976 were: WP: 805 000 ground forces, NATO: 731 00 without French troops in the FRG. If these, about 60 000, are added the difference is 14 000.

    Other, larger figures may also be presented but depend on interpretation. For instance, both sides have civilians taking care of certain logistic jobs like transport and communication, the West considerably more. Some countries keep a part of their reservists on very prompt alert and pay for this — how should they be included? The East may have a few per cent more but the troop balance is not far from parity. The withdrawals promised by President Brezhnev will further reduce the gap.

    NATO as a whole has more standing forces, more troops after full mobilisation, and a much stronger economic and industrial base. One-quarter of the Soviet troops are bound to the Chinese border facing a nation which, during a protracted crisis, can raise in addition to 4.4 million regular forces perhaps 100 million militia, some 10 million of them armed and fairly well trained in peacetime. Moreover, in case of a general war, China might be backed by Japan, a nation with a great military tradition, 1/4 million standing forces, 1 million professionally trained reserves and a sophisticated war machine.

The Warsaw Pact has perhaps 2.7 times more tanks and also more artillery and armed personnel carriers and fighter aircraft than the West, but the West has a considerable superiority in anti-tank weapons, helicopters and modern military technology in general. It is the Soviet doctrine based on offence, surprise and quick penetration which demands many armoured vehicles. The West has deliberately chosen different armaments and a different doctrine.

2 The Theatre Nuclear Weapons

NATO has superiority in numbers: at least some 6000 operational (and maybe an additional 1000 or 2000 retired ones) against perhaps 4500 Soviet weapons at present. NATO had 7000 in 1974, but the oldest and biggest bombs and missiles evidently have now been retired, or at least have been considered obsolete for the past five years. New ones have arrived, particularly many Lance missiles.

There is considerable uncertainty regarding the corresponding number of Soviet theatre nuclear weapons. For many years the IISS issued the magic number 3500. This number has probably increased to 4000–4500 with the introduction of more SCUD Bs at the Army level, the SS-21, some nuclear artillery (maybe 300 tubes) and more dual-capable aircraft. The Soviet battlefield capabilities have therefore considerably improved in the last few years.

This year the IISS published a special comparison of long- and medium-range nuclear systems for the European theatre[14] giving the Warsaw Pact an incredibly high 'inventory' figure — 5364 (4150 of them free-fall bombs). For NATO it gave only 2045, 366 of them missiles. Because of a lower serviceability and fairly low penetrability for aircraft the 'system utility figures' (warheads likely to reach their targets) are WP: 1209, NATO: 1065. Thus, the Warsaw Pact would have a 13 per cent advantage. But the accuracy of this estimate cannot be better than ± 30 per cent and we can speak of essential parity, or rough equivalence. If we also count the shorter range battlefield weapons, however, NATO has a clear edge in numbers. This was admitted even with such an authority as General Brown in 1978.[15] NATO may also have a qualitative superiority, and certainly will have it when the US modernisation programmes are completed, sometime in the mid-1980s. But numbers alone do not count and I would contend that they are not even the decisive factor in any comparison of efficiency. Both sides have more nuclear weaponry than they will have time to use before the world is blown up. Given the exorbitant stockpiles, it is the doctrines which will be crucial. Many other factors may also play a role — even psychological ones: nobody has any true knowledge or experience about how a nuclear battle would really be fought.

3 The Nuclear Doctrines

It is my opinion that NATO has never been able to work out a logical war-fighting doctrine for the use of its nuclear battlefield weapons. It claims to have a purely defensive doctrine: theatre nuclear weapons will be used in a restricted way against attacking enemy concentrations when the conventional defence begins to erode — perhaps after a few days' delaying operations in a friendly country, amongst tens of millions of fleeing civilians. To me this seems a purely political doctrine and militarily a hopeless one. It may have made sense when the USA had a clear nuclear superiority and the nuclear weapons played primarily a deterrent role, but it is a highly questionable doctrine for real war-fighting as the trend seems to be now in both sides.

The Soviets find no difficulty in assigning a clear role to nuclear weapons in their military thinking. Theirs is a purely military, Clausewitzian doctrine — perhaps derivative even from Sun Tzu. It is based on offence and surprise; artillery barrage; breakthroughs; fast, mobile and continuous attacks. The nuclear weapons bring about immeasurable chaos by being aimed simultaneously at the whole depth of the enemy forces. The chaos of the enemy, the defender, is the key to the success of the attacker. It is attained by pre-planned use of long-range nuclear weapons with centralised command.

From a purely military point of view the Soviet doctrine is certainly superior, and the Soviet Union has nuclear weapons that exactly match its doctrine. Thus, NATO is the stronger and richer Alliance but it feels itself weaker — and even may be so, because of organisational and doctrinal faults. Much of this inferiority complex derives from the fact that NATO attempts to solve its defence problems by applying nuclear weapons on every level, weapons which are not feasible tools for war-fighting.

FACTORS EXACERBATING THE PROBLEM OF EURO-MISSILES

The Euro-missile crisis is not primarily a military problem. Much of it rests on the fact that the United States feels it necessary to counter on the strategic level the Soviet/Cuban projection of military power into Africa and the general intensification of Soviet global politics (South Yemen, Vietnam, Afghanistan).

Particularly, the Soviet Union's open support of Vietnam's aggression to Campuchea and its direct military intervention into Afghanistan are turning the United States toward hard anti-communism: SALT II ratification probably will come into a new light; the United States will evidently re-evaluate the strategic situation in the region of the Indian Ocean; it probably will plan with its allies severe economic and political counter-moves. No doubt, *détente* is deeply disturbed.

President Carter has made known his foreign policy programme in his speeches at Wake Forest University and elsewhere. According to him the United States will counter the Soviet Union's global power projection 'through a combination of military forces, political efforts and economic programs'. The Carter Administration is increasing US strategic systems and the American defence budgets — it has just proposed an addition of $20 billion to the FY1981 budget. It urges its Allies (NATO, Japan and South Korea) also to increase their defence budgets, in the case of NATO by 3 per cent real growth annually. It plans establishing a mobile force of 110 000 for use in the Gulf and elsewhere. It negotiates for naval and air bases in the Gulf area. The 'China card' is also being used, although restrictedly so far. And the situation in Iran or Afghanistan may explode any day and lead to the most serious crisis since Cuba in 1962.

Evidently, believing that the 'correlation of forces' has turned to its favour 'the imperialism being doomed to perish' the Soviet Union is pursuing to erect communist states in strategic positions all over the world. Encouraged by the United States' loss of the Vietnam war and its apparent incapability to project its military power due to the split in US foreign policy authority, the Soviet Union challenges the United States, although the latter has a technologically and industrially stronger base and also a globally stronger strategic position. If this power game continues and no rapprochement takes place between the superpowers a real danger exists that the confrontation will culminate in the Third World War within a few years.

OUTCOME OF NATO MEETING ON 12 DECEMBER 1979

The goal of the NATO plan, the result of two years' intensive negotiations within NATO, was to decide by consensus deployment of 108 Pershing II missiles and 464 GLCMs after the SALT II protocol expires, beginning perhaps in 1983. The Pershing IIs would replace 108 Pershing IAs now deployed by American forces in Western Germany. The GLCMs would have been located in FRG, Italy, Great Britain, Holland and Belgium. However, when the Dutch Parliament decided on 10 December to postpone the decision on location by two years the United States withdrew its demand of consensus. Thus, the decision was made by majority.

WILL THE EURO-MISSILES INCREASE SECURITY IN EUROPE?

Will deployment of 108 Pershing II missiles in the FRG and 464 GLCMs in several NATO countries solve the 'perceived imbalance' regarding medium-range theatre nuclear systems? It is difficult to see that they could, except perhaps by persuading the Soviet Union to negotiate on a theatre nuclear balance. Militarily they are no counter to the SS-20. Their range is planned to be less than half of its range. The GLCM is a slowly moving, second strike weapon. Furthermore, they are not really militarily needed: NATO has enough other medium-range weapons. 400 Poseidon warheads are allocated to SACEUR and there are at least 700 nuclear-capable long-range fighter bombers in NATO Europe. Within two years 800 Tornados will start arriving. Poseidon SLBMs are practically invulnerable but fairly inaccurate and would be effective only against soft targets. But within two years 12 American Poseidon boats will have been refitted with Trident 1 missiles (the first is patrolling already). Trident I missiles have a good accuracy, CEP<500 m, and a higher yield, 100 kt. Why could not some of them be allocated to SACEUR? The first of at least 13 giant 24-tube Trident submarines, the 'Ohio', has been launched and becomes operational in 1981. Each of its SLBMs will carry eight accurate 100 kt MIRV warheads (= 192 per boat) until replaced by the much bigger Trident II SLBMs.

New aerial bombs are very accurate but the penetration of the fighter bombers is a problem. GLCM would facilitate the penetration problem but only if available in large enough numbers.

As for the linkage to the American strategic deterrence, it is difficult to imagine a US President preferring to push a GLCM-button rather than an SLBM-button in the case of nuclear war. The CM-use would be a much more complicated case to decide and would offer more political leverage to the opponent than the use of an SLBM. The small allied country from where the GLCM would be launched could be put under tremendous political pressure and face a nuclear response. But the Soviets would probably see little difference in which American weapon was used.

I do not think that the introduction of new, purely American-controlled medium-range weapons to Europe could correct the main problem, which is psychological: the ultimate security of the West European non-nuclear nations is in the hands of a transatlantic power and depends on its using measures which would risk its own society. This situation can only be corrected by improving Western Europeans' own conventional defence to the degree that Western Europeans feel confident that, together with the US forces, they can carry out an efficient conventional defence. The role of all tactical nuclear weapons should be slowly decreased and ultimately they should be withdrawn, first to second-line weapons like the chemical ones, then retired and removed from Europe. They cannot have any useful role in war-fighting. They would only cause huge losses of military forces (over 50 per cent lethalities in targeted units), losses of millions of civilians, and the irradiation of tens, even hundreds of millions (if ground bursts are used). Nuclear war-fighting can lead only to hopeless chaos, a rupture of order and possibly complete breakdown of the society. The only reasonable role for nuclear weapons is for them to serve as a deterrent to the use of nuclear weapons by anybody under any conditions.

The following programme for nuclear disarmament of Europe, proposed by this author in 1976 (see Note 10), still seems to be fairly up-to-date:

(1) After an agreement on troop reductions has been achieved in Vienna, the framework of the SALT or Vienna negotiations is widened or a new negotiation forum formed to cover all theatre nuclear weapons usable in Europe.

(2) Doctrines are unilaterally changed to 'non-first-use' of nuclear weapons. Because of psychological reasons such a change may be more easily achievable unilaterally than through a formal agreement. Some improvement of conventional defence may be deemed necessary and is possible, for instance, by applying new conventional technology.[16]

(3) A narrow non-nuclear weapon zone — let us say 80–100 km broad on both sides of the East–West border — could be useful as an initial step, as a confidence-building measure. It would not endanger

military security in any serious way but it would signal to the military leaders the changing course the military preparations have to take.

(4) The final goal must be complete elimination of the threat of the use of nuclear weapons in Europe even if a conflict were to break out. This could only be achieved through negotiations on a proper negotiating forum which includes all factors relevant to the military balance in Europe.

Any schedule for disarmament adopted must be flexible enough to allow changes in procedure if a stalemate is threatening.

Currently, Europe seems to be at a crossroads: either effective regional arms control or a spiral of European nuclear arms race. Not only the superpowers but the lesser nuclear powers, other members of the alliances and even the neutral and non-aligned states ought to be able to participate in the arms control negotiations in one way or another, because the risks of nuclear war threaten all of them equally. In the matters of nuclear weapons the neutral states might even be less biased than the members of the military alliances and, thus, in a better situation to find compromises which would be best for Europe as a whole.

NOTES

1. H. Schmidt, 'The Alastair Buchan Memorial Lecture' in *Survival*, Vol. xx, No. 1 (January/February 1978), pp. 3f.
2. Kissinger, H., 'The Future of NATO'. *The Washington Quarterly*, 2, No. 4 (Autumn 1979), pp. 3–17.
3. *United States Foreign Policy for the 1970s: A New Strategy for Peace*. A Report by President Richard Nixon to the Congress, 18 February, 1970 (London, United States Information Service, 1970); *President Nixon's Foreign Policy Report to the Congress*, 25 February, 1971 (n.p., United States Information Service 1971); *United States Foreign Policy for the 1970s: The Emerging Structure of Peace*. A Report to the Congress by Richard Nixon, President of the United States (May, 1973).
4. Remarks by James R. Schlesinger, Secretary of Defense, before National Jaycees, Twin Bridges Marriot Motel, Arlington, Va. (Saturday, 15 December, 1973) US Department of Defense news release (Washington, 1973) No. 605–73; and Remarks by James R. Schlesinger, Overseas Writers Association Luncheon, at International Club, Washington, DC (Thursday, 10 January 1974) US Department of Defense news release (Washington, 1973). Also in *Survival*, 16, No. 2 (March/April 1974), pp. 86–9.
5. James R. Schlesinger, *The Theater Nuclear Force Posture in Europe*: A

Report to the United States Congress in Compliance with the Public Law 93–365, p. 2 (Washington DC, April 1975).

6. M. Laird, interview, *New York Times* (16 April 1972).
7. *Military Balance 1975–76*, The International Institute for Strategic Studies (London, 1975).
8. Joseph D. Douglas, Jr., 'Soviet Nuclear Strategy in Europe: A Selective Targeting Doctrine?', *Strategic Review* (Fall 1977), pp. 19–32.
9. General Pierre M. Gallois, 'Western Europe: An Improper System of Defence', RUSI *Journal for Defence Studies*, 124, No. 3 (September 1979,) pp. 12–17.
10. Jorma K. Miettinen, 'Mini-nukes and enhanced radiation weapons' in *Tactical Nuclear Weapons: European Perspectives* (SIPRI, Taylor and Francis, London 1978), pp. 223–46.
11. Analysis of Arms Control Impact Statements for FY1978, prepared for the Committee on Foreign Relations, US Senate by the Foreign Affairs and National Defense Division Congressional Research Service, Library of Congress (Washington DC) April 1977, p. 128.
12. Fiscal Year 1980 Arms Control Impact Statements, Arms Control and Disarmament Agency (Washington, DC) March 1979.
13. Ibid.
14. *Military Balance 1979–80*, IISS (London, 1979).
15. G. S. Brown, USAF, Chairman, Joint Chiefs of Staff, prepared Statement in US Congress, Senate, Committee on Armed Services, Department of Defense Authorization for Appropriations for Fiscal Year 1979, Part 1: Authorization, Posture Statement, p. 407.
16. Miettinen, J. K., 'Can conventional new technologies and new tactics replace tactical nuclear weapons in Europe' in *Arms Control and Technological Innovation*, David Carlton and Carlo Schaerf (eds) (Croom Helm, London, 1977), pp. 52–69.

Part Three
The Baltic and the Arctic—
Regional Problems

10 Arms Control in Northern Europe: A Nordic Nuclear-free Zone?

PAULI O. JÄRVENPÄÄ AND KALEVI RUHALA

(This paper was originally published in Finnish in *Ulkopolitiikka*, January 1979)

The Finnish proposal for a Nordic nuclear-free zone has once again become the focus of a lively foreign policy discussion in Northern Europe. No doubt this round of debate was rekindled by President Urho Kekkonen's speech of May 1978 in Stockholm. The discussion was spurred on by the Swedish response outlined during Foreign Minister Hans Blix's visit to Finland in November, and it was further fuelled by the Soviet views presented under the pseudonym of Juri Komissarov in the December issue of the Finnish journal *Kanava*.

In general, the reaction to the Finnish proposal has been somewhat contradictory. The most impatient observers have started to see President Kekkonen's initiatives as the toils of Sisyphus: just as the rock is about to reach the mountain top, the sharp reactions of other Nordic countries make it rumble back to the valley. Some others have perhaps too readily regarded the idea of a nuclear-free zone as a remedy that will provide a fast cure for all Nordic security problems.

This article starts with the assumption that the proposal for the establishment of a Nordic nuclear-free zone is more relevant today than ever before. Reasons for its increased relevance are not hard to find. The Nordic sea areas are undeniably becoming more attractive to the superpowers for their strategic operations. The significance of these areas is augmented by the fact that the majority of the Soviet strategic submarine force is based in the vicinity of the Nordic countries and regularly patrols the Northern seas, as well as by the fact that in the event of a grave European crisis, the North Atlantic will provide a vital link between the United States and its European NATO allies. These two facts together will assure a growing great power interest in the Northern sea areas in the years to come. With good reason it can be argued, therefore, that it would be more desirable today than ever before to try to insulate the Nordic countries from the sphere of potential international tension.

The establishment of a Nordic nuclear-free zone would serve the interests of the states in the area in other ways, too. Arms control agreements have been traditionally seen as ways to reduce the probability of war, to decrease damage and suffering should war occur, and to diminish the costs and burdens of the arms competition. But such measures may have another useful function as well: they can also provide instruments for creating and fostering mutual confidence between nations.[1] Consequently, arms control arrangements could promote security by eliminating instabilities, by providing information about military activities, and by reducing uncertainties about the role of military configurations, with the ultimate goal of mitigating the impact of military power on politics between nations. The creation of a Nordic nuclear-free zone could be an essential component of that process.

The debate of the past year has once again revealed that the prospects for the realisation of the zone will have to be evaluated with both feet firmly on the ground; the conceptual distance between the Nordic reactions and the Soviet views as expressed in the Komissarov article remains wide. But paradoxically, perhaps, the fact that the contending positions have been so starkly drawn has opened up a new phase in the debate. It has now become exceedingly clear that the establishment of a Nordic nuclear-free zone will require reconciliation between the great power interests and the security objectives of the small Nordic nations. How this could be realistically done is a question that demands a careful examination. First, however, it is useful to take a closer look at the present debate over the Finnish proposal.

THE SCANDINAVIAN REACTIONS

The Finnish proposal for a Nordic nuclear-free zone was first introduced by President Urho Kekkonen in 1963. During the last decade and a half the proposal has matured from a mere expression of a political idea into a more fully articulated plan for political action. Many of the plan's elements have been presented in public in different forums over the years, but the concrete shape of the plan began to emerge more clearly than ever before during the past year.

From the Finnish point of view, the most important elements of the plan are expressed in President Kekkonen's speech of May 1978 in Stockholm.[2] According to the speech, the Finnish objective is to create a separate Nordic treaty arrangement that as completely as possible will isolate the Nordic countries from the negative effects of nuclear strategy in general and nuclear weapons technology in particular. The starting point for any Nordic arms control measures would have to be the existing security arrangements adopted and maintained by the nations in the Nordic area. In President Kekkonen's view, it would be natural — and for the prospects of the nuclear-free zone plan even critical — for the leading military powers to participate in negotiations over the zone from their very beginning. Another important aspect of the Kekkonen plan is the concept of 'negative security guarantees'. If the small Nordic countries will consciously and irrevocably decide to refrain from developing nuclear weapons and to promise not to allow these weapons to be stationed within their territories, it is only reasonable to expect that they will want to receive guarantees from nuclear powers affirming that these powers will not use nuclear weapons against states belonging to the zone, nor will they subject the zonal states to nuclear blackmail.

In reponse to President Kekkonen's speech, Swedish Foreign Minister Karin Söder maintained that just as before Sweden was ready to discuss the Finnish proposal, provided that other states concerned were willing to participate in discussions. For Sweden, the crucial question involves the areas to be included within the nuclear-free zone: 'It is our view that such a plan must take into consideration those tactical nuclear weapons in the vicinity of Scandinavia that can be used against targets in the area.'[3] The same reservation was expressed even more pointedly by Foreign Minister Söder's successor, Dr Hans Blix, in a speech on 1 November 1978 and repeated when he visited Finland later on in the same month. According to him, to be effective the Nordic nuclear-free zone will have to cover the total Baltic Sea area, or in other words, it should also include the Soviet Baltic republics and the northern parts of both the Germanies in the south, and the Kola Peninsula in the north.[4] In addition to the unsettled area question, another concern for the Swedish government seemed to be the impact of the proposed zone on the Nordic military balance. That, in the Swedish view, forms the background against which the idea of a Nordic nuclear-free zone has to be examined.

Other Scandinavian reactions largely followed the views already familiar from earlier rounds of debate. Prime Minister of Denmark Anker Jörgensen considered Dr Blix's ideas on extending the zone to include the Baltic Sea interesting but hardly realistic. The Norwegian response offered nothing basically new — except that perhaps the Norwegian way of saying 'no' was more polite than ever before. The Norwegian perspectives on the Finnish proposal will be analysed more fully later on, so it will be sufficient here only to note a recent official Norwegian position on the concept of a nuclear-free Scandinavia. The March 1978 Report prepared by the Defence Committee of the Norwegian Parliament makes the following arguments:

(1) The Nordic countries already form a *de facto* nuclear-free zone and no country in the area is planning to procure nuclear weapons. Furthermore, all Nordic states are parties to the 1968 Non-Proliferation Treaty.

(2) The proposal to establish a Nordic nuclear-free zone will have to be examined as part of a larger framework, e.g. in connection with the possibility of creating a nuclear-free zone in Central Europe.

(3) A nuclear-free zone will also have to set certain restraints on the actions of superpowers. In this connection, the Report points out that the Norwegians have long considered the Finnish proposal to be insufficient in that it fails to include the Kola Peninsula, the only area in the North that contains nuclear weapons today.[5]

A SOVIET VIEW

An article by Juri Komissarov in the December 1978 issue of *Kanava* can be seen as a well-timed response to the Swedish and Norwegian suggestions that the nuclear-free zone should cover a geographically larger area than the Nordic countries alone. It should be remembered, of course, that Komissarov's argument does not necessarily represent the official Soviet view, but at the same time the article no doubt closely reflects the general Soviet attitude toward the concept of a nuclear-free Nordic area.

Two sets of interesting arguments are advanced in the article. On one hand, Komissarov puts a great emphasis on certain inherent rights that in his view accrue to the nuclear powers by virtue of their sheer political and military significance. Therefore, he maintains that although the Nordic states themselves bear the primary responsibility for finding a workable solution to the problem of establishing a nuclear-free zone in Scandinavia, the interests of other states — particularly those of the most

closely involved nuclear powers — will have to be given due consideration. His remarks on the extension of the zone are straightforward
and unmistakably clear. It would be unreasonable, he argues, to expect
the Soviet Union to limit its military activities only because it happens to
border a planned nuclear-free zone:[6]

> It should also be taken into consideration that the Soviet Union is a
> nuclear power and, for that reason, neither its territory nor a part of its
> territory can be included in a nuclear-free zone or a so-called 'security
> zone' adjacent to a nuclear-free zone, nor shall the status of a nuclear-
> free zone prevent Soviet military vessels from transiting the Baltic
> straits, no matter what types of weapons they carry.

On the other hand, this exceptionally strongly formulated view on the
geographical limits of the zone is balanced in Komissarov's article by
remarks that are most likely intended to offer reassurance to those Scandinavian countries that have expressed the strongest reservations about
the Nordic nuclear-free zone. First, Komissarov emphasises that in the
process of establishing a nuclear-free zone each Nordic country will have
the right to see that 'the special features of its foreign policy position and
its security interests, as it defines them, will be respected'. Secondly, the
author of the article repeats an earlier Soviet promise that the Soviet
Union is ready, along with other nuclear powers, to grant so-called
negative guarantees to states belonging to the Nordic nuclear-free zone.
In other words, according to the article, the Soviet Union is willing to
promise that it will neither use nuclear weapons against the Nordic area,
nor will it threaten the Nordic countries with nuclear weapons. Finally,
referring to the Treaty of Tlatelolco, Komissarov points out that each
Nordic country could conceivably withdraw from the nuclear-free zone
treaty obligations should it decide that its supreme interests have been
jeopardised by extraordinary events.

Clearly, the Komissarov article is an interesting and articulate addition
to the discussion over the Nordic nuclear-free zone. Moreover, even in a
cautious assessment, it has introduced some new elements into the current debate. It would naturally be wrong to maintain that Komissarov's
comments would have in one grand stroke removed all the obstacles to a
Nordic treaty arrangement. After all, his ideas about negative security
guarantees provided by nuclear powers and a withdrawal clause attached
to the treaty do little more than restate previously advanced Soviet
arguments. However, it is his intimation that the Soviet Union might be
willing to give special consideration to Nordic security interests that

might offer a promising starting point for discussions and, in the best case, persuade the staunchest opponents of the Kekkonen plan to examine the proposal in a new light. If the discussion gets fresh wind in its sails, its central theme will most likely centre on the question of how the 'special features' of the foreign policy position and the 'security interests' of each Nordic country could in a balanced way be taken into consideration.

THE NORWEGIAN NUCLEAR OPTION

The key position in any security arrangement in the Nordic area is occupied by Norway. Without underestimating the opinions expressed in other Scandinavian capitals, it is useful to examine the Norwegian view more closely, particularly since over the years the staunchest opposition to the Finnish proposal has originated from Oslo. With justification it can be argued that the prospects of the Nordic nuclear-free zone stand or fall to the degree that Norwegian security requirements can be satisfied.

Norway's widely and thoroughly articulated security doctrine can be condensed into a single concept: the nuclear option. For Norway, the nuclear option refers to the possibility of requesting and receiving, in a grave crisis, NATO nuclear weapons in its territory. The Norwegian view has consistently been that the regular stationing of nuclear weapons in the country would be destabilising. However, according to a prominent Norwegian scholar of international affairs, through its linkage to the NATO Alliance, Norway has obtained 'special drawing rights' on the general balance of power between the superpowers on one hand and between NATO and the Warsaw Pact on the other.[7] The Nordic nuclear-free zone, as depicted in the Finnish proposal, would sever this linkage. But the Finns have tended to maintain that a nuclear-free zone would only formalise a *de facto* situation in the already non-nuclear Scandinavia, and that the zone would in no way change the basic premises of security policy in any country in the Nordic area. In the predominant Norwegian view the thrust of the Finnish proposal is seen to be just the opposite: by relinquishing its nuclear option Norway would radically alter the Nordic security balance and at the same time forfeit its own chances of seeking shelter under the Alliance nuclear umbrella in the event of Norway being severely threatened.

What are the circumstances in which Norway might want to exercise its nuclear option? Understandably the Norwegians have chosen not to spell out in detail the specific conditions for such a contingency, since they have wanted to retain their freedom of action in various crisis situations as long as possible. After all, nuclear deterrence aims at creating in a potential aggressor uncertainty about the results of aggression by posing a credible promise of unacceptable costs and risks. But although it is not possible to define a precise crisis threshold that would trigger the Norwegian nuclear option, it can nonetheless be inferred from the public record on the subject what kinds of conflicts the Norwegians regard as most likely.

The main Norwegian concern appears to be the Soviet military presence in the Kola Peninsula. The Norwegians have drawn attention to the fact that the Soviet-Norwegian military balance in the border area is highly asymmetrical. At the same time, however, they have repeatedly emphasised that they view the Soviet *nuclear* forces on the Kola area as part of the Soviet global military posture. It is, therefore, only in the context of a conflict between the superpowers that Norway might face a threat to its security. Although the possibility of a nuclear attack or nuclear blackmail against Norway is not wholly excluded, the main Norwegian scenario seems to depict a potential deployment of *conventional* forces from the Kola Peninsula against northern parts of Norway in a superpower conflict.

On the basis of this scenario an answer might be found to the question of why the Norwegians want to retain their nuclear option. It appears that the nuclear option is not primarily designed to deter a nuclear attack on Norway, the probability of which is considered to be low in any case. A more correct answer seems to be that the main threat is thought to be a conventional one, and Norway wants to retain its 'special drawing rights' in order to raise the conventional threshold. For Norway, the nuclear option is mainly an instrument of crisis control. It is possible that NATO tactical weapons might in some circumstances bolster defence after the war has started, but the nuclear option is mainly aimed at influencing behaviour in the period preceding the outbreak of hostilities. The Norwegian nuclear option is, therefore, profoundly political in nature: although its primary military purpose is to raise the threshold against a local conventional attack, it reminds any potential aggressor of the stakes involved and at the same time serves to reassure the Norwegians of their political linkage to the wider global and European networks of power.

CONSTRAINTS AND CONFIDENCE-BUILDING MEASURES

Critics of Norwegian security policy have at times contended that by choosing its present defence options Norway has looked after someone else's interests rather than its own. A necessary precondition for the establishment of a Nordic nuclear-free zone is, however, the recognition that the security perceptions of all participating countries will have to be taken seriously. There is no reason to assume the security concerns of a small country like Norway to be groundless. Indeed, it could be justifiably argued that the superpowers whose nuclear weapons greatly contribute to insecurity in the world bear a particular responsibility, and they should do their utmost to explore ways to dispel security concerns of non-nuclear nations.

Therefore, the realistic chances for the establishment of a Nordic nuclear-free zone can be crystallised in the following question: Is the nuclear option unequivocally a *conditio sine qua non* for Norway or could the legitimate Norwegian security interests perhaps be guaranteed through other arrangements? Judging from the rationales offered by the Norwegians for their nuclear option, it seems clear that Norway will be interested in a Nordic nuclear-free zone only if two conditions obtain: (i) if the potential for a NATO/Warsaw Pact armed conflict in Europe and especially in the Nordic areas is diminished; and (ii) if the alleged conventional threat posed to Norway by the Soviet military forces based in the Kola area is reduced. In other words, the Norwegians seem to regard their nuclear option as so valuable that any change in their present security arrangements would have to be compensated by considerably more concrete measures than by the negative guarantees and the 'no-first use of force' principle they imply.

It has often been pointed out by Norwegian observers that from Norway's point of view the basic weakness in the Finnish nuclear-free zone proposal has all along been the lack of a *quid pro quo*. Since the Norwegians seem to be most concerned about the Soviet conventional capabilities in the North, as outlined above, it is conceivable that Norway would be interested in concrete measures that would tend to eliminate or at least to ameliorate pre-emptive conventional instabilities in Northern Norway. An establishment of a series of arrangements with the explicit purpose of building confidence between the Soviet Union and Norway might contribute to this end, and at the same time make the proposal for a Nordic nuclear-free zone more palatable to the Norwegians.

In fact, there already exists a precedent for such arrangements. Norway has unilaterally accepted certain restraints on the deployment of military force within its territory. For example, NATO aircraft are not allowed to fly over territory in Norwegian possession on missions involving crossing the 24°E meridian. Similarly, NATO naval vessels are not permitted to call at ports east of that same meridian. Furthermore, there are regulations restricting the number of Alliance aircraft and warships that may be allowed to gather in northern parts of Norway at the same time, and Norway has set additional self-imposed limitations that apply to military manoeuvres in Northern Norway.[8]

The unilateral restrictions Norway has imposed on the NATO forces might serve as a model for bilateral restrictions on the deployment of military force between the Soviet Union and Norway. In order to demonstrate their peaceful intentions and to foster mutual confidence, these two countries might agree, as a point of departure, to the following measures:

(1) Constraints on the deployment of armed forces:
   (a) A demilitarised zone in the immediate vicinity of the Soviet-Norwegian border in which only lightly armed border troops would be allowed.
   (b) Adjacent zones on both sides of the demilitarised zone in which limited numbers of troops would be allowed. The number of troops would depend on an agreement between the parties.
(2) Confidence-building measures (to be applied e.g. in areas under jurisdiction of the parties north of the Arctic Circle).
   (a) Prohibition of military manoeuvres above an agreed number of troops.
   (b) Pre-announcement of all military manoeuvres (on land, at sea and in the air) and troop movements.
   (c) Exchange of observers during military manoeuvres.

It could be maintained, of course, that the narrow zone to be extended between the Soviet Union and Norway would by no means be militarily impermeable. For today's highly mobile troops a demilitarised or thinned-out zone would indeed be a minor obstacle. But at the same time it must be recognised that the most crucial function of the zone would be political, not military. The same can also be said about the possible confidence-building measures. A bilateral agreement, containing the proposed constraints on the use of force and some confidence-building measures, would in itself be a telling political signal to indicate that the participants take a responsible view of the security problems in the Nordic area.

A REGIONAL NON-ÁGGRESSION TREATY

Treaty arrangements prohibiting the use of force have gradually gained a noticeable role in international relations. The Charter of the United Nations, the Final Act of the CSCE, and various bilateral treaties established to normalise relations between states, for example, all included mutual commitments to refrain from the use or threat of force. Such arrangements may also be seen as components of regional arms control in Northern Europe.

The merits of treaty commitments prohibiting the use of force are substantial in principle, but their practical significance would undoubtedly increase if they could be more closely linked with regional arms control measures. One way of making the commitments more concrete might be to emphasise non-aggression treaties which have old — although admittedly not completely honourable — traditions in international relations. There are grounds for arguing that the situation is, however, better today than earlier, since the UN General Assembly in 1974 adopted the definition of aggression. This definition describes in detail those forms of action that member states condemn and from which they have in principle agreed to refrain when signing the UN Charter. With this definition serving as a starting point, the danger of misinterpretation would diminish and constraints on the use of force would consequently be strengthened.[9]

Traditional bilateral non-aggression treaties have a notable drawback: they contain a hidden reference to the fact that the treaties concern relations between potential enemies. A treaty that reminds parties of a confrontation hardly serves in the best possible way permanent pacification of interstate relations, and this being the case, such a treaty might not be politically the most successful approach.

On the other hand, a regional treaty of more than two parties that would comprise both members of military alliances and non-aligned countries would not expressedly emphasise antagonistic positions, provided that the treaty provisions equally concerned all the signatories. Such a treaty arrangement would most logically be established within a geographically uniform group of states. Northern Europe might conceivably be this kind of region.

The purpose of a North European non-aggression treaty would be to eliminate the use or threat of force as well as all acts of aggression between the signatories in accordance with the UN definition. As the first use of armed force by a State in contravention of the Charter constitutes *prima facie* evidence of an act of aggression, a regional non-aggression treaty would help pacify the borders of signatories from hostile activity and make it unacceptable to permit this activity from one's territory against the other parties.

Natural parties to a Nordic regional non-aggression treaty would be the Soviet Union, Norway, Sweden and Finland, but the participation of Denmark would also be appropriate as a consequence of its geographical and political status in Northern Europe.

Alliance commitments of some countries involved in the described arrangement may raise questions about whether the obligations of a non-aggression treaty would conflict with the treaty commitments of military alliances. Speculations on this question are, however, premature. At this stage it is sufficient to refer to those higher commitments concerning peaceful settlement of disputes the UN Charter imposes on its signatories. It is, furthermore, worth pointing out that in the Final Act of the CSCE the signatories have solemnly promised to regard each others' borders as inviolable and to refrain now and in the future from assaulting these borders.

The expression of the no-force principle on a regional basis in the form of a non-aggression treaty would not in itself constitute new international practice. Therefore, it is hard to find opposing arguments of a basic nature to such a treaty. In addition, a non-aggression treaty would significantly promote security and *détente*. The removal of the threat of aggression and military activity in general from the frontiers of the parties concerned would clearly decrease the need for military build-ups, and thus it would serve to strengthen political as well as military *détente* in Northern Europe.

CONCLUSIONS

Arms control measures are possible only if all states involved believe that the measures will enhance their security equally. This elementary but often neglected fact has been convincingly brought home by the recent round of discussion on the concept of a nuclear-free zone in Scandinavia. Some of the comments have once again reminded us of the practical limits of the Finnish proposal. But while the discussion has in part still echoed the old deeply entrenched arguments, there is some reason for guarded optimism: although the participants in the debate have reiterated their own security positions, at the same time the security perceptions of others seem to have received a fair hearing. It has been argued in this article that the discussion has opened up an opportunity to examine what kinds of elements are available for the establishment of arms control arrangements in the Nordic area. The ideas outlined here about the constraints on the use of force, confidence-building measures and the treaty of non-aggression are the result of an effort to see how such measures might provide building-blocks for regional arms control in Scandinavia, either by supporting and enhancing the prospects for a nuclear-free Nordic area or by augmenting security independently of that initiative.

It would, of course, be unrealistic to offer the ideas sketched out in this short paper as a panacea for Nordic security. The authors do not harbour any illusions about the potential obstacles involved in establishing the proposed arms control measures; neither do they expect that these measures alone would totally eradicate the possibility of the use of force in Northern Europe. However, there are grounds for arguing that the described arrangements would help diminish the possibility that Nordic areas would be embroiled in a military conflict — nuclear or conventional. Arms control is based, above all, on the notion that there exists a common interest between potential adversaries in reducing the likelihood for military conflict. In the Nordic context, it would seem that all nations, particularly the Soviet Union and Norway in their border area, would have an especially strong interest in dampening incentives to use military force in Northern regions.

The list of arms control measures discussed here is by no means exhaustive. Further constraints in the Nordic area could conceivably include a commitment by leading military powers to scale down their military presence in the Norwegian Sea. Pre-announcement of major naval manoeuvres and movements, restrictions on amphibious landing exercises, and limitations on the number of vessels allowed in the area might be worth considering. These measures, along with the ones sketched out earlier, would also help alleviate fears of pre-emptive use of military force in the Nordic area.

In Scandinavia, decisions on foreign policy matters are traditionally made on the basis of a thorough assessment of facts rather than on heated arguments of the moment. Cool and careful reasoning is no doubt sorely needed also when national security is sought through arms control. But as the experience with the Nordic nuclear-free zone proposal demonstrates, arms control will not advance on its own. The least that can be done in Scandinavia to get regional arms control on the road is to have an open-minded debate on how the available possibilities could be exploited. The debate might open up new dimensions for Nordic arms control; the avoidance of debate could signal an opportunity lost.

NOTES

1. For a recent elaboration on this theme, see Jonathan Alford (ed.), *The Future of Arms Control: Part III, Confidence-Building Measures, Adelphi Papers*, No. 149 (IISS, London, Spring 1979).
2. A speech by President Urho Kekkonen at the Swedish Institute of International Affairs, Stockholm, 8 May 1978. Reprinted in *Ulkopolitiikka* (February 1978), pp. 53–5.
3. *Internationella Studier*, 3 (1978), p. 130.
4. *Ulkopolitiikka* (April 1978), pp. 45–9 and *Helsingin Sanomat*, 17 November 1978.
5. Forsvarskommisjonen av 1974, November 1978: 9 (Oslo 1978), p. 74.
6. Juri Komissarov, 'Ydinaseettoman Pohjolan tulevaisuus', *Kanava*, No. 9 (1978), pp. 537–44.
7. The term 'special drawing rights' has been used in this context by Johan J. Holst in his 'Norwegian Security Policy: Options and Constraints', Holst (ed.), *Five Roads to Nordic Security* (Oslo, 1973), p. 81.
8. Ibid., p. 116.
9. For the definition of aggression, see e.g., *International Affairs*, 4 (1975), pp. 137–9.

11 Naval Confidence-building Measures (CBMs) in the Baltic

KALEVI RUHALA

In discussions about the future of confidence-building measures one of the ideas put forward has been to expand the prior notifications of military manoeuvres to include, in addition to land forces, other services as well. For many reasons, not least practical ones, naval manoeuvres seem to be a likely candidate for supplementing the CBMs with new components. In the Belgrade follow-up conference the neutrals and non-aligned as well as Romania proposed that consideration should also be given to the notification of naval manoeuvres. The idea seems to have gained the support of the Warsaw Pact countries as well. In his speech of 2 March 1979, Secretary General Brezhnev suggested expanding the notification practice: to notify in advance not only of manoeuvres but also of all major troop movements in Europe and major naval exercises if they are carried out in the vicinity of other CSCE-States. Since then the Warsaw Pact declarations have included the possibility of expanding the scope of confidence-building measures.

Expanding CBMs offers two main avenues of proceeding, within and outside the CSCE framework. In spite of the failure to expand CBMs in Belgrade their development within the CSCE process is being supported in many quarters. For instance Haass points out that one possible means of extending CBM to embrace naval forces might thus lie within the larger context of CBM within CSCE, where the advance notification requirement for manoeuvres could be expanded to include notification of the participation of naval and/or amphibious forces.[1]

Another approach which should be examined, particularly if insurmountable obstacles block promotion of the first one, is to develop CBMs in a regional context. The benefit of this approach undoubtedly is that in a limited geographical area CBMs might consist of relatively detailed provisions. In addition to manoeuvres of land forces this holds true with regard to naval exercises as well.

The Baltic Sea as a maritime region which is relatively free from outside operations might well serve as a test site of naval CBMs. The area of application would comprise all of the Baltic Sea and the measures to be agreed upon would concern all the Coastal States: Denmark, Sweden, Finland, the Soviet Union, Poland, the German Democratic Republic and the Federal Republic of Germany. The object of the CBMs would be naval exercises and movements of the coastal states as well as multinational manoeuvres. In this case the confidence-building measures might take the following forms.

(1) The coastal states notify each other in advance of naval and amphibious exercises as well as multinational naval manoeuvres. The size of the exercise to be notified would depend on an agreement between the parties concerned but could be defined so as to include all exercises of military-political significance. Notification should be given at least 30 days, preferably more, in advance of the start of the manoeuvre. Notification should contain (in accordance with the Final Act of the CSCE) at least information of the designation, the general purpose of and the States involved in the manoeuvre, the type or types and numerical strengths of the naval forces engaged, the area and estimated time-frame of its conduct. In addition, other relevant information, particularly that related to the components of the naval units, could be notified by agreement or provided voluntarily.

(2) Exchange of observers among the coastal states should also be possible, particularly in major naval manoeuvres. This may be arranged by inviting observers from other coastal states or by allowing the other coastal states to observe the exercise from their own vessels.

(3) Important movements of naval forces should be included within the CBMs. In this case notable movements are (a) transfers of naval units to the Baltic Sea or withdrawal of such units from the Baltic and (b) permanent positioning of new types of vessels, preferably also of new weapons systems, in the Baltic navies. Exchange of information among coastal states on these matters could substantially alleviate the anxiety that major movements and the appearance of new types of vessels have been seen to evoke.

(4) A long-range objective might consist of attempts to limit (a) the size and (b) the area of naval exercises, for instance, by agreement

that exercises should not be carried out in the vicinity of borders of other States (particularly amphibious exercises). Limits on the size of exercises would, however, not seem possible until sufficient experience has been gained from notifications of unlimited exercises.

In their present phase of development CBMs are a relatively primitive form of arms control. However, the record so far has been positive and justifies hope for further improvement. A logical step forward would be to set some commonly agreeable limits to military activities. Some thoughts have already been expressed on the desirability of not carrying out manoeuvres above a certain numerical level. In view of these ideas it may be possible that in the not too distant future the concept of limiting naval exercises might also gain support as a means of strengthening confidence and security.

NOTE
1. Richard Haass, 'Confidence-building Measures and Naval Arms Control', *Adelphi Papers*, No. 149 (Spring 1979) p. 28.

12 The Strategic Balance in the Arctic Ocean— Soviet Options

WILLY ØSTRENG

INTRODUCTION

Explorers and strategists have realised for decades that the Arctic had an immense, unutilised economic and strategic potential. This was not fully realised by governments, however, until after the Second World War. Changes in governmental attitudes have been gradual, but have resulted directly from new developments in *political circumstances, arms technology,* and, most recently, in the *exploitability of Arctic mineral resources.*

Changes in political relations between the United States and the Soviet Union from wartime collaboration to cold war antagonism have inevitably concentrated attention on the Arctic, the shortest air route between the two powers. Thus, inventions in weaponry, e.g. long-range strategic bombers, nuclear bombs, and intercontinental ballistic missiles, made the Arctic a core area for detecting the approach of bombers and missiles from across the Arctic Ocean, and consequently for preserving the strategic balance.[1] During the fifties both sides constructed interrelated radar detection systems facing northwards in order to achieve an early warning.

At present there seem to be three main reasons why the Arctic is the object of military interest: (i) the Soviet deployment of Delta-class submarines in an ever-expanding base area at the Kola peninsula; (ii) the sustaining of the early-warning systems on the North American and Eurasian continents; and (iii) the possible need for several countries to protect the activities of future economic exploitation. In this article, however, the only aspect dealt with will be the Soviet nuclear submarine deployment in the Arctic. The reason for this exclusive emphasis is the fact that the other two aspects have previously been discussed in some detail by others.[2]

For obvious reasons, information regarding military operations in the Arctic has, since the late forties, been a guarded secret in both Moscow and Washington. This, inevitably, confronts the researcher with the problem of providing sufficient documentation. Thus, it must be stressed as a qualification to the conclusions drawn in this paper that the data used have been taken from open sources only; they are to a large extent indicative, and logical deduction is the main method employed.

In 1975 it was reported that the Soviet Union was keeping its Delta-class submarines within the Barents Sea, safe beyond the detection range of US surveillance systems, rather than sending them on patrols off the American coast.[3] This 'change' of deployment can be interpreted in two ways: either it is a Soviet decision to put the Delta-class submarines through extensive training programmes before sending them on long patrols, or it might reflect a shift in Soviet SSBN deployment strategy to keep these vessels within the Arctic, close to home ports. Whatever interpretation is employed, no definite conclusion can be drawn at present given the sparsity of unclassified data available. However, on the basis of available data, the author feels that the reasoning introduced in this paper is sufficiently plausible to warrant serious consideration.

A glance at a world map will clearly illustrate the geographical disadvantages the Soviet Union has as a major seapower. Her access to the high seas is dependent on passage between her four naval theatres through straits which present huge transit problems. These passage areas can be covered with detection devices preventing the Soviet Fleet from operating without being observed and traced. Straits leading to and from the Soviet naval ports on the Pacific, the Black Sea, and the Baltic Sea can be controlled and even blocked in the event of war. To a lesser extent this also applies to the much wider Greenland–Iceland–United Kingdom Gap. Actually the Arctic is the only area where Soviet nuclear ballistic missile submarines (SSBNs) have direct access to the high seas, and where they can operate independently of the restrictive policies of countries controlling passage areas to and from Soviet ports. The simple fact that Murmansk can straddle *two* oceans with submarines — the Arctic Ocean and the Atlantic Ocean — has for long been underestimated in public discussion.

About 70 per cent of the Soviet SSBN fleet operates from bases in the Arctic.[4] The most frequently cited explanation for this deployment is the hypothesis that the purpose is to secure access of Soviet SSBNs through the GIUK Gap on their way to launch station off the east coast of the United States.[5] This explanation is both reasonable and possible but not necessarily exhaustive. It seems for instance to overlook the *operational capabilities*

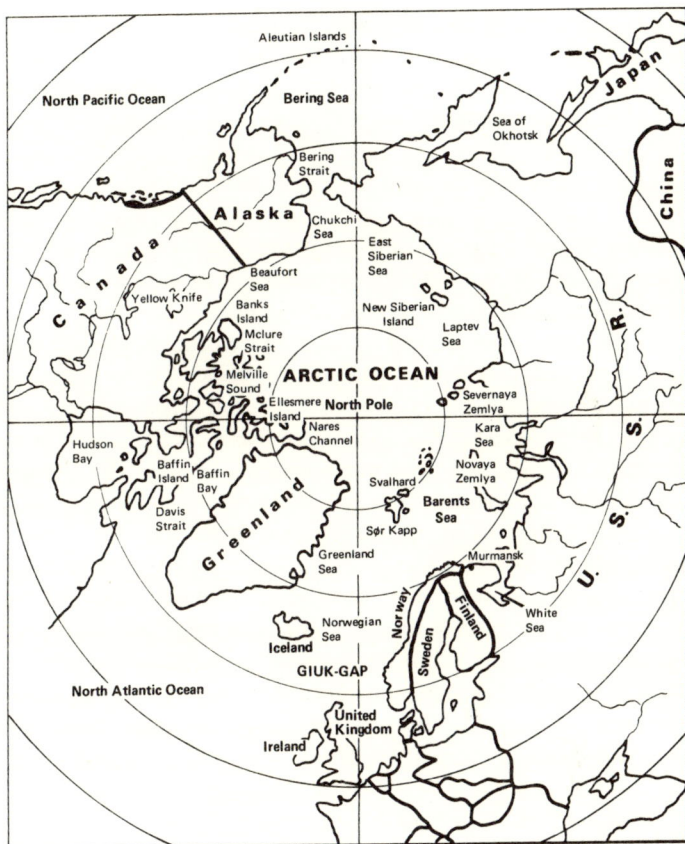

Fig. 12.1 The North Polar region

of SSBNs in the Arctic Ocean, and to underrate the *problem of passage* out of the region. The hypothesis of this paper is supplementary to the traditional explanation, and emphasises that the Arctic Ocean, favoured by tactically advantageous conditions of climate and geography, may have been serving the Soviet Union as an alternative transit and missile-launching area for some time. Indications further suggest that this will remain the case in the foreseeable future.

THE ARCTIC OCEAN AND THE SSBNs: OPERATIONAL CONDITIONS

The main factors pertinent to SSBN operations under sea ice are that they must: (i) be capable of surfacing through the ice; (ii) be capable of navigating safely; (iii) have the capacity to determine position in order to maintain their counter-city capability; and (iv) be equipped to communicate with military headquarters on land.

1. The Ability of SSBNs to Surface between/through the Ice

Contrary to popular belief the ice cover of the Arctic Ocean is not a static unbroken surface. It is constantly in motion, breaking into pieces, and building up pressure ridges above and below the surface where floes grind together. Because of the cleavage of the sea-ice canopy, leads and areas of open water (called polynyas) and thin ice (called skylights) constitute from 5 to 8 per cent of the total area of the Central Arctic Ocean (about 4.7 million km² in area) during the winter season (Table 12.1), and approximately 15 per cent of open water during summer.[6] This is equal to 235 000–376 000 km² of polynyas and skylights during winter, and approximately 705 000 km² of open water in summer. By way of example the open space available to a submarine in the Central Arctic Ocean during the summer season is about twice the total size of the Caspian Sea. In addition to this, a large proportion of the marginal sea (e.g. the Laptev Sea, the Beaufort Sea) is usually ice-free for several months each year. In the words of Horace Wilson, a Canadian meteorologist: 'during the summer, when the Arctic pack is broken into floes, the Arctic Ocean becomes dominantly marine in character . . .'[7]

TABLE 12.1 Percentage of completely open water in 1962–63

Season (months)	Canadian basin	Eurasian basin
Spring (June–July)	6	6
Summer (Aug.–Oct.)	12	7
Autumn (Nov.–Dec.)	6	5
Winter (Jan.–May)	12	11

SOURCE W. I. Wittman & J. J. Schule, 'Comments on the Mass Budget of Arctic Pack Ice', in J. O. Fletcher (Ed.), *Proceedings of the Symposium on the Arctic Heat Budget and Atmospheric Circulation* (California, 1966).

The distribution and frequency of polynyas and skylights is random, but they seem to appear with sufficient frequency to satisfy the operational needs of nuclear submarines.[8] Even in the vicinity of the North

Pole polynyas are formed throughout the year.[9] Captain James Clavert amply confirms this in describing a surfacing in the Arctic Ocean in August 1958: 'Only 40 miles from the North Pole we found the largest polynya of our cruise — nearly half a mile in diameter.'[10] Two years later the USS *Seadragon* found open water at the very Pole.[11] And since that time the North Pole has been the surfacing spot of more than ten US submarines.[12] This is not to say that ice conditions do not differ between areas. Generally, polynyas appear less frequently the closer one gets to the North Pole. It has for instance been noticed that:

> On the Pacific side of the Arctic Ocean Basin, series of water openings may appear in summer . . . these are often large enough for fleets of submarines. Such favourable ice conditions offer nuclear powered submarines a protective canopy of sea ice and, at the same time, holes in the canopy suitable for surfacing or for submerged launching of ballistic missiles.[13]

In winter a submarine usually must break through ice skylights to surface. The superstructure of a SSBN can withstand damage from contact with skylight ice. Breaking through one metre of ice has been accomplished by SSBNs several times. In order to surface through an ice skylight the submarine must rise vertically at sufficient speed to break the ice sheet by the impact of the ship's momentum.[14]

The thickness of the ice-sheet in the Arctic Ocean varies from a few inches to about 100 feet at places where the ice has piled up into ridges. So far there is no reliable information available about the proportion of different ice thicknesses. Such information is difficult to obtain in any case, since ice conditions vary from year to year and between seasons. However, Swedish sources have estimated that the area of the Arctic Ocean covered by ice thinner than 4–5 feet is 30 per cent or more.[15] This estimate is partly confirmed by ice-sheet measurements conducted by American scientists in the early sixties (Table 12.2). If these measurements reflect the true distribution of different ice thicknesses, it should not be too difficult for a submarine to find a place to surface for a missile launch. On the other hand, if ice conditions are too prodigious at one particular place, there is always the possibility of blasting an opening in the ice with torpedoes.[16] Both the Russians and the Americans have conducted experiments on blowing up the ice-sheet.

Table 12.3 gives measurements of the ice conditions confronting a nuclear submarine operating in the Arctic Ocean in 1971.

TABLE 12.2 Relative percentage[a] of different ice thicknesses in most of the Arctic Ocean[b]

Season (months)	Polar ice (aver. 10 ft)	Thick winter ice (1–8 ft)	New ice (0–1 ft)
Winter (Jan.–May)	62	26	12
Spring (June–July)	62	33	5
Summer (Aug.–Oct.)	56	23	20
Autumn (Nov.–Dec.)	58	23	18

SOURCE Wittman & Schule, 'Comments on the mass budget of the Arctic pack ice', J. O. Fletcher (Ed.), *Proceedings of the Symposium on the Arctic Heat Budget and Atmospheric Circulation* (February 1966, California).
[a] The percentage is based on the following numbers of observations: Winter — 1413; Spring — 447; Summer — 857; Autumn — 421.
[b] The Kara and Laptev Seas are not included. Instead the Greenland Sea and Baffin Bay are included.

2. About the Possibility of Safe Under-ice Piloting

Under-ice piloting is done almost entirely by sonars in correlation with a certain knowledge of the bathymetry and ice conditions of the operating area. During the period 1957–62, the submarine forces of the US Pacific and Atlantic fleets conducted about 50 000 km of under-ice operations with the help of sonars.[17] No serious accidents due to the malfunctioning of sonars were reported during these years.

Specialised sonars were, and still are, used to guide the submarines around under-ice obstacles, and to locate suitable places for surfacing through the ice.

In January 1960 the US nuclear submarine *Sargo* entered the Arctic Ocean by way of the shallow Bering Strait, and during a period of thirty-one days transited a distance of 6000 miles across the Bering and Chukchi Seas.[18] *Sargo* navigated these shallow areas[19] by means of sonar, and at times was no more than 25 feet above the sea-bottom.[20] In 1959 the USS *Skate* partly navigated the same area to a point as close as 100 miles from the New Siberian Islands.[21] The navigability of the Canadian Arctic Waters was similarly tested in the early sixties. In August 1960, the USS *Seadragon* followed the Northwest Passage from east to west. The route was through the Lancaster Sound, the Melville Sound, under the ice to emerge in the Beaufort Sea.[22] In July/August 1962 the USS *Skate* made a more hazardous trip entering the Arctic Ocean by way of the narrow and ice-ridden Nares Strait between Ellesmere Island and Greenland.[23] After having examined the data available concerning navigability

TABLE 12.3 Measurements taken from beneath the ice on the return voyage of HMS Dreadnought from the North Pole to the ice edge in March 1971

Latitude °N	Level ice mean draft[a] in metres	Level ice equivalent thickness[b]	Per cent of track with < 30 cm ice	Number of ice keels per 100 km track				
				Draft 10–15 m	15–20 m	20–25 m	25–30 m	Total
89–90	2.3	2.6	1	172	29	1	0	202
88–89	2.1	2.4	1	164	24	8	0	196
87–88	2.1	2.4	2	249	55	6	2	312
86–87	2.2	2.5	9	217	37	8	0	262
85–86	2.2	2.5	5	143	18	2	0	163
84–85	2.3	2.6	4	168	31	13	1	213
83–84	2.2	2.5	4	152	30	8	0	190
82–83	2.5	2.8	15	162	35	8	2	207
81–82	2.4	2.7	3	126	37	8	2	173
80–81	2.4	2.7	10	116	23	3	0	142
79–80	2.1	2.4	3	38	2	0	0	40
Mean 80–90N°	2.3	2.6	5	167	32	7	0.7	206

SOURCE Charles Swithinbank, 'Arctic Park Ice from below', *Sea Ice Conference Proceedings* (Reykjavik, 1972), pp. 246–254.
[a] 'The level ice mean draft' is only the thickness of level ice, and does not include ice keels and pressure ridges above and below level ice.
[b] 'The level ice equivalent thickness' is the *true* mean thickness of the sea ice canopy taking into account pressure ridges and ice keels.

through and around the Canadian Arctic Islands, General Dynamics reached the conclusion: '. . . that submarines would be useful throughout most of the region'.[24] This applied to big submarine freighters (170 000–250 000 DWT), and so must also be valid for the much smaller SSBNs (8000–10 000 DWT) with that much greater margin of safety. Estimates concerning the absolute *minimum* of waterspace necessary for submarine operations in the Arctic Ocean show that the most recent generation of American SSBNs need at least 60 feet of water to accomplish their mission.[25] Needless to say, such conditions greatly 'influence operations, requiring careful piloting and accurate, detailed knowledge of the bathymetry and sound conditions of the area during transit'.[26]

During the early sixties US submarines gained experience in Arctic operations under the following conditions:

I. Minimum ice cover (summer, 5 to 25% open water): submarine surfaces in open polynya in deep water, II. Maximum ice cover (winter, 0 to 10% open water): submarine must break through ice in deep water, III. Maximum dark period (no sunlight or twilight): submarine must break through ice without benefit of light overhead, IV. Shallow waters: submarine must transit at a depth less than maximum draft of the ice canopy and dive vertically in bottom-limited waters, V. Icebergs: submarine must detect ice masses extending below operating depth at maximum speed, VI. Channels: island passages under an ice canopy possibly containing icebergs.[27]

It must be taken into account that these expeditions were carried out 11–15 years ago, and that the capability of nuclear submarines to operate beneath the ice has without doubt improved since that time. This conclusion applies equally to US as well as to Soviet nuclear submarines.

3. About Preserving the Counter-city Capability of SSBNs in the Arctic Ocean

Since the first under-ice passage of *Nautilus* in 1958 the Ships Inertial Navigation System (SINS) has been used and has proved reliable for use in submerged sailings in the Arctic Ocean. The navigator in charge during the *Nautilus* trip stated after its termination:

Sufficiently accurate and safe navigation in the Arctic Ocean up to and including navigation at the Geographic North Pole is a reality using present day equipment, both conventional and inertial. Now that we have seen what the equipment will do and have operating experience, we would not hesitate to operate in an unrestricted manner in these waters.[28]

This statement related only to safe piloting, and not to position determination to achieve a counter-city capability. If, for instance, in the early sixties, the SSBNs had been compelled to rely on SINS alone, with no external guidance, they would probably have lost all counter-city capability within a relatively short time of entering the Arctic Ocean. The *Nautilus* experience may once more serve as an example. During her under-ice crossing in 1958 three back-up systems of navigation were used. The main system was SINS, the other two were based on two different types of naval gyrocompass. After four days beneath the ice a solar fix was taken in open water, and the position of the vessel was found to be within ten miles of that estimated by the three systems.[29]

During the next ten years the inertial navigation systems underwent radical technological improvement. A specialist in submarine navigation at the Norwegian Defence Research Institute stated:

By modern technology it has been possible to develop inertial navigation systems of such a quality that a Polaris submarine can navigate independent of other systems in one month before an error of one nautical mile is accumulated.[30]

Generally, this assessment seems to be valid. But compared to the more recent literature on inertial navigation, it seems to overestimate the independence of these systems over other navigational systems. It is, for instance, widely accepted that present-day inertial systems, from time to time, have to be updated by external sources to be effective — perhaps more so in the Arctic Ocean than elsewhere. At present this may be provided by different types of Very-Low-Frequency systems (VLF), and by satellite navigation, separately or in combination.

VLF systems have been found to provide reliable signal circuits, relatively little affected by auroral and geomagnetic disturbances in the Arctic. Of particular significance is the range, which for the large VLF systems is many thousands of kilometres.[31] The Omega system is an example.[32]

Omega is a worldwide general purpose low frequency navigation system (10.2–13.6 kc/s) for military and commercial aircraft and ships. It consists of eight widely separated transmitting stations. According to the US Navy Electronics Laboratory (NEL), Omega is well suited for submarines because:

> its low frequencies penetrate sea water to appreciable depths. They also travel through sea ice. Thus, a completely submerged submarine can be guided through any seas, including those that lie beneath the frozen polar regions.[33]

The US Navy Electronics Laboratory assumes that the Omega system will provide: 'Accurate position fixes (rms errors of ½ nautical mile during the day and 1 nautical mile at night)'.[34] These position estimates have been confirmed by several other sources.[35] However, position fixes obtained through the polar ice pack are known to be less precise than those obtained in ice-free waters. On the other hand, a Swedish study concludes that: 'heavy ice, which is mostly free of salt . . . facilitates the receiving conditions of submerged submarines', especially as regards depth penetration.[36]

The Soviet Union is known to have a navigation system comparable to the US Omega system. The signal coverage of this system takes in the northern part of Canada, and there are indications that all or most of the Arctic Ocean is within its range.[37]

The best known external position fixing information is obtained by satellite.[38] The US transit system is composed of five satellites, all in polar orbit. Errors as low as 50 feet have been reported, and consequently a fix obtained by satellite can be regarded as being nearly perfect.[39] Under the ice cover, signals from the transit system can be received by hovering an antenna through a polynya or skylight. If this cannot be accomplished the SSBN might surface. Satellite fixes can be obtained almost continuously in the Arctic Ocean, because a transit satellite passes above the Arctic horizon every 22.5 minutes.[40] The Omega system, or any other VLF-system, could be used in between satellite readings to improve the accuracy of continuous navigation. It is for instance known that the British submarine *Sovereign* used the Omega system in correlation with SINS during her under-ice cruise in the Arctic in October 1976.[41]

Obviously, VLF navigational systems, like satellites, are entirely vulnerable to first strikes and sabotage actions. Consequently, the SSBNs have to be self-sufficient with regard to navigational aids in order to preserve their deterrent capability. Besides SINS, this might be achieved by the use of beacons (transponders) or navigational landmarks on the seabed. If necessary the SSBN might even surface to take a celestial fix. Such exposure to the environment in remote and desolate areas represents a risk to the survivability of the SSBN, however slight.

The Circular-Error-Probability (CEP) of the Soviet SS-N-8 missile is thought to be in the range 1.5–2 km.[42] The warhead of this missile is in the one megaton class and will demolish brick buildings within an area of about 50 kilometres from the point of explosion.[43] Consequently, a missile aimed at a city does not have to be very accurate to retain its counter-city capability, since the destruction will be immense no matter where in the city it lands. With regard to the Arctic Ocean this means that even if the error in the navigational systems were 4 or even 5 km, the SSBNs would maintain a deterrent function.

The conclusion to be drawn from this discussion is that the navigational aids on hand in the Arctic at present would seem to be sufficiently accurate to provide the Soviet SSBNs with a counter-city capability. However, the combined effects of the inaccuracy of navigational data obtained in the Arctic and the relatively high CEP of known Soviet SLBMs seem to be too large to fulfil the requirements of a counter-force capability. That is, the capability to destroy US JCBMs inside reinforced concrete silos from launch position in the Arctic Ocean.

The early warning system is one more reason why it is not in the interests of the Soviets to use the Arctic Ocean for counter-force strategy. The Ballistic Missile Early Warning System (BMEWS) in the Arctic gives the retaliatory forces of the United States a warning time of 15–20 minutes, enough of a time-lag to allow the United States to launch US ICBMs and SLBMs against Soviet targets, but not to evacuate cities.

4. Radio Communication between Military Headquarters Ashore and SSBNs beneath the Ice

The last operational aspect to be mentioned, albeit briefly, is that of communication between shore stations and SSBNs. At present SSBNs routinely receive radio VLF signals while submerged under the ice. For transmission, however, the submarine must surface.[44] As well as communication, VLF stations might also be used for navigational purposes.[45]

Today, 18 years after the first nuclear submarine cruise in the Arctic Ocean, it can be concluded that both superpowers now have sufficient operational knowledge to be able to carry out operations under the ice.

5. Strategic and Tactical Prospects: Predictions

After the *Nautilus* cruise in 1958 it was assumed that a new era in Arctic strategy had been opened up. Hanson Baldwin of the *New York Times* pointed out that:

> nuclear submarines operating in the Arctic Seas have an important deterrent capability. . . . This is the region from which missiles with nuclear warheads could dominate most of Russia.[46]

It was also assumed that the 'major Soviet use of the Arctic might be as a protected missile launching area'.[47] The tactical advantages of operating in the Arctic Ocean were acknowledged by US submarine commanders. The *Nautilus* cruise, for example, was assessed in these terms:

> A submarine can remain undetected indefinitely, drifting on the surface in an open lead, camouflage painted white to blend with the ice, cruising under the ice, or lying quietly stopped against an adequately thick ice floe just as submarines have previously lain immobile on the bottom of the sea. From its position in the ice, the submarines can emerge to fire missiles within a few minutes of receiving a signal to do so.[48]

The performances of nuclear submarines indicated that 'strategists of naval warfare (should) . . . add the Arctic to their thinking and planning'.[49] The basic premise behind these statements was obviously the fact that the physical conditions of the Arctic Ocean by and large met the operational requirements of SSBNs. However, from the Soviet point of view this alone could hardly be the most important reason for making the Arctic Ocean a SSBN deployment area. A more compelling reason could be the fact that the Arctic Ocean, in the same way as the Soviet mainland, is 'locked' in by landmasses partly controlled by US-aligned countries. To some extent the Soviet problem of exiting from the Arctic might be compared with her problem of passage in the Pacific, Baltic and Black Seas.

THE SOVIET PROBLEM OF ARCTIC NAVAL EXIT

1. The GIUK Gap

The Greenland–Iceland–United Kingdom Gap (GIUK Gap) is known to be a rather effective ASW barrier connected to the comprehensive US Navy Sound Surveillance System (SOSUS).[50] According to a report on ASW from Harvard University, SOSUS is so reliable that 'in the North Atlantic there is very high confidence of knowing where every submarine is' most of the time.[51] It has been assumed that the SOSU system can detect a nuclear submarine anywhere in the Atlantic and localise it to within a 50 nautical mile radius.[52] This conclusion is supported in a more general assessment made in a recent monograph published by the Stockholm International Peace Research Institute (SIPRI):

> According to unofficial estimates, the United States could under favourable conditions detect and localize most of the Soviet missile carrying submaries on station or in transit most of the time, using presently available area defence ASW systems.[53]

Additional systems now under development, e.g. the Moored Surveillance System (MSS) and the Suspended Array System (SAS), will increase the ability to detect and track submarines in the North Atlantic. The Suspended Array System, which is based on acoustic transducers mounted on a high submerged tripod tower, will be of such size and power, 'that just one such installation will be capable of surveying an entire ocean'.[54] Dr Kosta Tsipis at the Massachusetts Institute of Technology concludes that with the establishment of the MSS and SAS:

> the survivability of hostile submarines in this area will become more problematic. And the end effect of all these surveillance systems may be to effectively discourage the Soviet Union from deploying SSBNs in this ocean basin.[55]

In a recent article by Dr Jim Bussert in *Defence Electronics* it is contended that if under-water tracking equipment were produced in the quantities needed: ..., 'the United States has the technology available to track a Soviet sub from the time it leaves home port until it returns...'[56]

An interesting fact in this respect is the rather low percentage of Soviet SSBNs usually deployed in the North Atlantic.[57] The fact that the Delta-class submarines have not been detected in leaving the Barents Sea and Greenlands Sea for southern latitudes ever since the first deployment in 1972, may illustrate the credibility of Dr Tsipis' prediction.

By far the most effective weapon against a nuclear submarine is another nuclear submarine. On the other hand, by concentrating ASW efforts on natural barriers such as straits and confined sea areas, even diesel-powered submarines may prove to be a valuable counter-SSBN weapon. If the conventional submarine fleets of US-aligned countries littoral to the passage areas under consideration operate in co-operation with the ASW forces of the United States, and if they are particularly suited for the geographical region in which they are patrolling, they might serve as effective anti-SSBN weapons. As regards the GIUK Gap, the SSBN fleet operating from the Kola peninsula can be denied easy access to the North Atlantic by seasonal ice, Norway's navy, or by the contributions of other countries (e.g. Great Britain) to barrier forces in this area.[58] The killing potential of a concerted NATO submarine attack on Soviet SSBNs in the GIUK Gap clearly cannot but add to the rather efficient US ASW capabilities at present in this area. In time of war, or even threat of war, this aspect of passage will obviously be part of Soviet military concern and planning. Soviet leaders also have to consider the possibility that:

> the northern passages to the Atlantic can be sealed with anti-submarine minefields rather than with the enormously expensive barrier of SSNs, landbased patrol aircraft and surface ships assisted by ocean surveillance arrays now deployed. The Captor mine is specifically designed for that purpose.[59]

2. The Bering Strait and the Davis Strait

SOSUS also covers the oceanic approaches to Alaska.[60] The only 'gateway' from the north to the world oceans which may not be kept under surveillance by the United States at present seems to be the Davis Strait. But even here a 'closure' may come about. In the Canadian White Paper on Defence of 1971, the Trudeau government states that:

> Although Canada has a good capability to detect submarines in the temperate zone, it has only very limited capability to detect submarine activity in the Arctic. It might be desirable in the future to raise the level of capability so as to have subservice perimeter surveillance, particularly to cover the channels connecting the Arctic Ocean to Baffin Bay and Baffin Bay to the Atlantic.[61]

A part of the reason for this concern was probably given by Associate Assistant Deputy Minister of the Canadian Department of National Defence, R. H. Falls, in 1973:

To the extent that the ability of the West to detect and track submarines coming through the Greenland-Iceland UK passages improves, alternate routes to the Atlantic through the Arctic become more attractive.[62]

In May 1977 it was reported that: '. . . the Danish Ministry of Defence now believes that Soviet subs can passage between Ellesmere Island and Greenland and, furthermore, that Soviet submarines . . . station themselves under Arctic ice.'[63]

Establishment of a surveillance system in the channels connecting the Arctic Ocean to the Atlantic may turn out to be successful. Contrary to the rather high level of ambient ocean noise measured at the boundary between ice and water,[64] and the highly varying noise level measured beneath the moving sea-ice canopy in the Central Arctic Basin,[65] the ambient noise present in these channels generally seems to be quite low. Allan R. Milne at the Pacific Naval Laboratory concludes, after having carried out measurements of ambient noise under shorefast ice in the Barrow Strait, that:

in the audio range the background noise level was lower than that experienced by the author on any occasion during numerous deep sea operations (in icefree oceans). There was almost a complete absence of popping or cracking noises which could be associated with the motion of the ice.[66]

Obviously, the level of ambient noise will vary with the seasons[67] but it would seem safe to conclude that hydrophones emplaced on the sea bottom in this area would be useful in detecting submarines attempting to transit these channels.

The growing need for Arctic defence measures is clearly recognised in Canada. New airfields are already under construction in the Canadian Arctic, while old ones are being improved. Air surveillance has been stepped up and Arctic military exercises are being staged every year. In 1970 a new military headquarters was established in Yellowknife to administer tasks in the Arctic.[68] The question of acquiring nuclear hunter-killer submarines to provide for Arctic defence has also been a topic of discussion for some time in Canada.[69] Furthermore, the Maritime Command of Naval Forces has staged its first major anti-submarine exercise in Hudson Bay since 1961.[70] These efforts are not all directed solely against SSBNs operating in the Arctic Ocean, they are primarily related to all possible consequences of the new economic development in the region. As a matter of fact, as stated in the Canadian White Paper, the general policy of the government is that:

> the present degree of emphasis on antisubmarine warfare directed against submarine launched ballistic missiles will be reduced in favour of other maritime roles.[71]

This also applies to the Arctic. Nevertheless, military improvements of the kind mentioned are quite new to the Arctic and consequently cannot but add to the high-latitude ASW capability of Canada.

With surveillance and ASW technology at the present levels, in the event of war NATO could not possibly succeed in tracing or intercepting all Soviet SSBNs trying to penetrate the GIUK Gap.[72] The *probability* of detection, however, is relatively high, and continues to increase as new and improved surveillance systems are established. At stake is the survivability of 70 per cent of the Soviet SSBN fleet. Obviously, the Soviets are well informed about the performances of US underwater surveillance equipment and systems in the GIUK Gap[73] and are fully aware of the potential threat these systems pose to free submarine movement. Consequently, there is no logical reason why they would imperil a substantial part of their second strike capability when in a position to avoid it. This has been acknowledged by Rear Admiral John Charles, Deputy Chief Controller General of the Canadian Armed Forces, when he stated in 1970 that a Soviet submarine might use the Arctic as a 'refuge' should allied surveillance activity in the North Atlantic become too intensive.[74]

CONCURRENT SOVIET REASONS FOR AN ARCTIC SSBN DEPLOYMENT

Western observers seem to agree that the Soviet Union is at present lagging five to ten years behind the United States in ASW technology. It is a fact that Soviet SSBNs — especially first-generation ones — are noisier and consequently more susceptible to detection and destruction than their American counterparts. The Soviet Union could partially counteract this situation by heavy SSBN deployment in the Arctic, where the possibility of using ASW devices in an effective manner is considerably less. To ASW forces the Arctic Ocean presents severe barriers.[75]

The sea-ice canopy, cold weather, and reduced visibility hamper ASW aircraft surveillance missions. Surface ASW units have to limit their operations to the fringes of the Arctic, and active and passive sonars may, in the Central Arctic Ocean, be of little use, due to the screwing sounds and constant motion of the ice.[76] At times, the screwing sounds of the ice are so high that it may be difficult to separate submarine signals from oceanic background noise. Thus, the only effective weapon against a SSBN beneath the ice seems to be a hunter-killer submarine.

Since the Soviet Union has no location available for forward bases, a lot of time is wasted getting submarines to the launch station. This means that she has a problem maintaining the same deterrent force operational at any one time. It could be partly alleviated, however, if she were to use the Arctic Ocean — the shortest route between the territories of superpowers. The distance from Murmansk to New York via Nares Strait is less than the distance via the GIUK Gap.

Until recently the short range of the Soviet SLBMs meant that their submarines had to operate fairly close to the US coast in order to be able to strike inland targets (Table 12.4). Soviet submarines were thus more vulnerable to US ASW systems than vice versa. Existing surveillance barriers such as the GIUK Gap made the tracking and detection of Soviet SSBNs comparatively easy. The tracking capacity of the SOSU-system was very soon evident when during the first journey of *Nautilus* she was tracked by SOSUS for six to seven days at a distance of over 1300 miles.[77] This encouraged the quietening of later American submarines and led to further improvement in underwater sonar arrays. To compensate in some measure for this, Soviet submarines in the Arctic could avoid the US surveillance system by traversing beneath the ice cap.

The Hudson Bay approach north or south of Greenland seems to have been the first course of attack through the Arctic that was considered by Moscow.[78] In the late fifties and early sixties Soviet military writers discussed this approach in some detail.[79] Moscow Radio even warned the United States that missile-bearing Soviet submarines could enter Hudson Bay from under the Arctic ice and bombard the industrial heart of North America.[80] If one considers the time this threat was issued — 1959 — it could have been nothing but pure propaganda. Even if the Soviets had had an operational nuclear submarine at that time, they almost certainly did not have a SLBM long-ranging and accurate enough to be able to carry out such a threat. The air distance from Hudson Bay to for instance Ottawa is about 1000 miles. It is another 400 miles before the prime target of New York is reached (Table 12.4). And so, the

TABLE 12.4 SLBMs (in nuclear subs) of superpowers

	United States				Soviet Union		
Type	Max range miles (stl), km	First deployed	No. deployed July '78	Type	Max range miles (stl), km	First deployed	No. deployed July '78
Polaris A3	2880 miles 4875 km	1964	160	SS–N–5	750 miles 1270 km	1964	33
				SS–N–6	1750 miles 2963 km	1969	528
Poseidon	2880 miles 4875 km	1971	496	SS–N–8	4800 miles 7788 km	1972	306[a]
C4 Trident 1	4590 miles 7400 km	1979		SS–N–18	5530 miles 8900 km	1978	88[a]

[a] Uncertain and approximate numbers
SOURCE *Military Balance* (IISS, London)

Hudson Bay approach as a course of attack could at best have been only a Soviet prospect or futuristic dream. It could not in fact have materialised until the deployment of SS-N-6 in 1969. Canada actually staged her first major anti-submarine exercise in Hudson Bay as early as 1961.

The current range of the Soviet SS-N-8 and the basing of Delta-class submarines in the Murmansk area,[81] have reduced the recent Soviet need to exit any of the three gateways, and have enhanced the strategic significance of their Arctic deployment. As shown in Table 12.7, Soviet SS-N-8s can now threaten cities almost anywhere on the North American continent from submarine positions in the Arctic Ocean. As a matter of fact these missiles can hit vital US targets from Russian territorial waters along the Siberian coast, from where they also cover Europe and vital parts of China. This has been acknowledged by R. H. Falls: 'as the range of their [the Soviets] submarine-launched ballistic missiles increases, they do not really need to use the Atlantic Ocean for their deployment.'[82]

Since the advent of nuclear submarines the Soviet Union has gradually acquired SSBN weaponry to partly alleviate her geographic disadvantages. The former need of the Soviet Union to assure the access of her SSBNs to the North Atlantic has gradually diminished. The Arctic Ocean concurrently has become a realistic deployment alternative to the Atlantic and Pacific Oceans. To the degree that this hypothesis is true, it

TABLE 12.5 Deployment pattern of Soviet submarines (1978).

Type	Northern fleet	Baltic fleet	Black Sea fleet	Pacific fleet	Total
Ballistic missile submarines (N)[a]	48	—	—	20	68
Ballistic missile submarines (D)[b]	10	6	—	6	22
Attack submarines (N)	52	—	—	35	87
Attack submarines (D)	79	32	30	39	180

SOURCE The table is based on computations from: John Kristen Skogan: 'Nordflåten: utrikling, status, utsikter' in *Internasional Politik* no. 3B (1978), p. 494.
[a] Nuclear.
[b] Diesel.

TABLE 12.6 Number and types of Soviet SSBNs (July 1978)

Type	No. and missile types in each SSBN	Building rate per year
15 D–1–class	12 SS–N–8	6–8
13 D–2/3–class	16 SS–N–8/–18	
33 Y–class	16 SS–N–6	
1　Y–class	12 SS–NX–17	
7　H–class	3 SS–N–5	
1　H–class	6 SS–N–9	

SOURCE *Military Balance* 1978–79.

TABLE 12.7 Distance from two positions in the Arctic Ocean to cities in the United States

Launch station	Target	Distance in km from launch station to centre of target
Sørkapp (a small island	New York	5650
south of Spitsbergen).	Key West	7570
Position: 16°32′53″ east,	Los Angeles	7350
76°28′47″ north	Seattle	5900
	Chicago	5880
North of Banks Island.	New York	4450
Position: 120° west,	Key West	5990
75″ north	Los Angeles	4560
	Seattle	3020
	Chicago	4030

must affect the strategic significance traditionally assigned to the North Atlantic and the Norwegian Sea in this respect.[83]

In 1963 it was announced that the first Soviet nuclear-powered submarine, the *Leninsky Komsomol*, had reached the North Pole. Later Captain Zhiltsov — commanding officer during the trip — gave this account of the voyage:

> It was an ordinary trip. We have made such cruises before as well. We had taken part in exercises, carrying out tasks which had not been new to us. But the fact that in the course of the exercise we had to pass under the Pole made the trip not quite ordinary.[84]

The underlying military assumption in this statement was confirmed by *Izvestia*:

> The main mission of the ship lay in quickly reaching the North Pole and there barring the path of enemy missile carrying submarines which had been penetrating the Barents Sea.[85]

According to one Soviet journalist the reason exercises like this were being held was because:

> other submarines . . . are creeping up to the North Pole from the other hemisphere. They are looking about for places from which *Polaris* missiles could be launched.[86]

In his most authoritative book, *Soviet Military Strategy*, Marshal V. D. Sokolovski confirms that US submarines were thought to be deployed in launch positions in the Arctic Ocean at the outbreak of war between the superpowers.[87] Captain Christer Fredholm of the Royal Swedish Navy wrote in 1972:

> Through exercises simulating attacks against Soviet territory, Moscow became fully aware of the significance of the . . . Polaris submarines which regularly patrolled the Arctic Regions.[88]

Thus, *Leninsky Komsomol*'s trip to the North Pole in 1963 and similar trips may have been part of an overall exercise programme aimed at preventing attacks on Soviet territory from beneath the ice. Consequently, the possibility should not be overruled that the Soviet Union, apart from her need to use the more sheltered routes beneath the ice-cap to launch station, has also acquired a preparedness to counter US submarines operating under the ice. The Soviet Arctic submarine deployment may thus fulfil two military purposes in the Arctic Ocean — a *strategic offensive* one, and a *purely defensive* one.

SUMMARY AND CONCLUSION

Three relatively distinct periods might be singled out with regard to the Soviet Union's potential and need to utilise the Arctic Ocean.

1. The Sixties

In 1964 the Soviet Union deployed her first SS-N-5 missile with a total range of 1270 km. With the proven ability of Soviet SSBNs to operate beneath the ice-cap, the Soviet Union may have chosen to use the sheltered routes through the Arctic Ocean and the Canadian Arctic to avoid the US surveillance system in the GIUK Gap and the Bering Strait, thereby gaining optimal protection and surprise, and consequently enhancing the real deterrent value of their SLBM force.

The material at hand further indicates that Soviet strategists may have initiated an exercise programme beneath the ice-cap aimed at countering US SSBNs operating in the Arctic Ocean.

2. 1969–72

In 1969 the Soviet Union deployed her first SS-N-6 missile with a total range of 2960 km. With this range the long discussed Hudson Bay approach could become a reality. From launch positions in Hudson Bay and in the Davis Strait, New York was within reach. To a certain extent this reduced the previous need of Soviet SSBNs to penetrate the GIUK Gap to reach launch station off the east coast of the United States.[89]

3. 1972–

With the deployment of the SS-N-8 missile in 1972 the Soviet Union drastically reduced the need of her SSBNs to exit the Arctic Ocean. From almost anywhere in the Arctic Ocean Soviet SS-N-8s could now hit vital US, European, and Chinese targets. Taking into account the long range of this missile (Tables 12.4 and 12.7) the Soviets may already have assigned the Barents Sea their main missile-launching area in the Arctic Ocean. On the other hand, the Soviets may have chosen to spread out their SSBN fleet over the entire Arctic Ocean to minimise the risk of substantial destruction through concerted attack by US and NATO ASW forces on the Barents Sea area. As a matter of interest, the Soviet Union has more strategic options available today than ever before. What choice she has had — or is likely to have in the future — can only be guesswork given the sparsity of data available.

This development and the numerous uncertainties it entails, will obviously receive close attention by US military authorities, who may try to counteract the Soviet achievements by fuelling their present efforts to achieve a sufficient readiness to conduct defensive as well as offensive actions beneath the ice. Since 1975 the US Navy has annually conducted at least one submarine mission in the Arctic. In the years to come the Arctic Ocean may well become an area of importance toward the maintenance of a strategic balance.

As a supplement to the most frequently employed theory stressing the Soviet need to secure her SSBN fleet access to the high seas to achieve a deterrent capability, my hypothesis is that part of the Soviet SSBN fleet at present in Murmansk may to a certain extent fulfil its strategic mission by operating within the Arctic Ocean. This is not to say that the Soviets are supposed to rely exclusively on the Arctic Ocean in this respect. Soviet SSBNs will certainly continue to operate on a global basis, and to exit the GIUK Gap, both for *military* and for *political* reasons. The point is simply that the Soviets are making their presence even more global by also operating in and from the Arctic Ocean.

BRIEFLY ON FUTURE POSSIBILITIES

There is every reason to assume that the US Navy has not yet established the same submarine 'presence' in the Arctic Ocean as has the Soviet Union. However, in US Navy circles there seems to be a growing awareness that this situation cannot go on, 'considering the strategic importance of the area and its military potential'.[90] During a marine conference in Washington in 1970, Rear Admiral C. A. Richmond stressed that: 'There is a growing awareness nationally of not only the economic importance of the Arctic but of the strategic importance of the Arctic'.[91] This attitude is also reflected in the US Navy Arctic research programme, the purpose of which is to:

> formulate and implement an adequate Arctic and Cold Weather Program that will ensure suitable information, material and equipment, techniques, and trained personnel for the prosecution of warfare in the ice covered ocean and seas, and to maintain the Navy in the highest state of readiness to conduct defensive and offensive actions in these areas.[92]

The need for environmental information by surface ships, aircraft, and submarines has dictated the priority of investigations so far.[93] Among other things, the 'Arctic and Cold Weather ASW Project' to develop the capability to penetrate ice by air-dropped particles, may serve as an example of the US Navy research efforts in the Arctic.[94] The latest Soviet achievements in SLBM weaponry and the increasing strategic importance of the Soviet Union's Arctic SSBN deployment cannot but hasten the present US efforts to adjust to all aspects of underwater warfare in the Arctic Ocean. Actually, a change in the utilisation of the Arctic Ocean may occur due to developmental trends not solely related to the Arctic.

If the ongoing SALT negotiations do not end up with an effective agreement on qualitative ASW limitations, the possibility of a technological ASW breakthrough will always be open. Professor Harvey Brooks at Harvard University puts it this way: 'Almost anything in the area of strategic ASW can be done at a cost, but can also be defeated by counter-measures at a cost.'[95] The mere likelihood of an ASW breakthrough in the future may provoke the superpowers into reaching an agreement on SSBN survivability, knowing that the strategic balance theoretically might be at stake in the timelag between the deployment of new ASW systems and the procurement of counter-measures. One line of approach has been the idea of establishing ASW-free areas (so-called submarine sanctuaries) to safeguard the SSBN fleets of the superpowers. Two types of sanctuary have been proposed: those that might be established on the high seas and those that might be established in the territorial seas or the coastal zones of the United States, the Soviet Union, or a third state. In the general debate on this issue the potential of the Arctic Ocean as a sanctuary has not been part of the discussion. Considering that most of the arguments against the idea do not fully apply to the Arctic Ocean, this fact is astonishing. First of all, converting the Arctic Ocean into a sanctuary would not, for the moment at least, interfere with international sea routes. Secondly, the number of countries capable of using tactical ASW against SSBNs in the Arctic is small. With the exception of Canada, and to a lesser extent Norway and Denmark, no other country would have any reason to feel provoked by a sanctuary arrangement in the far north. Thirdly, as both the United States and the Soviet Union are littoral to the Arctic Ocean, their respective SSBNs could operate out of bases in the area, thus eliminating the problem of transiting ocean areas (i.e. between home ports and the high seas sanctuary) where strategic and tactical ASW are not abandoned.[96] Obviously, an Arctic sanctuary could cause problems for the circumpolar countries and thereby jeopardise the arrangement. The point to be made, however, is simply that some of the traditional counter-arguments do not apply to the same extent to the Arctic, this in itself suggesting that the region may have 'refuge' potential if the sea-based deterrent capability is at stake in other oceans. This potential seems to be acknowledged in the Soviet Union.

NOTES

1. For the purposes of this paper the Arctic Ocean is the total ocean area north of the North American and Eurasian continents. It is made up of two main geographical parts: (1) *The Central Arctic Ocean* (4.7 mill. km² in area), which is covered by a sea-ice canopy throughout the year, and (2) *The marginal Arctic seas*: The Chukchi, the East-Siberian, the Laptev, the Kara, the White, the Barents, the Beaufort Seas, and the Canadian island waters. The total area of the Arctic Ocean as defined here is 10.35 million km². Delineation between the Arctic Ocean and the North Atlantic follows the delimitation between the Barents and Greenland Seas, and further north-westward along the Yermak Rise to Greenland. Delimitation between the Arctic Ocean and Baffin Bay follows the 80°N latitude, but includes the Canadian Arctic waters. On the Pacific side the Bering Strait is the line of delimitation. See Patrick D. Baird, *The Polar World* (London, 1963), pp. 90–1.

2. See, for instance, Sayre A. Swarztrauber 'Alaska and Siberia: A Strategic Analysis', *Naval Review*, US Naval Institute, 1965; T. J. Laforest, 'Strategic Significance of the Northern Sea Route', *US Naval Institute Proceedings*, Vol. 93, No. 12 (Dec 1967); Stuart Kirby, 'Considering Siberia', *Rusi-Journal* (June 1973); Anthony Harrigan, 'Northern Defence Frontier', *Military Review*, Vol. XLIX, No. 12, (1969); Richard Boyle, 'Arctic Passages North America', *US Naval Institute Proceedings* (January 1969); Lawrence Griwold, 'The Cold Front', *Sea Power* (Dec 1972); and Gerald E. Synhorst, 'Soviet Strategic Interest in the Maritime Arctic', *US Naval Institute Proceedings* (May 1973), *Naval Review Issue*; Willy Østreng: 'Polhavet i internasjonal Politikk (The Arctic Ocean in International Relations)', Study AA: HO12 (The Nansen Foundation, 1979), 489 pages.

3. See *International Herald Tribune*, 29 April 1975: 'Russians Keeping Missile-Subs Beyond US Tracking Range'.

4. Johan Jørgen Holst, 'The Soviet Union and Nordic Security', *Cooperation and Conflict*, Vol. VI, Nos. 3–4 (1971). See also Table 12.4.

5. See, for instance, Johan Jørgen Holst, 'Northern Europe in the Process of European Security', *NUPI/N-45*, May 1973.

6. Arthur E. Molloy, 'The Arctic Ocean and Marine Science in the North Polar Region', *Oceans*, Vol. 1, No. 2 (1969). For a discussion of the distribution of polynyas and skylights in the Arctic Ocean, see also Charles Swithinbank, 'Arctic Pack Ice from below', *Sea Ice Conference Proceedings* (Reykjavik 1972).

7. Quoted from Donat Pharand, *The Law of the Sea of the Arctic with Special Reference to Canada* (Ottawa 1973), p. 154.

8. Dr Robert E. Kuenne does not agree with this conclusion in his book, *The Polaris Missile Strike. A General Economic System Analysis* (Ohio, 1966),

pp. 88–101. He believes that the frequency of leads and polynyas is not as great as one would think from the more 'enthusiastic' nuclear submarine literature. His scepticism is based on the following three examples: First, in 1958 Captain Anderson of the USS *Nautilus* concluded that polyn'yas were not 'frequent enough to allow a conventional submarine to "jump" from polynya to polynya'. Secondly, the USS *Seadragon* on one occasion in August 1960 searched for twelve hours and nine minutes before finding an opening through which to surface. Thirdly, the most extreme and serious experience was made during the voyage of USS *Skate* in January/February 1960, when the crew discovered only one polynya in twelve days. Obviously, such experiences would be of the utmost importance in deciding whether SSBNs could operate in and from the Arctic Ocean and still preserve their deterrent function. They do not necessarily verify Dr Kuenne's conclusion, however. Compared with the scientific literature on the Arctic ice-pack, Dr Kuenn's conclusions seem to be incorrect. Today it is an established fact that polynyas are more frequent than originally believed in the early sixties. The problem Dr Kuenne describes may be explained by the fact that in the early sixties a submarine had to pass almost directly beneath a polynya before being able to recognise it. The upwards directed sonar continuously measuring the sea-ice canopy was restricted in its capacity to recognise polynyas in the vicinity of the track followed by the submarine. Consequently, the problem in finding polynyas did not necessarily reflect the frequency of water openings, but instead the restricted capabilities of early sonar equipment. Today submarines are equipped with sonars which can cover areas hundreds of metres on either side of the submarine.

9. Waldo Lyon, 'The Submarine and the Arctic Ocean', *The Polar Record*, Vol. II, No. 75 (1963).
10. James Calvert, *Surface at the Pole. The Extraordinary Voyages of the USS Skate* (New York, 1960), p. 127.
11. James L. Dyson, *The World of Ice* (London, 1963), p. 114.
12. *US Navy Press Release*, concerning the USS Flying Fish's North Pole, Baffin Bay trip, March–May 1977.
13. Ragnar Thorén, *Picture Atlas of the Arctic* (Amsterdam, 1969), p. 32.
14. See John E. Sater, *The Arctic Basin* (Washington, 1963), p. 235. See also the 1969 edition of the same book.
15. Ulf Samuelson, 'The Arctic and its Role in World Affairs'. Unpublished manuscript, London 1970, pp. 58–60.
16. Ibid. Ulf Samuelson is a Commander in the Royal Swedish Navy.
17. John E. Sater, op. cit., rev. ed., pp. 265–74.
18. *The Polar Record*, Vol. 10, No. 66 (Sept 1960), p. 279.
19. The average depth of the Barents Sea is 229 m; that of the Kara Sea is 118 m, the Laptev Sea 519 m, the East Siberian Sea 58 m, and the Chukchi Sea 88 m.
20. Waldo Lyon, op. cit.
21. Tønne Huitfeldt, 'A Strategic Perspective on the Arctic', *Cooperation and Conflict*, Vol. IX, Nos. 2–3 (1974), p. 90.
22. *The Polar Record*, Vol. 10, No. 66 (Sept, 1960), p. 390.
23. Waldo Lyon, op. cit.
24. John L. Helm, 'Freighter Submarine Tankers', *Fifth National Northern*

Development Conference Proceedings, 4–6 Nov 1970, Edmonton, Alberta, p. 124.

25. G. E. Synhorst, op. cit., p. 98, fn. 7.
26. Waldo Lyon, op. cit., p. 700.
27. John Sater, op. cit., rev. ed. p. 262.
28. S. M. Jenks, 'Navigation Under the North Pole Icecap', *US Naval Institute Proceedings*, Vol. 84, No. 12 (Dec 1958).
29. *The Polar Record*, Vol. 9, No. 61 (Jan 1959): 'Under-Ice Crossings of the Arctic Ocean: USS *Nautilus* and USS *Skate*', 1958. See also S. M. Jenks, op. cit.
30. Knut Endresen, 'Ubåtnavigasjon' *Forsvarets Forum*, No. 2 (1969), p. 11.
31. R. Thorén, *Picture Atlas of the Arctic* (Amsterdam, 1969). See also J. E. Sater, op. cit., pp. 289–307.
32. In this paper the Omega system is discussed purely for the purpose of illustrating different VLF navigation systems which *could* be used in the Arctic Ocean *if* the authorities in the countries concerned found it advisable and necessary. Technically speaking, there is, for instance, no reason why the Soviets, the British, or other nationalities should not use the Omega system for submarine navigation. A modified version of their already installed VLF communication equipment would probably serve such a purpose. Furthermore, the Omega system provides a good illustration of the Arctic capabilities of VLF systems in general, for instance, the US Navy VLF communication system and the Soviet Omega-like system, on which not much information has been released. The exemplification does not imply any assumption on my part that Omega receivers have been installed in US SSBNs.
33. US Navy Electronic Laboratory, 'Omega Navigation System', *Bureau of Ships Journal*, Vol. 14 (Jan 1965), p. 8. See also R. Thorén, op. cit., and J. E. Sater, op. cit.
34. Ibid., p. 7.
35. See, for instance, Knut Endresen, 'Ubåtnavigasjon', *Forsvarets Forum*, No. 2 (1969); Owen Wilkes, *Omega: Nuclear Warfare Subsystem or International Navigation Aid*, Mimeographed April 1969, Wellington; and Professor R. N. Gould, 'Omega: A Military-Political Analysis', *Comment* (Oct 1968). It should be noted, however, that other sources point out that the average inaccuracy of the Omega system lies in the range of 1–2 nautical miles. See, for instance, Philip J. Klass, 'Navaid Competition Grows Keener', *Aviation Week and Space Technology*, 10 Dec 1973, pp. 55–9. However, the differences observed here do not in any substantial way affect the conclusion drawn in this paper.
36. R. Thorén, op. cit. Thorén proceeds: 'As an example, the depth of penetration in saltfree ice at about 15 kc is about 100 times greater than in sea water with a salinity of 30% . . . Because of this, receiving conditions at a specific diving depth will be more favourable if the submarine leaves open water and moves in beneath an ice field.'
37. Philip J. Klass, 'Soviets Using Omega-like Navaid System', *Aviation Week and Space Technology*, No. 22, 1971.
38. See *Jane's Weapon Systems*, 1973–74, p. 152.

39. W. Blanchard, 'Navigation by Satellite', *Wireless World*, February 1975.
40. John D. Nicolaides, 'The Navigation Satellite', in Fredrik I. Ordway III (ed.), *Advances in Space Science and Technology*, Vol. 5 (New York, 1963), p. 167. The frequency of navigational signals received by a ship at the North Pole, as computed by Nicolaides, is based only on four satellites in polar orbit.
41. Peter Wadsham: 'A British Submarine Expedition to the North Pole, 1976' in *Polar Record*, Vol. 18, No. 116 (1977), pp. 487–91.
42. Manne Wängborg, op. cit., p. 78. *SIPRI Yearbook on World Armaments and Disarmament*, pp. 110–11, claims that the CEP-value most often assigned to the SS-N-8 missile is approximately 1 mile or 1.8 km. It should also be noted that the Soviets during the US/Soviet Summit in 1974 assumed that the United States underestimated the accuracy of Soviet missiles. The Soviets assumed that the CEP-value of present-day Soviet missiles was within the range of 500–800 m. However, the most recent US figures in this respect do not seem to have been affected by this 'correction'.
43. SIPRI, *Offensive Missiles*, Stockholm Papers, August 1974, p. 11.
44. John E. Sater, op. cit., p. 265.
45. See Phillip J. Klass, op. cit., p. 58. It should be noted that VLF stations intended to provide vital communication with *Polaris/Poseidon* and other strategic forces present a problem to continuous navigation because they are shut down individually, and change transmissions periodically.
46. *New York Times*, 3 March 1958, 'New Role for the Arctic. A Discussion of the Region's Military Value in Age of Missile and Atom Submarine'.
47. Gordon W. Brown, 'Arctic ASW', *US Naval Institute Proceedings*, Vol. 88, No. 3 (March 1962).
48. R. D. McWethy, 'Significance of the Nautilus Polar Cruise', *US Naval Institute Proceedings*, Vol. 84, No. 5 (May 1958), p. 35.
49. W. J. Ruhe, 'Seapower in the Seventies', *US Naval Institute Proceedings*, Naval Review, 1969, p. 29.
50. *SIPRI Yearbook of World Armaments and Disarmaments*, 1969/1970, pp. 148–52.
51. *Report on Workshop on Anti-Submarine Warfare*, 11 April 1974, sponsored by the Program for Science and International Affairs and Center for International Affairs, Harvard University.
52. Kosta Tsipis, 'Antisubmarine Warfare — Fact and Fiction', *New Scientist*, 16 January 1975.
53. *Tactical and Strategic Antisubmarine Warfare*. A SIPRI Monograph, 1974, p. 42.
54. Ibid., p. 30.
55. Kosta Tsipis, op. cit., p. 147.
56. Jim Bussert; 'Computers Add New Effectiveness to Sosus/Caesar', *Defence Electronics* (Oct 1979) p. 64.
57. *Report on Workshop on Anti-Submarine Warfare*, op. cit.
58. This point has also been made by Gene La Roque, 'The Nth Country Submarine ASW Problem', in Tsipis, Chan and Feld (eds.), *The Future of the Sea-based Deterrent* (Cambridge, 1973).
59. *Tactical and Strategic Antisubmarine Warfare*, op. cit., p. 36.
60. *Report on Workshop on Anti-Submarine Warfare*, op. cit.

61. *White Paper on Defence: Defence in the 70's*, Ministry of National Defence, Canada 1971, p. 18.

62. R. H. Falls, 'Security in the North' in Nils Orvik (ed.), *Policies of Northern Development* (Kingston, 1973), p. 138.

63. C. G. Jacobsen; 'Soviet Strategic Interests and Canada's Northern Sovereignty', Orea Extra-Mural Paper No 4, February 1978, Department of National Defence, Ottawa, Canada, p. 47.

64. O. I. Diachok and R. S. Winohur, 'Spatial Variability of Underwater Ambient Noise in the Arctic Ice-water Boundary', *Journal of Acoustical Society of America*, Vol. 55, No. 4, (1974). See also R. J. Urick, 'The Noise of Melting Icebergs', *Journal of Acoustical Society of America*, Vol. 50, No. 1 (1971).

65. A. R. Milne and J. H. Ganton, 'Ambient Noise under Arctic Sea Ice', *Journal of the Acoustical Society of America*, Vol. 36, No. 5 (1964). See also Charles B. Greene and B. M. Buck, 'Arctic Ocean Ambient Noise', *Journal of the Acoustical Society of America*, Vol. 36, No. 6 (1964), and Robert J. Urick, *Principles of Underwater Sound*, 2nd ed. (McGraw-Hill Book Company, 1975), p. 201.

66. Allan R. Milne, 'Shallow Water Under-Ice Acoustics in Barrow Strait', *Journal of the Acoustical Society of America*, Vol. 32, No. 8 (1960). Square brackets mine.

67. See, for instance, A. R. Milne and J. H. Ganton, op. cit.

68. *Government Activities in the North. Advisory Committee on Northern Development. 1972 Report and 1973 Plans*, Information Canada, Ottawa, pp. 95–104.

69. See *Toronto Globe and Mail*, 5 June 1970, 'Atomic Submarines proposed for Arctic Defence'.

70. Robert McNeill, 'New Look at the North', *Arctic*, Vol. 23, No. 4 (1970).

71. *Defence in the Seventies*, op. cit., p. 28.

72. If, for instance, Soviet SSBNs operate at shallow depths and at low speed, the possibility of their not being detected by the SOSU-hydrophones is fairly good. Soviet SSBNs might even slip through the Denmark Strait beneath the ice. Furthermore, it has been pointed out that if a submarine operates in the interface of fresh and salt water by the Norwegian fiords, acoustical anomalies are so difficult to overcome that any submarine is fairly well protected from detection (see Farooq Hussain, 'Omega's Role in Missile Launching', *New Scientist*, 16 October 1975). The noise generated by oil-drilling activities in the North Atlantic may also be utilised by Soviet SSBNs for the purpose of avoiding detection.

73. See, for instance, B. Tepelinsky, 'America's Naval Programmes', *Survival*, March/April 1973; and *Translation on USSR Military Affairs*, No. 1063, pp. 1–6, National Technical Information Service, Springfield 1974.

74. See *The Montreal Star*, 24 April 1970, 'Reds in Arctic — Ottawa Silent'.

75. For a more thorough discussion of ASW problems/possibilities in the Arctic Ocean, see Ulf Samuelson, op. cit., pp. 60–2, and Gordon Brown, op. cit.

76. A. R. Milne and J. H. Ganton, op. cit., p. 863, and R. J. Urick, op. cit., p. 201.

77. Kosta Tsipis, op. cit. See also *SIPRI Yearbook of World Armaments and Disarmament, 1969–1970*, Stockholm, pp. 148–54; Jim Bussert,

'Computers Add New Effectiveness to Sosus/Caesar' in *Defence Electronics* (Oct 1979), pp. 59–64.

78. *Montreal Daily Star*, 18 Aug 1959, 'Reds Issue Hudson Bay Threat'; *Ottawa Evening Journal*, 11 Aug 1958, 'New Danger in the North'.

79. Gordon Brown, op. cit.

80. *Montreal Daily Star*, op. cit.

81. *Jane's Fighting Ships*, 1974–75, p. 531.

82. R. H. Falls, op. cit. See also Manne Wängborg, *Militär doktrin och politikk i Sovjetunionen* (Stockholm, 1974), pp. 77.

83. This aspect is thoroughly discussed in Jan Ingebrigtsen, *En studie av Norskehavets strategiske betydning som funksjon av sovjetmarinens nordflåtes operasjoner*. Mimeographed Oslo (NUPI).

84. Quoted from Norman Polmar, *Atomic Submarines* (New Jersey, 1963), pp. 163–4.

85. Quoted from G. E. Synhorst, op. cit., p. 91.

86. J. Nekhamkin, 'On Board a Nuclear Submarine', *Soviet Union*, No. 19–59, 1963.

87. V. D. Sokolovski, *Soviet Military Strategy* (Santa Monica, 1963), p. 442.

88. Christer Fredholm, 'The North Atlantic: The Norwegian Sea, a Scandinavian Security Problem', *Naval War College Review*, Vol. xxiv, No. 9 (1972), p. 58.

89. Given the extreme sparsity of unclassified data we cannot at present conclude whether Soviet SSBNs have negotiated this route, on a regular basis, occasionally, or even at all. The indications at hand are *general*, *vague*, and *uncertain*. Two 'facts' may be established however: (1) In the late sixties and early seventies there were no under-the-ice sonar barriers in the Canadian Arctic, nor any other immediate way of monitoring illicit SSBN passages (see John Gellner, 'A Canadian Viewpoint', *The Soviets and Northern Europe* (Paris, 1971), p. 58; and *Defence in the 70s, White Paper on Defence*, Canadian Department of National Defence, 1971), (2) According to the Canadian press a number of reported sightings of undersea craft were *reported* in these waters during the same period (see for instance *The Montreal Star*, 24 April 1970, and *The Globe and Mail*, 19 Feb 1970). According to the *Montreal Star* a few of these sightings were classified by Canadian defence authorities as 'probables', while others were dismissed as being without foundation. None, upon investigation, has been definitely confirmed. One of the problems in verification is that by the time the aircraft arrives over the spot, the submarine — if there was one there — will have moved on. Another problem is to establish the real identity of the submarine.

90. Davidson Luehring, 'The Never-Never Sea', *US Naval Institute Proceedings*, Vol. 95, No. 8 (Aug 1969).

91. Quoted from *Globe and Mail*, 30 June 1970, 'Arctic's Strategic, Economic Importance Stressed at Washington Marine Conference'.

92. *Arctic Bulletin*, Intergency Arctic Research Coordinating Committee, Vol. 1, No. 3 (Winter 1974), p. 125.

93. Ibid., pp. 124–33.

94. Ibid., p. 126.

95. *Report on Workshop on Antisubmarine Warfare*, op. cit.

96. See Tsipis, Cahn and Feld (eds.), op. cit.

13 The Arctic Resources' Possible Part in Future Energy Politics

JØRGEN TAAGHOLT

Recent international crises involving energy and raw material resources have prompted recognition that today's known reserves cannot continue to satisfy a rising demand for raw materials and energy, particularly oil. At the same time, recognition of the need to alter priorities of raw material and energy use has prompted conscious limitation of consumption and an expansion of recycling. The use of potential raw materials and energy resources in relatively inaccessible Arctic areas may soon become reality despite the investment required. In this context the great potential for raw materials and energy resources in the Arctic deserves increased attention.

MINERAL RESOURCES

In the northern part of the Soviet Union today mining of minerals as well as oil and gas production take place. The Kola Peninsula in Arctic USSR has gone farthest in industrial development with significant production of nickel and platinum and other metals. In Alaska there is no substantial mining, but in Canada's Yukon and Northwest Territories significant mining, mainly of zinc, lead, silver and copper, is carried on. Production of zinc and lead ore, and the export of kryolite occurs in Greenland, which also has large deposits of iron ore. In Scandinavia there is sufficient iron ore production together with the mining of copper, molybdenum, zinc and sulphur. The polar regions contain approximately 78 per cent of the globe's fresh water reserve, most of which is in the Antarctic. However, the great amount in the Arctic area could easily satisfy a large demand if transport problems could be solved economically.

ENERGY RESOURCES

Coal

Coal is the oldest industrially utilised energy source. Significant deposits of coal are found in the Arctic region, evidenced particularly by extensive Norwegian and Soviet mining activity at Spitzbergen in Svalbard, where each of these countries mines approximately 450 000 tons of coal a year. Approximately 58 per cent of the Soviet Union's total reserves, calculated to be among the world's largest, are found north of the 60th parallel. There are definite coal deposits on the east and west coast of Greenland as well as at Nordøstrundingen. Deposits in east and north Greenland have not been more closely investigated, but they may be significant. Geological surveys and an evaluation of the extent and quality of the coal mines in relation to shipping possibilities are yet to be accomplished.

At Disko Island in west Greenland coal has been mined from 1924 to 1972, both for internal use in Greenland and for export. New and substantially larger deposits have been found at Nugssuag peninsula. However, Arctic coal production can make sense only when production costs enable the coal to compete on the world market. The decision to begin mining depends upon transportation possibilities and the quality, especially the heating value of the coal itself. Given a sufficiently high heating value, the coal potentially could be used in local iron works or exported for electricity production.

Increasing coal consumption causes demand for new coal mines which, as well as rising energy prices, can accelerate the use of the Arctic coal resources.

Uranium

The total amount of coal and oil consumed globally from the year 1900 until now, would today only meet approximately five years' demand. Within only a few generations, oil reserves will be used up. Therefore, new energy possibilities, such as nuclear power based upon uranium, continue to attract investigation.

Norway apparently does not have substantial uranium deposits. Swedish deposits are not of particularly high quality. It is estimated that the Soviet Union has rich uranium reserves. The largest deposits have been found in southern Russia, but large deposits have also been discovered in the Arctic area.

The first Russian atomic energy plant commenced production of electricity in Moscow in 1954 with an output of approximately 5 MW. The largest operating atomic plants in the Soviet Union today have an output of up to 1500 MW and are situated in areas where there are no other available energy sources.

Canada produces a large amount of electricity through the Canadian-developed CANDU reactor which uses natural, non-enriched uranium. Canada also produces and exports uranium in significant amounts. Today 80 per cent of the Canadian uranium production comes from mines in southern Canada. Large uranium deposits have been found in the Northwest Territories, but constraints have been placed on mining by the federal governments' latest restriction on foreign control for Canadian uranium production and on uranium exports.

In Greenland uranium deposits have been known for many years. Since 1978 the Danish Government has conducted intensive geological prospecting at the Narssaq deposit which today shows an occurrence of approximately 43 000 tons of uranium. Additionally, a pilot production of 20 000 tons of ore has been started as well as comprehensive environmental investigations.

These proven deposits near Narssaq, with its year-round port, are most likely to be first used depending on the Greenlandic–Danish political decision. Since 1973, however, the Danish Government has used aircraft to investigate large areas in north and east Greenland with some positive results. Deposits of thorium and other radioactive minerals in Greenland may be a valuable energy resource as additional fuel for future generation of the CANDU reactor.

It might be that the coming generation will not blame us too severely for the introduction of nuclear power stations and the difficulties of storing radioactive waste. However, this problem must be taken seriously. Environmental groups throughout the world have made the authorities aware of the nuclear waste problem. However, from an environmental point of view, nuclear power stations today are the cleanest and most trouble-free sources of energy we have. An intriguing possibility for the disposal of nuclear waste is the use of the Polar regions for this purpose. The slow iceflow in the ice-cap in the Arctic regions thus opens up possibilities for storing radioactive waste on Arctic ice-caps. The flow pattern in the Greenland ice-cap shows a drift-time from the centre and out to the edge of about 100 000 years. Maybe even better results could be found in the totally unpopulated Antarctic. If, however, due to unforeseeable reasons, the waste has to be moved away, huge technical and financial problems will arise.

On the other hand, I feel sure that future generations will blame the people of the twentieth century for using too large a percentage of the world's oil reserve for heating and production of electricity, and today causing too much air pollution by uncritically changing to the use of coal.

Oil

Oil production in Siberia from 1980 onwards is expected to be approximately 300 million tons a year. The Soviet Union is presumed to have the largest oil and gas reserves in the world. Soviet research generally indicates that about 50 per cent of the world's oil reserves are found north of 60°N (see Figure 13.1).

The central area of the northern Soviet Union illustrates that large energy deposits by themselves may have no practical significance in this century because of the great technical and specialised transportation problems involved in exploiting them. Today, about 40 per cent of Russia's oil is transported by railroad at a cost almost three times as great as that for transport by pipeline, which itself is substantially more expensive than transport by oil tanker. Drilling activities are currently under way at sites near the Arctic Ocean which are suitable for shipping by oil tanker. Today the Soviet Union has the leading expertise in the navigation of Arctic ice-covered sea.

It can be asserted generally for the Polar regions that where oil deposits in the Middle East are unique from a geological point of view, the new discoveries, which are made in other places, such as Alaska, are less and at the same time more difficult to utilise. In Alaska the yield of the average well is decreasing, while the energy consumption per production unit is increasing. It can be mentioned that the US has increased yearly investment in oil prospecting by 20 per cent and production during the same period has decreased by 7 per cent annually. After some internal conflicts in the USA and especially in Alaska, the 1264 km-long pipeline from Prudhoe Bay to the shipping port of Valdes was placed in operation in 1977.

Natural Gas

Large amounts of natural gas are extracted with the oil in a proportion of up to 25 litres of natural gas per litre of oil. Significant amounts of gas are pumped back into the oil wells because the new American laws do not permit the gas to be burned. Experts claim that this solution will not work

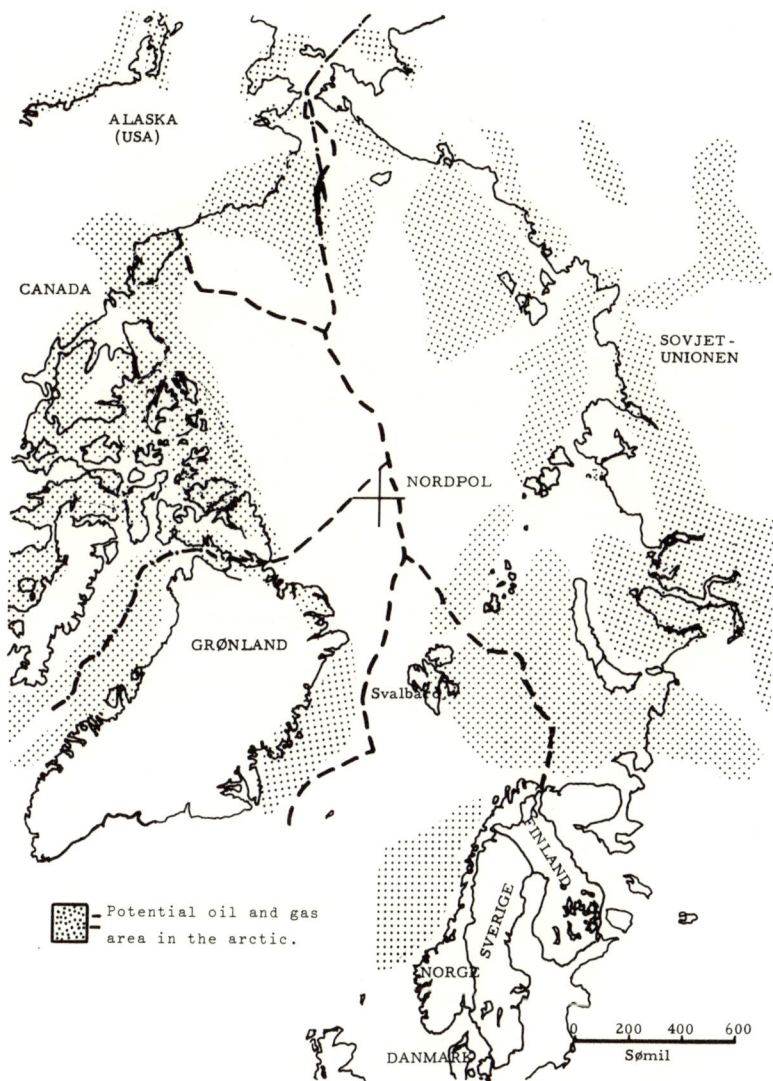

FIG. 13.1 Potential oil and gas area in the Arctic.
SOURCE Bach and Taagholt, *Udviklingstendenser for Grønland*, Commission on Scientific Research in Greenland (Copenhagen, 1976), based on a map made by the US Government, 1974

for more than few years, but a planned gas pipeline from Prudhoe Bay via Mackenzie Valley is now under construction.

The first oil strike in Canada was made well over 100 years ago, but Canadian oil production, dominated today by the central provinces, did not begin until after the Second World War. In 1973 Canada acknowledged its need for an active national policy regarding the environment, the economy, and the export of natural resources when the Canadian Ministry of Energy, Mines and Resources promulgated a 'Canadian National Policy', asserting that the mere continuation of current energy exports would demand an additional investment of approximately $42 billion. Now there is a growing tendency to increase export duties and to export finished goods rather than raw materials — electricity rather than uranium, chemicals rather than oil, etc.

Prospecting activities take place in Canada on land as well as in the continental shelf areas, including the Arctic regions. The discoveries of oil and natural gas on and near the Canadian Arctic islands are of great interest since many of these deposits stretch under the ocean close to Greenland. The cost of prospecting is still large, but in comparison to the capital required to produce and transport oil of Arctic origins, the amount is small.

Based upon relative intensive investigations including seismic tests over a large sea area, the first offshore drilling in Greenland was conducted in 1976, with four during 1977, but all five drillings were dry. No further drillings are planned at present.

Hydrographic measurements at the sea areas east of Greenland show that a continental shelf runs the entire length of east Greenland to a width of 100 to 200 km. It is geologically plausible that the area from Scoresbysund to Kronprins Christian Land consists mainly of sediment deposits identical to those off Norway's west coast.

During 1979 the Danish Government conducted investigations including aeromagnetic observations and seismic tests over a large sea area at the southeastern Greenlandic continental shelf with rather positive results, giving bases for planning increasing activity.

In north Greenland only initial exploration of oil has been undertaken and it is not possible to predict when oil prospecting will be resumed in here. It is apparent, however, that north Greenland, geologically related to the Canadian Arctic islands where oil and natural gas have been found, one day will again be subject to further prospecting. The technical conditions related to prospecting in north Greenland are favourable in that the cold summer is long and very dry; some of the largest ice-free areas in Greenland are found there (see Figure 13.2). If a resumption of prospecting leads to discovery of oil deposits, the greater problem of transporting oil to the ultimate refineries will remain. Production itself is not likely to present great difficulties.

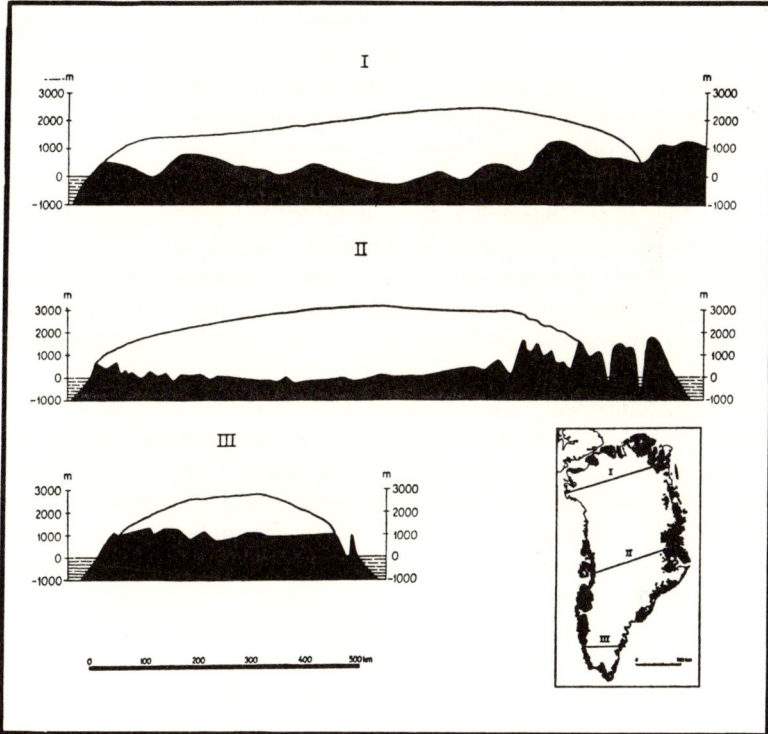

Fig. 13.2 Cross-sections through the Greenland ice sheet. These are based on measurements made by Jean-Jacques Holtzscherer. I. Section from Thule Air Base to Kap Georg Cohn. II. Section from Disko Bugt to Cecilia Nunatak. III. Section from J.A.D.Jensens Nunatakker to Skjoldungen. Vertical exaggeration approx. 1:40
SOURCE Børge Fristrup, *The Greenland Ice Cap* (Rhodos, Copenhagen, 1966)

HYDROELECTRIC POWER

Hydroelectric power is a very attractive, regenerative, clean, energy possibility, already utilised extensively in the Soviet Union, Norway,

Iceland and Canada. For example, hydroelectric power installations provide about two-thirds of the entire Canadian electricity production. For the most part, production capabilities have been reached in closely populated industrialised areas. New, larger hydroelectric plants demand great capital for construction, dams, etc., and require expensive distribution systems from production sites to consumer areas. But environmental concerns, the determination to limit the use of non-reproducing resources, and technological developments in transporting high-voltage current over great distances may in the future lead to our building hydroelectric rather than nuclear plants.

In 1972 Canada constructed one of the Western world's largest hydroelectric plants at Churchill Falls, Labrador. The precipitation from a 100 000 km² relatively level field collects in a large natural lake complex with a falling height of approximately 300 metres to the installed turbines. Their collective capacity is 5225 MW. The maximum yearly output of 34 500 GWh corresponds to about 13 per cent of the total Canadian electricity production, or twice Denmark's production in 1974. The output is channelled to south Canada and to the US. A still larger hydroelectric plant at James Bay in Canada is now under construction.

Similar favourable conditions for hydroelectric production exist in other Arctic areas, particularly in the Soviet Union and southern Greenland, where heavy annual precipitations combined with favourable topographical conditions open possibilities for some smaller hydroelectric plants.

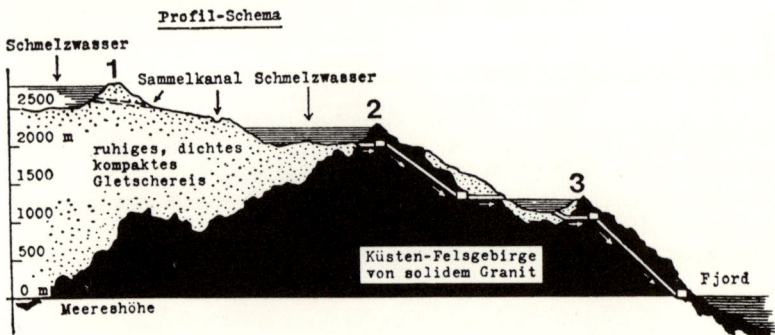

FIG. 13.3 Swiss proposal for hydroelectric power plants in Greenland
SOURCE Kollbruner and Stauber, *Gletscherkraftwerke in Grönland* (Institut für bauwissen schaftslische Forschung, Zurich, 1972)

After the energy crisis in 1973 site evaluations for hydroelectric plants in Greenland increased. In 1975 the Greenland Technical Organisation presented sixteen possible locations for construction based upon traditional techniques with a production capacity of up to 500 MW for the larger plants and a total yearly production capacity of up to 10 000 GWh (see Figure 13.3).

In Scandinavia the national power distribution system connects Denmark, Norway and Sweden, and yields maximum use of the hydroelectric production capacity in Norway and Sweden. Such international co-operation helps to cut down consumption of non-regenerate energy sources.

CONCLUSION

Traditional trade areas have been more or less intensively mapped and investigated; the Arctic has undergone only slight and sporadic geological survey, but with promising results. There is a good chance that the Arctic may contain substantial mineral and oil deposits. When Middle East oil production comes to an end in the next century, Arctic oil deposits will be important as a basis for chemical industries and as fuel for transportation. The future use of oil for heating or for production of electricity is less certain.

Any expanded use of Arctic deposits is tied closely to the resolution of technical problems and the discovery of still richer deposits which need not have commercial worth in this century. No matter how rich the deposit, however, the most pressing technical problem will be the transport of energy resources from one geographical region to another.

Arctic pipelines are already a reality. Many, but not all favourable, experiences have occurred in the Soviet Union. The permafrost tundra areas in particular are considered to be almost prohibited from further development.

In Alaska, after Canadian environmental legislation halted experiments with tanker ships in the Northwest Passage, the trans-Alaskan pipeline has become a successful alternative, now followed by the construction of a gas pipeline via Canada. Conditions for shipping oil by tanker are more favourable in Arctic Europe because the warm Gulf Stream makes year-round sailing possible up to the Kola Peninsula. Large icebreakers render more of these waters navigable on a year-round basis (see Figure 13.4).

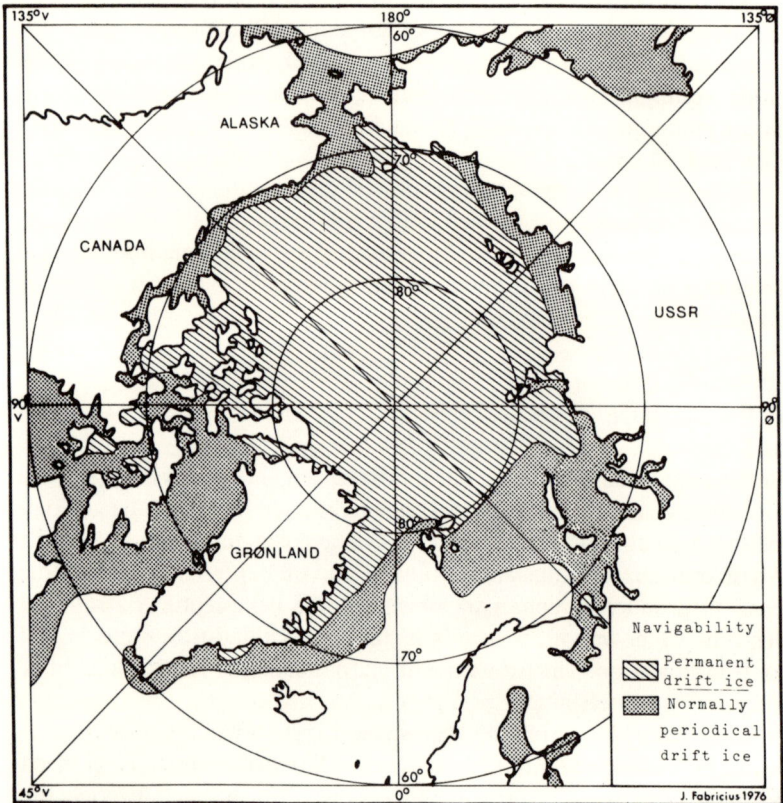

FIG. 13.4 Navigability in the Arctic Ocean
SOURCE Bach and Taagholt, *Udviklingstendenser for Grønland*, Commission on Scientific Research in Greenland (Copenhagen, 1976) from a map made by J. Fabricius, Danish Meteorological Institute

The Soviet Union has shown superiority with respect to surface navigability in the polar seas by going from Taimyr Peninsular direct to the North Pole and back to Murmansk in August 1977 with the nuclear-powered icebreaker *Arktika*, followed by the sistership *Sibir*'s transpolar assistance to the merchant cargo ship *Kapitan Musjovski*, which during May/June 1978 crossed the Polar Sea from Murmansk to the Bering Straits within 17 days.

At present Canada, with the Arctic Pilot Project, plans to transfer liquid natural gas from the Arctic Canadian archipelago via Baffin Bay to the industrial area in southern Canada, using special LNG (liquified natural gas) tankers built for heavy ice.

In a world which, to an increasing degree, is experiencing energy shortages, and where energy production in many cases leads to adverse effects on the environment, it is already unreasonable to let regenerative energy sources flow unused into the Arctic Ocean. Enormous potential energy is involved; one Swiss calculation placed possible hydroelectric production in south Greenland on a scale of millions of megawatts. Danish investigations show that the theoretical potential may be 500 TWh/year which has to be seen in relation to a total electric consumption in Europe in 1976 of 1700 TWh and the proposed realistic utilisation in Greenland of about 10 TWh/year.

Clean local hydroelectric plants in Europe can deliver a significant part of the total local energy requirements, thus reducing the number of oil- and coal-driven power stations, and also reducing pollution. Advanced high-tension current transmission techniques will probably enable the transport of large amounts of energy over thousands of kilometres from energy centres to consumer centres without too much loss *en route*. Already there is an energy production centre on the Churchill River in northern Labrador that, because of its location at the southern rim of the Arctic, supplies consumer centres in Canada and the US. It is reasonable to assume that projects on a similar scale in these peripheral areas will increase in years to come, among them transportation of hydroelectric power using hydrogen transported as liquid gas.

Ideally, energy-demanding heavy industries — those involved in producing fertilisers, aluminium, copper, steel, zinc, lead, PVC, polyethylene, fibreglass polyesters, etc. — will be built in energy-rich regions away from population centres and using up-to-date technology to minimise pollution. Mines will be placed where the combination of materials, energy and transportation is favourable. Plastics industries will locate where natural gas and electrical energy are readily available. In this way energy consumption can be decreased substantially in the population centres.

Exploitation of the riches of the oceans and the ocean floors, especially in the Arctic regions, may require extensive use of huge nuclear-powered icebreakers for supporting the surface bulkcarrier or tanker transport or large submarines capable of carrying raw and energy materials from places of production to consumers in various industrial countries. Their routes under the surface of the ocean may entirely transform the present navigational pattern on the oceans of the world. It is likely that the greatest change will take place in the Arctic Ocean where, up to now, it has been impossible to employ the ordinary units of the Merchant Navy. (Development trends are shown in the US Marine Technology Forecast, see Figure 13.5.)

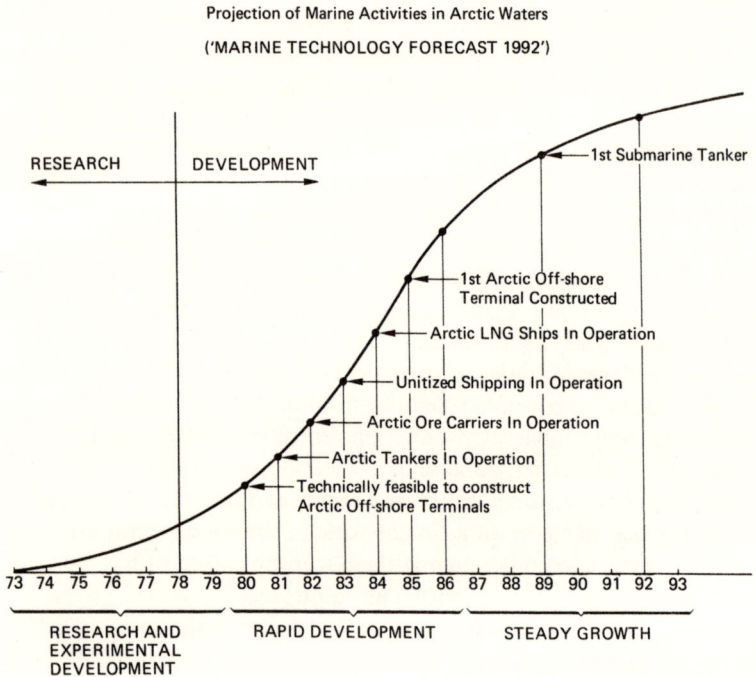

Projection of Marine Activities in Arctic Waters

('MARINE TECHNOLOGY FORECAST 1992')

FIG. 13.5 From US National Academy of Science 'POLAR-GARP' Projections of specialised shipping activities in Arctic regions. Adapted from Arctic Marine Commerce Study by the Arctic Institute of North America under sponsorship of the US Maritime Administration (1973). LNG refers to liquified natural gas SOURCE Bach and Taagholt, *Greenland and the Arctic Region, in light of Defence Policies* (Danish Defence Command, 1977)

Future problems will be technical, commercial and political. To guide the development of the Arctic it would be beneficial to encourage mutual frankness regarding the exchange of technical and scientific knowledge among the Arctic nations, so that the international research capacity invested may be co-ordinated.

The political problems presented by this need for co-operation are not limited to East–West relations. A general international understanding between North and South is also needed. Developing countries, too, have to appreciate the global nature of environmental problems; strong national desires to expand economically and industrially should be adopted to a co-ordinated international plan for the protection of the environment. Finally, environmental considerations must be more than mere restrictions on expanded activity in the Arctic; they must be consistent and highly regarded guides, so that development of energy sources in the Arctic will not result in destruction of the Arctic environment.

NOTES

The more objective information in this paper is mainly based upon the following books, which contain extensive references:

Bach and Taagholt; *Udviklingstendenser for Grønland.* (*Development trends for Greenland. Resources and environment in global perspective*), published by the Commission on Scientific Research in Greenland, Nyt Nordisk Forlag (Copenhagen, 1976), 248 pp.

Bach and Taagholt; *Greenland and the Arctic Region, in light of Defence Policies.* Published by the Danish Defence Command (1977), 56 pp.

The more subjective comments and recommendations express my own personal opinions and cannot be taken as expressing any Danish governmental attitude.

14 Non-living Natural Resources of the Arctic Ocean, Particularly North of Europe

IVAR HESSLAND

Among the main natural sea-bed resources (oil and gas, metals, coal, calcareous matter, gravel and sand) oil and gas are now of paramount importance to the world economy and the contribution of these offshore sources to total world production will increase. The enormous quantities of certain metals in subsea polymetallic nodules will predictably be exploited in the future.

Investigations of the natural resources of the Arctic Ocean bed have started only recently and our knowledge is generally scanty or, for vast areas, non-existent.

Metallic nodules have been observed in Arctic areas but in restricted quantities. In any event, their content of valuable base metals, such as copper and nickel, seems to be low so their commercial value is obviously small. On the other hand, onshore metal and coal deposits should be considered in this context, in conjunction with adjacent offshore oil and gas, since these components together constitute a favourable constellation of prerequisites for local production of ore concentrates. These prerequisites seem to be present in the Canadian Arctic archipelago.

The main interest in the Arctic region for the north of Europe will be focused on the Barents Sea, the Svalbard and Franz Josef Archipelagos and the coastal areas of Norway and the USSR adjoining the Barents Sea. As a rule in estimating potentialities of natural resources, it should be borne in mind that only deposits of great potential are of commercial interest. This is particularly true for Arctic regions.

Large quantities of oil, gas, coal and metals occur in the Soviet section. Comparable quantities are not present or can hardly be expected in the Norwegian sector. Iron, copper, nickel and molybdenum are among the metalliferous deposits of the Kola Peninsula (no oil, gas or coal). Big deposits of phosphates are also present there. Metal-bearing deposits occur in the coastal area between the Kanin Peninsula and the Ural Mountains as well as in Novaya Zemlja. The Pechora Basin (a triangular area between the Timan Mountains and the Ural Mountains) is of exceptional interest because of the presence of enormous coal reserves (estimated at some 350 000 million tons) and a great many giant-sized oil and gas fields. This basin extends into the Barents Sea but its seaward extension is not known. The geology-geophysics of the eastern parts of the Barents Sea are still too little known to allow estimates of oil and gas reserves, but extrapolations of onshore oil and/or gas-bearing geological structures indicate that they could be very considerable. Rather shallow water facilitates exploration and exploitational operations.

Considering onshore northern Norway and the Svalbard and Franz Josef archipelagos, Norway has some copper and a sizeable iron ore deposit. No metal-bearing deposits have been found in the Svalbard–Franz Josef archipelagos but coal is present in both of these areas. The estimated recoverable coal reserves in Svalbard are 115 million tons.

Oil prospecting has taken place on Spitzbergen for about twenty years but with no positive results. Norwegian investigation crews pay special attention to the southern subsea continuation of Spitzbergen, called the Spitzbergen Bank, which includes Beeren Island (Bjornoya) in the Southwestern part. These investigations are being carried out very actively. This area will be under Norwegian jurisdiction but the countries which signed the special Spitzbergen Treaty in 1920 may claim certain oil and gas exploration and exploitation rights.

There is a general belief that the natural resources of the Arctic region (metalliferous deposits, coal, oil and gas) are enormous. This may be so, but the fact is that we really do not know, because the geology of the Arctic has not been studied in great detail so far, except for some areas, such as Spitzbergen and Greenland. The reasons why the geology of the Arctic region has not been sufficiently studied yet are obvious. Those areas are hostile and accessible for investigation only during a restricted period every year. As far as the geology of the Arctic sea-bed is concerned, geophysical instruments for such investigations have been available for some time but they have not yet been used extensively. For this reason the sea-bed of the Arctic region is an almost entirely white area on the global geological map. There is, however, reason to believe that knowledge of the

Arctic sea-floor geology could soon increase because of new and re-latively quick survey techniques. Geological sections of sea-beds can be produced by continuous reflection seismics. Continuous profiling by means of magnetometry and gravimetry can also be done. This is a much more pleasant method than hammer and boot geology in a hostile, snow-covered, mountainous Arctic land environment. The possibilities of in-terpreting the magnetic, gravimetric and acoustic spectra have increased substantially. It is possible, at least to a great extent, to judge, for exam-ple, whether the fillings of structural traps are hydrocarbons or salt water. That, of course, is very important because less has to be spent on trial borings which are the most expensive element in a prospecting budget.

By way of comparison the North Sea floor was a white spot on the geo-logical map only twenty years ago, but today it is geologically one of the best known areas in the world.

Only very large quantities of natural resources can be exploited. Many deposits are subeconomic because they are not big enough and have to be left untouched. The scale prerequisite is especially important when deal-ing with Arctic natural resources. Among other things, labour and trans-portation costs are high and export of the products can only take place during part of the year. This means that Arctic natural resources should be particularly big in order to compete with those in other geographical regions where the exploitation costs are lower, to be exploited eco-nomically. Ore and coal deposits in the Arctic should not only be big but they should also be of high grade; mining conditions should be fa-vourable and transportation costs from the mine sites to export harbours relatively low.

It is of prime importance to lengthen the shipping season, preferably to all-the-year-round shipping. This is not feasible by means of the present type of cargo carriers, but other types of ships specially built for Arctic shipping must be developed. Such work is being done in Sweden.

The Soviet Union and Canada share the main part of the Arctic region but they have great quantities of minerals in other parts of their countries which are more easily accessible so it is natural that these are exploited first. However, the Soviet Union has well-established mining activities on the Kola Peninsula and Canada is planning to increase Arctic mining.

Denmark, on the other hand, has no mining industry but is presently operating one mine in Greenland — not without economic success. The search for natural resources in Greenland is quite active. Norway has mineral deposits but no coal which, however, is transported from Norwegian coal mines in Spitzbergen to northern Norway where it is used as an energy source and for metallurgical purposes.

The ores that may be mined in the Arctic will certainly not be exported as raw materials but as processed products in order to reduce shipping costs. Ore concentrates are being produced already in Greenland and Canada. In future the processing may be carried further so that refined metals may be produced. This means that great quantities of energy are needed. It is obvious that the areas which have the best chance of exploitation are those where energy sources plus coking coal for ferrous metallurgical processes are present. Several areas in the Arctic region seem to qualify in these respects.

It is also very probable that natural gas will be transformed into LNG (Liquified Natural Gas). Refineries are likely to be built in the Arctic.

Revolutionary ideas have been put forward with regard to processing plants and harbours, namely that they should consist of mobile floating modules which could be put together according to local needs and moved from one site to another as the access of raw material changes.

It may also be mentioned that other raw materials are present in the Arctic in addition to energy-producing natural resources and ores, namely sand and gravel. There is an increasing need for such materials in Europe.

There is also reason to consider one particular natural resource in the Arctic which has hardly been thought of before, namely the hydroelectric power that could be produced from ice-dammed lakes.

There is reason to believe that exploitation of natural resources in parts of the Arctic region takes place now for other reasons than economic revenue. Why, for instance, is the Soviet Union mining coal in Spitzbergen? The estimated recoverable coal reserves in the Norwegian coal fields are about 115 million tons. The reserves in the Soviet sector are hardly likely to be greater. This means that the Spitzbergen coal deposits being worked by the Soviet Union are negligible compared to those which are present in the Soviet coastal areas of the Barents Sea, namely in the Pechora Basin, where the coal reserves have been estimated to be some 350 000 million tons. In the northern part of this basin there are, additionally, some very large gas fields and in the southern part some big oil fields.

In the Siberian section of the Soviet Arctic coast area there are several other regions of the same or even higher potentialities with regard to coal, oil and gas.

In Alaska several metallic ore deposits have been found and coal deposits are obviously considerable. Uranium has been observed in several places. Exploration of importance has not yet taken place but prospecting may increase, partly influenced by Japanese interest. Onshore oil and gas from N.Alaska is being piped to Southwest Alaska for further transportation. Offshore prospecting activities along the Polar coast of Alaska will increase and there are geological reasons for believing that they will be successful.

In Canada the main metalliferous deposits are located in the middle and southern part of the country. They are already extensively exploited, and Canada is ranked fourth in the world for ore extraction.

Canadian geologists were until recently rather pessimistic with regard to metalliferous deposits in the Arctic part of the country. Until after 1968 no metalliferous deposits of importance had been discovered in the Canadian Archipelago. Today several such deposits (both iron ores and sulphide metalliferous deposits) have been located and some are being exploited or considered for exploitation. The Canadian government, in co-operation with private enterprises, is studying the special problems (technical, social and other) connected with mining operations in this Arctic environment.

Great quantities of coal are present in the Canadian Arctic but they have not yet been evaluated and developed for production. Gas and oil have been found in several places (onshore and offshore) in Arctic Canada and the problem of connecting them with the Canadian pipeline system is being studied. Their exploitation has not started yet.

In Greenland there is some coal. Several metalliferous deposits have been located and one lead-zinc deposit is presently being mined. Offshore oil exploration is being carried out off the west coast and some areas off the east and north coasts are being considered for investigation. On Spitzbergen coal deposits are being exploited by Norway and the Soviet Union. No metalliferous deposits are known. Oil exploration has been made onshore during the last twenty years but so far without success. The present offshore exploration is being done in the entire western part of the Barents Sea.

In Arctic Norway, several small deposits of sulphide ores have been found and one copper deposit is being mined. An iron ore field (Sydvaranger, the largest ore field in Norway) is being exploited. It is located close to the Soviet border. Coal deposits cannot be expected in Arctic Norway, but there may be offshore oil.

On the Kola Peninsula, phosphate deposits of great importance have been found; there are also several metalliferous deposits, including nickel at Patsamo and large deposits of iron ore which is mainly exported by rail to a steel plant near Leningrad.

The Pechora Basin is significant for very large coal deposits and oil and gas fields. Its extent under the Barents Sea has not been determined: though in general it is clearly within the Soviet sphere, Norway may be able to contest the ownership of some of it.

In Siberia, there are several huge basins containing large coal fields and enormous quantities of oil and gas. These basins extend into the Arctic Sea but, like the Pechora Basin, the limits of their seaward extensions are not known. The very long Arctic shelf area of the Soviet Union is incompletely known with regard to geological structural composition and, consequently, all its offshore oil and gas potentialities. Judging by extrapolation of onshore structures they should be considerable. Lack of appropriate geophysical instrumentation may be one reason why these areas have not been sufficiently investigated.

The most westerly of the basins (the West Siberian Basin) is one of the largest producers of gas and oil in the world and there is no doubt that the Kara Sea which covers the undersea parts of this basin will soon (probably in the 1980s) be included in the gas and oil production of the onshore part of the basin.

The easterly basins (including the Laptev Sea area and the East Siberian Sea area) will probably not be taken into practical account before the end of this century. As in the Pechora Basin the energy resources in these basins are surrounded by metalliferous deposits. Further investigations will certainly show that such deposits are more common than is known today.

The development of the natural resources of the Arctic will depend on increased shipping facilities and the prices and the availability of corresponding natural resources in other parts of the world.

Gas and oil are still cheap products at the source, although the prices have increased considerably since 1973/1974. At a certain price level the Arctic oil and gas may be able to compete. The price of Arctic oil and gas depends on many parameters of which shipping costs is a major one.

With regard to metals, iron can be produced in great quantities and at low prices in many parts of the world, so Arctic iron ore deposits are not likely to be able to compete for the time being unless a very favourable local constellation of energy resources and coking coal is present in the vicinity of sites with great quantities of high-grade ore.

Copper, nickel, lead and zinc are the most important sulphide metals. Certain predictions have been made which claim to show that the world should run out of these metals within a few decades. New finds are being made continuously, however, and there is no reason to believe that there will be a shortage of these metals for a long time to come. The harvest of deep-sea polymetallic nodules (mainly in the Pacific) could result in a heavy surplus of copper and nickel. There is thus no reason for an immediate rush for Arctic base metals although, as with iron, favourable local access of suitable energy sources would increase their chances of being exploited.

Part Four
Threats to Global Stability and Public Confidence in Europe

15 Potential Threats to European Stability

DAVID CARLTON

In October 1944 Winston Churchill and Anthony Eden visited Moscow for talks with Joseph Stalin. Without the knowledge of the Americans, the British and the Soviet leaders appear to have reached an informal agreement for the division of much of Europe into spheres of influence —the so-called percentages agreement. According to the first draft of the record by Sir Archibald Clark-Kerr, then British Ambassador in Moscow,

> *The Prime Minister* [Churchill], then produced what he called a 'naughty document' showing a list of Balkan countries and the proportion of interest in them of the Great Powers. He said that the Americans would be shocked if they saw how crudely he had put it. Marshal Stalin was a realist. He himself was not sentimental while Mr. Eden was a bad man. He [Eden] had not consulted his cabinet or Parliament.

The percentage shares proposed by Churchill were:

Rumania

Russia	90%
The others	10%

Greece

Great Britain	90%
Russia	10%

Yugoslavia   50–50%

Hungary   50–50%

Bulgaria

Russia	75%
The others	25%

At first Stalin was inclined to quibble. According to Clark-Kerr

> Marshal Stalin reverted to the Balkans and asked for the figures about Bulgaria on the 'naughty document' to be amended and suggested that our [i.e. British] interest was not as great as the Prime Minister claimed.[1]

But after more haggling a broad understanding appears to have been reached. One early result was that the British had a free hand from Moscow at the end of 1944 in crushing the pro-Communist forces in Greece. The Americans made high-minded protests but Stalin had no complaints at the British crushing of the Greek Communists.

After the war the Americans took the lead in protesting at the establishment of Communist governments in Eastern Europe. The British, consistent with Churchill's 1944 policy, were more interested in preventing Communism spreading to Western Europe or the Mediterranean. True, Churchill himself proved an exception for in March 1946 he delivered an extreme anti-Soviet speech at Fulton — causing much annoyance to Foreign Secretary Ernest Bevin. But Churchill was out of office in 1946. Once restored to Downing Street in 1951 he reverted to his approach of 1944 and tried hard to obtain a *modus vivendi* with Moscow. The Americans, however, disapproved. In January 1952 Churchill and Eden were due to visit Washington. Recently released material in the Archives of President Harry S. Truman is revealing. An Interdepartmental Steering Committee, advised by the Joint Chiefs of Staff, prepared a paper for Truman containing this judgement:

> . . . by virtue of a complex of factors, of which its geographic position and its special history in European power relationships are perhaps predominant, the UK may differ with us over the tactical methods to be followed in realizing our objectives. In sum, the UK may tend (1) to put a more optimistic interpretation on the imminence and extent of the Soviet threat than we do; (2) to place more faith in the feasibility and desirability of making arrangements with the Soviet bloc in the 'spheres of influence' tradition; and (3) consequently to place more emphasis on the value of direct negotiations with Soviet leaders.

Another paper from the same Committee is also of interest:

> The British will tend to question the necessity or desirability of political warfare operations. They are inclined to accept the present *status quo* in Eastern Europe and do not desire to engage in activities which they consider not only will be calculated to increase East-West tension, but which might even provoke the Kremlin to acts of aggression. The British, in short, appear to believe that the immediate dangers of provocation over-balance the long-term deterrent results of political warfare carried on within Moscow's own orbit . . . The Soviet Union . . . is endeavouring to create disunity, tensions and weakness in the free world. In the face of this massive attack, we believe we cannot adopt a defensive and passive position but rather must counter-attack by political warfare activities directed against the USSR itself and against the Soviet satellites of Eastern Europe with the objective of increasing the discontent, tension and divisions known to exist in the Soviet orbit. The Iron Curtain must be pierced to bring home to the Kremlin's subject peoples the fact that they have friends and allies in the free world. In addition, such activities are designed to form the political bases and operational nuclei for resistance groups which, we hope, would weaken the Soviet regime in case of armed conflict.
>
> We consider that, on balance, this positive activity will operate to deter rather than to provoke the Soviet Union to military aggression . . .[2]

The Americans thus clearly saw Churchill's desire for Summit talks with the Soviets as likely to undermine these policies. Gradually during the ensuing two decades the Americans were won over to the British view. The first Summit was held in 1955 and they have since been held with increasing frequency. American talk of rolling back Communism in Eastern Europe largely ceased after their failure to take any action with respect to Hungary in 1956. Finally came *détente* and the Helsinki Agreements. The Americans finally recognised the post-war frontiers, recognised the German Democratic Republic and committed themselves to the process known as *détente*.

The present strategic position in Europe is one of considerable stability. The chances of either the Warsaw Pact or NATO deliberately initiating a major war in that continent are generally thought to be slight. The real bones of contention are now relatively few. Perhaps the future of Yugoslavia after Tito represents the only major issue on which no tacit understanding exists. We are thus living in the most stable European environment since the beginning of this century — perhaps even since

Metternich. There is of course a price to be paid for this stability and the concommitant low probability of war. Several countries in Europe have had unprecedented limitations placed upon their sovereignty. Finland and Austria, for example, could not join a military bloc. Again, the two German states cannot unite. There must also be real doubt whether any Western European state could in practice join the Warsaw Pact. Collective economic pressure from other Western countries would probably suffice to prevent it, though the precedent of Cuba in another Continent means that we should not perhaps entirely rule it out. But it is not clear, either, that Moscow would actually welcome any new applicant for Warsaw Pact membership if that appeared likely to heighten tension in Europe as a whole. The failure of the pro-Moscow Communist Party to take power in Portugal may be illuminating in this connection. The Soviets appear to have given much more practical help to Marxist forces in the newly independent former Portuguese colonies in Africa than to similar forces in Metropolitan Portugal. Was this perhaps a symbol of a greater degree of East–West understanding applying to Europe than to other continents? Finally, we may note that in Eastern Europe various countries are still subject to a form of Soviet control that was even elevated to the level of a formal doctrine — that of limited sovereignty for members of the Socialist Commonwealth as enunciated by Leonid Brezhnev in 1968 to justify the invasion of Czechoslovakia. The West shows little willingness to offer a central challenge to this doctrine. For example, its formal renunciation was not made a Western precondition for the Helsinki Agreements — a more significant point in reality than high-minded rhetoric, included in the various baskets, that appeared to point in the direction of increased rights for small states. The Europe of the 1980s looks likely to bear more resemblance to the wishes of NATO and the Warsaw Pact than to those of Bucharest, Belgrade, the supporters of Charter 77, the so-called Euro-communists or the Western neutralists. Many Europeans will regret the limitations on national freedoms involved. But it is equally clear that very few Europeans wish to see new outbreaks of the warfare that so scarred the Continent in the first half of the twentieth century and which might well result from any drastic disturbance to the present power relationships.

What are the threats to this Metternichian Europe of the 1980s? Some relate to Europe itself. For example the leaders of the superpowers may change course. A future American Government might go isolationist and withdraw from Europe. Alternatively, a future President may carry forward President Carter's 'Human Rights' campaign to such an extent as to be seen to be intended to 'destabilise' various Communist Governments with the consequence that *détente* and the tacit spheres of influence arrangement would be brought to an end. Or, to take another example, new Soviet leaders may abandon all restraints in seeking to promote revolutionary activities throughout Europe. Again, so many smaller countries in Europe may attempt simultaneously to abandon their alliances with Moscow and/or Washington that one or other or both superpowers may be unable or unwilling to maintain the *status quo* — thereby increasing the chances of coming into conflict with one another in the fluid environment thus created. But none of these developments appears particularly likely to happen in the early 1980s.

It is in extra-European conflicts that the greatest threat to European stability would appear to lie. There has never been any systematic division of Africa, Asia or the Middle East into superpower spheres of influence. And any attempt now to do this would evoke much stronger practical resistance from the Third World states than any of the smaller European states have offered to 'spheres of influence' arrangements since 1945. With demands for a new world economic order gathering strength, the influence of both superpowers in the Third World may indeed be expected to decline rather than increase. But the superpowers cannot simply retreat into a Northern Laager. For they face a future of increasing dependence on the Third World for vital raw materials and, above all, energy resources. In the short term it is the West that stands in greatest need — principally with respect to Middle East oil. But the Soviets might be unwise to seek to exploit Western difficulties in this respect. For in the longer run they, too, will need to import oil. And it is not clear that if more Middle East states follow Iran along an anti-Western path the Soviets would necessarily benefit. For resurgent Islam on the Iranian model might be as anti-Soviet as anti-Western and maybe more so because of Moscow's official commitments to atheism. Again, the Soviet Union contains 30 million citizens who might conceivably look more to Mecca than to Moscow if a new Islamic revival should develop. Thus increasing competition between Moscow and Washington for influence in the Middle East may be damaging to both and may also heighten tension in Europe. But if the Soviets show restraint in not seeking to promote threats to Western oil supplies in the Middle East, they may reasonably feel entitled to increased Western technological cooperation in developing the vast resources of Siberia.

Moscow and Washington may also find it prudent to limit their competition in Southern Africa. Here again mineral resources are at stake. And too bitter a fight for exclusive influence may lead to the effective exclusion of both superpowers in the long run.

The rising power of China provides yet another possibility for increased tension between Washington and Moscow which may in turn disturb the present stability in Europe. The Americans may be tempted to play the 'China card' in some contingencies. But many Europeans will wish them to weigh most carefully whether such a policy might not do more harm than good to the interests of European security.

Clearly the extra-European concerns of the Warsaw Pact and NATO powers are complex and numerous. Moscow may appear to have an advantage in one area, Washington in another. But the reality is that all spheres are linked to one another. Attempts at the compartmentalisation of extra-European problems will in most cases be doomed to failure. And if East–West tensions should increase in the extra-European sphere, we must expect that the prospects for European stability will thereby be jeopardised.

NOTES
1. *Inverchapel Papers*, FO 800/302, Public Record Office, London.
2. *Steering Committee Negotiating Papers*, 3 and 6 January 1952, Harry S. Truman Papers, Box 116, Truman Library, Independence, Missouri.

16 Further Confidence-building Measures: The Reduction of the Military Threat to Peace

WILLIAM GUTTERIDGE

The Final Act of the Helsinki Agreement connected the need for confidence-building measures not only with certain aspects of security and disarmament but with *détente* generally. The causes of tension between peoples and states are at least as much a matter of mutual confidence as of the level of armaments and armed forces. Armed conflict is even more likely to arise from misunderstanding or miscalculation of military activities and developments, than it is from deliberate and direct threats to peace.

It was for these general reasons that the Helsinki Final Act paid particular attention to such practical matters as the exchange of observers by invitation at military manoeuvres as a way of promoting contacts and mutual understanding between military establishments. An important step taken at that time, which has been to some extent realised, was to promote the notification of major military manoeuvres to other states through diplomatic channels. These military manoeuvres as defined in the Agreement, were to be those exceeding a total of 25 000 troops, but provision was made for notification of forces of less than that number if desired. The Agreement also specified the distance of such manoeuvres from the frontier shared with another state and in fact provided that prior notice need be given only of such exercises within 250 kilometres of the geographical frontier of another state. As has been said, this provision has in large measure worked. The question is what purpose it effectively serves and in what way the thinking which led to this stance could be extended in order more effectively to diminish the undoubted perception of threat which exists in a number of quarters.

The well-publicised attendance of observers at each others' military manoeuvres may make some contribution to bringing home to the public consciousness the intention of the countries concerned to establish better international relationships. It is not, however, at this level that the greatest problem exists. The real difficulties are those of popular attitudes as influenced by politicians who may be tempted to exploit for other purposes the fears of their supporters.

Any attempt seriously to tackle this problem requires a degree of public frankness on the part of leaders of major states which has not so far been evident. They need to appreciate that, unless they are as open as considerations of military and national security really allow, they will always be suspected of having ulterior motives. Thus the reported deployment in new areas and apparently for new purposes of armed forces, (armies, navies or airforces) provides continual fuel for suspicion. Such movements of military forces are regularly associated in the public mind with the whole question of national survival — by, for example, raising the possibility of being deprived of essential food, energy or raw materials. The world is today facing a situation in which the growing scarcity of various essential commodities is likely to lead to increased competition for access to them. This applies as much within existing organisations for economic co-operation as it does between the member countries of different power groupings. In short the degree of competitiveness and rivalry is increasing and is likely to continue to increase unless international means are found of pooling resources and of guaranteeing access to them.

Not long ago this problem was thought most likely to lead to conflicts on a North–South basis — that is to say between the developed countries and the less developed countries who nevertheless have within their boundaries potential supplies of essential raw materials. It is now apparent that even within Europe there is likely to be increasing competition for access to scarce energy supplies.

This may seem a long way from the kind of confidence-building measures which featured in the Final Act of the Helsinki Agreement. But *détente* does not apply only to relationships across national boundaries in Europe and there are at least three areas in which if even a small amount of progress was made the rewards in terms of a growth in mutual international confidence would be great.

(1)   The pre-notification of military manoeuvres on a short-term basis is of little popular concern; what does concern the mass of the population is the reported, apparently routine, redeployment of

large military forces not only in Europe but outside it and in the seas around the other continents. These require at least some public explanation if they are not to generate suspicion. As in the end most of them have no prospect of being kept secret, an agreement to notify substantial movements, even soon after the events, would help to allay fears about ulterior motives.

(2) Connected with this are the frequent reports over the years of intervention directly or by way of military assistance by foreign forces from the northern hemisphere in the less developed parts of the world. A code of conduct for military aid and support (perhaps along the lines of that proposed for the transfer of technology) would in itself be a form of restraint, especially if all countries agreed to report to the UN military activities of any kind outside their own borders.

(3) Linked to both (1) and (2) is the question of access to resources. There will not be lasting peace even within Europe if one group of countries fears that another is attempting to deny or wrest from them supplies essential for their survival not only as military entities but as viable societies. This situation is not yet acute but the European countries throughout the continent are in a strong position for many reasons to begin to discuss the pooling of resources and the rational allocation of them. A broad-based approach to these problems would provide a sound rationale, for example, for joint research and development of alternative sources of energy and the maximum use of hydroelectric and other forms of power: it could provide a model for a realistic approach to a modified international economic order.

17 The Impact of Current Developments in Southern Africa on International Security and Co-operation Generally and in Europe in Particular

WILLIAM GUTTERIDGE

The oil crisis of 1973 focused attention on the problem of energy resources but only recently, following the crisis in Iran, has there been discussion of the possibility of international conflict arising from scarcities in this field. A US Senate subcommittee report (quoted in the *Guardian* 16 April 1979), however, predicted a 'fierce political and economic struggle' among the industrial nations over scarce oil supplies.

The fact is that there is now the prospect of international competition not only with regard to energy resources, but eventually for food and metallic mineral raw materials. Provided fertilisers can be manufactured (subject to the availability of the necessary energy supplies) and land can be reclaimed for agricultural use, the supply of food may prove sufficiently elastic. Minerals are, however, in a real sense finite, even though for some time ahead substitutes may be found, new reserves prospected and material effectively reused.

Oil scarcity and even grain supplies have already been manipulated for political ends. Are there other natural materials to which the same might apply? Eventually uranium, if not continually reprocessed or recycled, might come into this category. There are also certainly some metals, which, for military or chemical industry purposes, seem to be in this category and are recognised as being so by authorities in the United States, the Soviet Union, Western Europe and Japan.

Such considerations lead inevitably to the world's major powers beginning to think of scenarios for the not so distant future which involve the possibly catastrophic consequences of global population pressures on supply, leading to international rivalries and conflict. One area of the world particularly involved is Southern Africa where several countries including Rhodesia/Zimbabwe and South Africa have both the capacity to produce food surpluses for export and important mineral production and reserves. The attitudes of major powers towards Southern Africa as a whole from Zaire southwards seem to be influenced more by strategic interests then by a genuine concern for peace and for the development and freedom of peoples and countries which are economically deprived and politically oppressed.

In Southern Africa — and in Africa generally — there is competition for influence on the part of foreign powers which, while it may be rhetorically related to liberation and justice for oppressed peoples, is primarily concerned with access to resources, the possibility of, when deemed necessary, denying them to others, and with commercial and strategic advantage.

Southern Africa thus reflects closely the crude realities of international politics. Without a recognition of these and a deliberate attempt to reconcile the different national interests involved moves towards fundamental disarmament measures on a global basis are bound to be frustrated. National defence policies involve the protection of raw material supplies through stockpiling, through the creation or maintenance of friendly alliances and through the establishment of trading connections and economic relationships which reap diplomatic benefits. These policies are ultimately concerned on one level with those raw materials, including food supplies, which cannot be dispensed with in wartime.

The catalogue of strategic raw materials is constantly changing but there is no denying that Western Europe, Japan and, for some commodities, even North America are dependent upon imported minerals for industrial development if not directly for military purposes. The question which has arisen in relation to Southern Africa is whether raw materials from that quarter might be denied, for example, to NATO countries when Warsaw Pact countries are for the time being largely self-sufficient for minerals.

The perception of threat in these circumstances, and the potential for conflict, is understandable and likely to inhibit the approach to disarmament. But this is not the only consideration: much more important is the tendency, as a result, to disregard the needs of the African peoples in question. Some of them, in South Africa in particular, have yet to achieve any real political freedom; all of them are dependent on the need to develop the resources of their lands and trade on equitable terms with the rest of the world. They require the security of stable markets and fair prices on which to base economic and social development. They cannot be well served, for example, in a situation which encourages sporadic stockpiling.

International rivalry for control and influence in Africa has enabled the South African government to exploit the apparent dependence of the Western nations on South Africa as a supplier of many of the world's strategic minerals. In several cases, e.g. platinum, the major alternative supplier is known to be the Soviet Union. The generation of a belief in the indispensability to Western countries of the South African resources tends to discourage prospecting in other parts of the world and the consequent growth of less developed countries. Mining companies with major investments in South Africa are encouraged to maintain in the West the impression that South African mineral resources are vital to their survival and must at all political costs be kept viable. This is reinforced by the emphasis in the Soviet press and on Radio Moscow on the value of Southern Africa's minerals supplies and by the well-publicised movement of naval contingents.

The overall effect of international tensions and rivalries on Southern Africa has been to inhibit rather than to encourage rapid peaceful political change there, especially in the interests of the black populations in Zimbabwe, Namibia and South Africa. Chrome in Zimbabwe, uranium and diamonds in Namibia, platinum, vanadium and manganese in South Africa have all acquired an undue importance and at least covertly proved obstacles to political change by peaceful means.

If the Southern African situation is not to remain a factor affecting *détente* and global security and co-operation then a number of decisions have to be taken internationally. Major powers and less developed countries, especially those in Africa need:

(1) to agree that they will always seek peaceful solutions to political problems, however serious the situation may be perceived to be;
(2) to respect the economic and social needs, especially of the less developed countries, when making industrial and commercial plans;
(3) to consider, in the interest of moves towards global peace and in the face of the potential exhaustion of the world's natural

resources, some system of allocation and sharing which would not discriminate against the economically weaker countries and would provide reasonable access for all countries to materials in scarce supply.

The Southern African situation, precisely because of its serious racial character, more-or-less in microcosm provides an opportunity to rehearse possible approaches to or alleviations of the problem of competition for resources which, when it becomes acute, will otherwise ultimately cause direct conflict and nullify attempts at disarmament.

The possibility that major powers will attempt to resolve the problems arising exclusively amongst themselves as a basis for mutually improved relationships has to be obviated. It is time for an initiative, including offers of massive economic co-operation, aimed at the recognition of the genuine freedom, economic and political, from external intervention of African peoples. International rivalry in the area is likely to serve only to consolidate the subordination of the black African to white domination in Southern Africa and at the same time to endanger the evolution of *détente* outside Africa.

NOTE
This was written a year before the elections in Rhodesia in February 1980.

Part Five
Economic and Technical Co-operation in Europe

18 East–West Economic Co-operation in Europe: Real Premises and Military Obstacles

NANSEN BEHAR

Economic co-operation between countries with different social orders is closely linked to their political relationships. On one hand, the economic interests of the separate countries encourage political contacts and arrangements of the international relations between them. This tendency dominated in the first half of the 1970s when trade between Eastern and Western Europe grew dynamically, leading to a general desire for the rationalisation and improvement of international arrangements between the two systems in Europe which was expressed by European Security and Co-operation in Helsinki and the Final Act of that conference.

On the other hand, political and military relations between the separate states have a considerable influence on their economic relations. Not by accident the West German professor of political science Gerda Zellentin called the state of the economic relations between Eastern and Western Europe an indicator of the political climate. The economic relations and the military and political relations between the states are in a correlative retro-action, although in the realisation of this relation are involved many factors of economic, ideological, social and geographical nature.

The disparity between the political and military *détente* in Europe reflects itself in a particular way on economic co-operation. In the 1970s important political agreements were reached which contributed to the change for the better of the political climate in the world. Such were the agreements between USSR and the Federal Republic of Germany (FRG) and Poland, USSR and France, the four-power agreement on

Berlin, the contract for the basic interrelations between the German Democratic Republic (GDR), the FRG and many others. These agreements paved the way for political understanding between the countries of different social order, created the basic political premise for the process of *détente*, which in its turn opened the way for the extension of economic co-operation. At the same time, and mainly in the years after Helsinki, the military expenditure of the world and Europe continued to grow and the arms race was given a fresh impetus. This disparity between political and military *détente* reinforced once more the signs of distrust between the governments, revived attitudes from the period of the 'cold war' and slowed down the rate of development of economic interrelations in Europe as compared with the early 1970s.

Thus there is a contemporary paradox. The years after Helsinki, during which logically military *détente* needed to be realised in line with political *détente*, turned out to be a period of dynamic growth of military expenditure in the world at large and in Europe. Indirectly this contributed to a limitation of the commercial, scientific and technical contacts between the countries of the two main social political systems. It is evident that some reactionary forces saw in the decisions of Helsinki and in the possibility that these decisions would be consolidated at Belgrade a 'threat' to their interests. There are reasons for believing that between Helsinki and Belgrade, and after Belgrade, elements in the military industrial complex, mainly in the United States, were activated in all spheres in order to nullify the achievements of Helsinki. In the American press there appeared information about the role which militarist forces played in preventing the normalisation of economic relations between the USA and USSR and in maintaining discrimination in economic policy by the USA towards the socialist countries. The gradually evolved campaign in some capitalist countries directed against the socialist system under the slogan of 'the rights of man' and the attempt to establish the requirement that foreign trade policy be made conditional upon 'democratisation of the political system in the socialist countries' had a considerable negative effect on economic relations between the two systems. Moreover, while the political and military factors reflected reacted on the economic relations between the USA and USSR, some circles in the United States also tried to impose on their partners in Europe a similar link between politics and trade.

In Europe there are all the objective economic, natural and institutional premises necessary for a complete and dynamic unfolding of economic and scientific and technical co-operation. This was underlined many times in Helsinki, as at Belgrade. The existing economic relations between the two social systems in Europe, however, do not correspond to the possibilities of the separate countries, to the achieved degree of development of their economic and scientific and technical potentialities. One of the basic reasons for this disparity is the whole military system existing in Europe, the increase in the armaments drive, which along with the other factors impeding the development of economic co-operation, creates mistrust and tension on the continent.

A considerable proportion of the business interests in Western Europe are convinced that they can have a lasting and mutually advantageous arrangement in the field of international economic relations with the socialist countries. The basic prerequisite for this is the presence of stable economies and an extensive socialist market. But in line with this, some right-wing circles in Western Europe affirm that from bilateral economic relations the socialist countries alone secure an advantage. These circles call on the West not to develop economic relations with the East, as this 'increases' the military potentiality of the socialist countries, which are in need of advanced technology. The viciousness of similar affirmations was revealed in the statements of a number of authoritative political men such as Helmut Schmidt, Valéry Giscard d'Estaing, Bruno Kreisky and others, who have underlined the bilateral advantages of the development of economic relations. In Western Europe alone as a result of trade and co-operation with the socialist countries it is estimated that employment for about 1 300 000 men is provided, which, especially in the conditions of economic stagnation, is of great importance from a social point of view.

A basic objective economic argument for the development of inter-relations between the two systems is the evolving and deepening of international division of labour. As in the case of scientific and technical progress it becomes more and more difficult for a country to produce independently the whole spectrum of means of production and consumer goods necessary for its development. This affects in the first place the small and middle-size countries, like those in Europe, but it is becoming more and more valid also for large countries such as the United States or the Soviet Union. Autarchy of national economies in contemporary conditions is becoming impossible, an anachronism. Even within the frame of the integrationist groups exchange between them and the 'outside world' is becoming a rational necessity. Thus, for example, the countries of the Common Market need to import technology in order to fill the 'technological gap' between them and the United States, as well as raw materials and energy. The proposition of CMEA to the Commission of EEC for the development of economic relations between the two groups is founded on concern for the consolidation of co-operation and security in the world and for the maximum utilisation of the potentialities of an international division of labour and of the resources of the European continent.

The military circumstances are, however, a strong impediment for scientific and technical and economic co-operation. The military need the most advanced technology (for missile construction, electronics, instrument-building and so on), but their need for secrecy prevents exchange of valuable information. We again come up against paradox imposed by the forces of militarism — those branches of scientific knowledge, which need the highest degree of international exchange of scientific and technical information and cadres, are subject to the greatest limitations in this respect.

The energy and raw material crisis in the world should also stimulate the development of economic contacts between the two groups of countries in Europe. In the present situation the eyes of business circles in Western Europe are directed to the rich raw material and petroleum reserves in the Soviet Union and this encourages them in the search for new forms of economic interrelations. This economic, mutually advantageous co-operation in the sphere of raw material policy could transform the European continent into a region to a large extent independent of world markets of raw material. Western Europe is rich in iron ore, coal and some other raw materials, and in the territories of the member countries of CMEA are 80 per cent of the world reserves of manganese ore, 65 per cent of nickel, wolfram and asbestos, 50 per cent of copper and zinc and 40 per cent of natural gas.

However, in this sphere the military factors hamper the solution of the all-European energy problems. On one hand, the mutual distrust concerning the solution of the problems of energy policy, dictated not least by considerations of 'military security', hinder the joint treatment in the important sphere of energy. On the other hand, the military budgets absorb huge resources, which could be utilised for the solution of energy problems. According to official data the overall budget of the European countries for scientific research and development for military purposes is nearly six times higher than the budget for research in the sphere of energy.

Last, but by no means least, ecological factors should encourage co-operation in Europe. The pollution of the environment is increasingly a global problem. It is more and more difficult for attempts to cleanse and conserve the environment to be fully effective if they are confined by national boundaries. Clean air and water are essential, especially for a continent of limited area such as Europe. Co-ordinated steps for conservation and against pollution require scientific, technical and economic co-operation.

The maintenance of a huge military machine in Europe further complicates the problem of the environment. For Europe is to a smaller degree affected by the problem of radioactive pollution of the atmosphere arising from Chinese nuclear experiments, than are, for example, Japan and the USA. But according to data published in the SIPRI *Yearbook* (Stockholm 1977) for the period 1966–76, in Europe and the seas around it there have been twenty-seven great or smaller accidents with aeroplanes or submarines carrying nuclear weapons. During the period January 1976 to February 1977 alone there were twenty major military exercises in Europe which damaged much fertile land.

Europe has to solve great problems connected with the economic and social development of a number of backward regions in the southern part of the continent; the energy problem; the fight with pollution of environment and many others. All these problems require projects on an all-European scale with considerable financial backing. One possible source of funds would be the reduction of the military budgets and armaments in Europe. Regretfully however, in recent years the reverse tendency has been apparent — military expenditure in Europe has tended to grow. According to data from SIPRI, while in 1974 the total amount of European military expenditure (constant prices, 1973) was $121 billion, in 1976 it had increased to $125 billion. In 1977 European military expenditure (according to preliminary data) increased by $15 billion. Moreover, while for the period 1969–77 the military budget of the Soviet Union has remained approximately on the same level, the member countries of NATO have nearly doubled their total military budget.

The economic relations between the countries of the two systems and *détente* in the military sphere arc linked in a complex fashion. The objective premises and factors more and more impose in international life the development of co-operation between countries of different social order for the solution of the global problems of humanity. Whoever opposes these tendencies is in essence resisting the tide of events in the world. Protagonists of increased military establishments and the adherents to armaments in Europe and the world are in this position. Proclaiming themselves against any considerable major steps towards disarmament and peace, in essence they become an obstacle to economic and social progress. And vice versa, the struggle for peace and disarmament is not only concerned with the elimination of the danger of war, but also incidentally opens the way for social and economic progress in the world.

19 European Collaboration in Science and Technology After Helsinki

MARTIN KAPLAN

An assessment of increased science and technology collaborative activities between Eastern and Western European countries after Helsinki does not give much satisfaction to the high expectations at the time of the 1975 Agreement. Let us scan briefly the different fields that were proposed for such activities. I shall not repeat the admirably phrased expressions of intentions, which could scarcely be improved upon, but stick to the content of the recommendations in broad outline.

The main conclusion I derive is that activities in practically all the fields cited have not changed to any appreciable degree, quantitatively or qualitatively, pre- and post-1975. The question is whether there are now any specific suggestions for increased collaboration in any of the fields which would represent, say, an order of magnitude greater than heretofore accomplished, and would thus correspondingly enlarge the contribution of science and technology to European security. The following are possibilities in the different fields.

AGRICULTURE

Research into new technologies for increasing crop cultivation and animal husbandry including machinery, irrigation and genetic breeding; for example, a greatly intensified effort in genetic engineering aimed at transfer of nitrogen-fixing gene(s) to common cereals.

ENERGY

New technologies of production, transport and distribution of existing fuels, hydroenergy, nuclear, thermal and geothermal energy; for example, massive combined efforts in fusion and solar energy research and development including commonly built and operated research centres and experimental reactors.

TRANSPORT TECHNOLOGY

International, national and urban transport networks.

CHEMISTRY

Collaborative research in electrochemistry, polymers, metals and alloys.

METEOROLOGY AND HYDROLOGY

Weather and hydrology forecasting; collection, evaluation and transmission of data.

OCEANOGRAPHY

Air/sea interactions.

SEISMOLOGY

Forecasting of earthquakes.

GLACIOLOGY, PERMAFROST, AND LIFE UNDER CONDITIONS OF COLD

COMPUTER, COMMUNICATION AND INFORMATION TECHNOLOGIES

Telecommunications and information systems.

SPACE RESEARCH

Remote sensing, satellites, rocket probes.

MEDICINE AND PUBLIC HEALTH

Cardiovascular, tumour and virus diseases, molecular biology, neurophysiology, new drugs, pediatrics, gerontology, organisation of medical services; for example, construction and sharing of commonly operated laboratories and centres with P3 and P4 categories of safety facilities for work in genetic engineering and dangerous pathogens.

ENVIRONMENTAL RESEARCH

Health effects of pollutants, collection and sharing of data on environmental hazards and degradation effects including industrial processes on air, water, soil, marine life etc.; for example, much more intensive development of monitoring networks.

In implementation of co-operation for these fields, general recommendations were made in the 1975 Helsinki Declaration for exchange of information in fundamental science, the creation of a 'Scientific Forum' of wise scientist statesmen to forward activities and exchange of information, increased collaboration in the humanities and social sciences, and in education, especially in history, geography, foreign languages and culture generally.

We cannot and should not be satisfied with the routine activities of the UN and its specialised agencies and other international activities which have gone on in the last three years, and which in all likelihood would have occurred with or without the Helsinki Agreement. An increase in the scale of co-operation would necessitate a corresponding increase in funds and manpower by the governments concerned in addition to pious expressions of goodwill on both sides.

The vexed question of human rights featured largely at Helsinki and Belgrade. There was a strong move by a group of eminent scientists to boycott a world congress on cancer, scheduled to be held under the auspices of the International Union Against Cancer in Buenos Aires in

September 1978, because of repression of scientists in Argentina. Such action is now being urged with respect to international scientific conferences and even to visits of scientists and exchange of information with countries presumed to repress scientists and scientific freedom in any significant way. It is obvious that the interpretation of what constitutes repression, and the truth of such allegations, varies greatly. Also, some scientists believe that such a boycott would be counter-productive, that direct lines of communication between scientists should be kept open, and that the universality of science is above 'politics'. Clearly, however, a basic moral and ethical dilemma is involved in the minds of many scientists, the repercussions of which threaten scientific collaboration in Europe and elsewhere.

20 European Co-operation in the Area of Electric Power

R. E. BOTZIAN

INTRODUCTORY REMARKS

The Final Act of the Conference on Security and Co-operation in Europe, signed in Helsinki on 1 August 1975, enumerates within the framework of Basket Two several points of departure for possible co-operation.

Among them the 'Projects of common interest' play an important role. Under this heading primary and secondary energy are quoted as explicit examples with special reference to 'exchanges of electrical energy within Europe with a view to utilising the capacity of the electric power stations as rationally as possible'.

Indeed, using electric power as a kind of 'guinea pig' for co-operation offers some advantages. The slogan 'electricity knows no borders' used by some utility companies in advertising their multinational activities, now must be seen in the light of the fact that the era of abundance, where the generating and selling of electrical energy allowed for a basically egocentric attitude in spite of all declarations of internationality, seems to be definitely over.

On the other hand, electrotechnology constitutes a well-established field where most of the inventions, the credit for which might be claimed by the leading nations, were made before the First World War. The two major European grids in East and West represent a total installed capacity of about 190 GW (electrical giga-watts) and constitute a storehouse of practical experience and innovative potential. Nevertheless, a comparison with the United States figure of more than 500 GW calls for intensified European endeavours.

ORGANISATIONS

The Helsinki Final Act also recommends active participation by existing bodies. Here one should mention first of all the international organisations dealing with the practical tasks of running large internationally interconnected grids in 'parallel operation', i.e. all power-generating machines working in a synchronous rhythm. Such organisational tasks are especially the clearing of energy deliveries, the balancing of peak loads, and mutual assistance in cases of the disturbance of supply. The 'Union pour la Co-ordination de la Production et du Transport de l'Electricite' (UCPTE) takes care of a grid comprising almost all West European countries and Yugoslavia. NORDEL accomplishes the analogous task for the Scandinavian countries and the 'Central Control Administration of the United Power Grids Peace' for the European members of the Council for Mutual Economic Assistance (CMEA), though only partially in the case of the Soviet Union.

All-European electrical co-operation is not new. Between the two World Wars the 'Union Internationale des Producteurs et Distributeurs d'Energie Electrique' conducted feasibility studies of an interconnected grid in central Europe. Today UNIPEDE is still concerned with the general prospects of electric power. Among its members are included almost all the central European countries and Poland, in particular.

The Committee on Electric Power of the United Nations Economic Commission for Europe is a genuine all-European body dealing with general problems, among them the integration of large generation units including nuclear power plants into the grid.

TECHNICAL POSSIBILITIES OF
AN ALL-EUROPEAN GRID

Two courses of action are feasible. Firstly a 'strong interaction' between the two systems in Eastern and Western Europe could be strived for. It would require strong and high-voltage interconnecting lines capable of carrying 5–10 GW in each direction. An interesting proposal in this direction was submitted to the ECE by the Soviet Union and Romania in 1971. According to a study, a transcontinental line from Kursk (SU) via Poland and Czechoslovakia to Laufenberg (Switzerland) would be the backbone of the parallel operation of the entire system and would allow for an overall saving of about 2–3 per cent of the installed power which is not insignificant in view of the difficulties of finding sites for new power plants.

Some objections have, of course, been raised. One of them, however, does not appear to be valid, namely that stability can no longer be guaranteed in cases of local disturbances as soon as the entire power system (the 'short-circuit power') becomes too big. But a partitioning of the system at appropriate interfaces is an effective remedy, and certainly a large all-European power system would be a reality today were it not for the consequences of the Second World War.

Other aspects to be discussed are:

(1) Different standards in East and West concerning the tolerable deviation from the mean frequency (i.e. the usual 50 Hertz of alternating current) render a stable parallel operation of both systems difficult.

(2) The high-voltage line (three versions ranging from 750 to 1150 kilovolts have been studied) would require a new technology. It would have to be duplicated to provide a reserve.

(3) A 'unit construction system' is not possible. These considerations lead to uncertainties as to final costs.

(4) The radial distribution at the terminals of the line would require additional investments.

(5) The actual 'give and take' among the participants of a parallel-operated system cannot be pre-determined exactly. Since there are always some residual amounts to be settled in cash, different economic and monetary systems in East and West would require special arrangements of prototype character.

Secondly, a 'weak coupling' between East and West is already under way. It has been the practice for some time to separate a single power plant for a definite interval from one grid and to the other. But only recently have definite plans been made to couple both systems continuously. Here the agreement between Poland and Austria (Czechoslovakia participates as a transit country), concluded in September 1977, is a remarkable pioneer achievement. The coupling between the Eastern and Western grids, each using alternating (three-phase) current, is effected by a special conversion element using direct current in an intermediate step ('high-voltage direct coupling'). It offers the following advantages:

(1) There are no unforeseeable variations in the delivered power.

(2) There are no problems with frequency instabilities being 'exported' from one grid to the other. In the first stage, due in 1983, a transmitting power of 0.4 GW will be available which might be

easily increased unit by unit up to 1.5 GW. Yugoslavia, which is operating its very modern high-voltage grid parallel with the UCPTE, also has connections with the CMEA grid (i.e. at the Iron Gate Hydroelectric power plant run as a joint venture together with Romania) and is planning to follow the Austrian example with a high-voltage direct coupling unit near Nis. Logically a third interconnection between the CMEA and UCPTE grids would be desirable in the North. This would have to be something like a project still under discussion involving the connection of Lower Saxony with power plants near Kaliningrad.

COMMON ENTERPRISES

As stated in the CSCE final document, a basic principle of co-operation has to be the balancing of 'give and take' with the aim of a common advantage. In the technical domain, for instance, the Eastern side could offer experience in the fabrication and operation of very high-voltage (750 kv and more) lines and certain electrotechnical machinery, whereas the Western side could make available nuclear and semi-conductor technology. In economic terms an equation between energy resources and modern technology brought in by the parties would be the basic issue.

Of course, a great deal of research and development would have to go into this, for instance:

(1) Further studies of concepts for long-distance transmission lines: different voltages, alternating versus direct current, diminishing of losses, enhancing of reliability.
(2) Design of a comprehensive network of lines (hierarchical system of different voltages for long- medium- and short-distance power distribution).
(3) Studies of possibilities of saving installed capacities (mutual access to reserves, taking advantage of different local peak times) and on contingency planning to cope with breakdowns (the Electricité de France, for instance, has a computer-based simulation model for national purposes).
(4) Standardisation of technical equipment (e.g. semi-conductor elements for high-voltage direct coupling and of grid operation, especially frequency deviation tolerances (harmonisation of stand-

ards in general are an important precondition for all successful technical co-operation as stated in the Helsinki document).

POLITICAL ASPECTS

As mentioned earlier, the present political situation is not such that the establishment of an extensive all-European power grid rests upon nothing else but technical and economic criteria. In following the proposals made in Helsinki it should be acknowledged that there are political traps that have to be identified and overcome as early as possible.

One major stumbling block seems to be the question of political dependence as a consequence of the possibility that energy supplies might suddenly be cut off. This problem was raised, for instance, in connection with the project for interconnecting Kaliningrad with Northern Germany — especially with regard to the position of West Berlin. Some technical arrangements have been proposed as a safeguard. But the main pillar of mutual confidence cannot be technical gimmicks. It can only be a politically anchored code of conduct. Where there are potentially so many points of interdependence at which disruption could cause grave consequences, it would be unwise to concentrate on technical efforts to eliminate what is really a single political risk.

Long-time successful co-operation can only be based on a spirit of partnership. It would be counter-productive in the long run, if one side claimed to be dominant. In that context the weak coupling between the two grids would be the best starting position, because directives to stabilise the frequency (in severe cases with the consequence of sudden disconnection of major consumers) cannot be imposed mutually and breakdowns where a 'culprit' is looked for cannot be exported from one system to the other one. It would not be good practice for one side to attempt to exploit the economic needs of the other by, for example, selling power plants with lower standards of operational and environmental security than normally required. Partnership means imposing on the other side only those risks one accepts for oneself.

Another political problem arises if common enterprises are to be started with pooled funds. The European Community has had some sad experiences with participants wanting to withdraw their share from funds for national projects. If that situation prevails, co-operation means nothing but an increase in bureaucracy. Here the Utrecht research facility of the Union Internationale de Chemins de Fer might serve as an

interesting model bearing in mind that there are many structural anal-
ogies between electrical and traffic techniques. The UIC, basically an all-
European institution, assigns research and development tasks to single
members in such a way that the commercial benefits of the results are
made available to all of them.

In any case it should be noted that there is a long European tradition of
attempting to interconnect build-up of economic infrastructures and the
establishment of political structures. As early as in 1904 the Russian
Prime Minister Count Witte, a learned railway engineer, strongly urged
collaboration between Russia, Germany and France based on mutual
economic advantages and — at that time regrettably out of reach — com-
pensation of political interests. What else is that *mutatis mutandis* in
almost the same regional context but the philosophy of the three CSCE
baskets?

CONCLUSION AND PERSPECTIVES

The most promising way of promoting all-European co-operation in the
field of electrical power could be to start by intensifying the mode of
'weak coupling' between the two grids. If by following the example given
by Poland and Austria the two other interconnections in the North and
South were established, this could lead to a considerable exchange of
power totalling several GW.

This should be a good way of aiming in the long run at strong coupling
with a uniform frequency adjustment. Starting all activities as early and
as comprehensively as possible would be advisable, because in the energy
field especially one has to allow for several years of planning time if the
demand is not to overtake supply.

A first step would be to team the existing international institutions in
the most effective manner, i.e. the UCPTE and the CMEA electricity of-
fices where the more everyday-life issues are handled, the UNIPEDE
with its longer term orientation and, of course, the ECE, representing a
truly all-European forum. A somewhat different model would rest upon
the interesting fact that it was Switzerland as a neutral country and a
traditional promoter of intergovernmental activities which took the initiative in connecting the French, West German and Italian grids as the
nucleus of the UCPTE and which still renders good services to the
organisation (e.g. adjusting the common frequency in such a way that
electrical clocks remain on time). Therefore, it appears worthwhile to
consider assigning the task of a kind of 'secretary general' for the all-

European electrical activities to one or two of the non-allied neutral participants in the Helsinki Conference.

Of course the interdependence of the electrical field and other requirements of co-operation have to be taken into account. Environmental protection and transport are two such elements. As mentioned above, we might learn a great deal from the planning procedures employed in the railway domain. One might, for instance, refer to the all-European 'infrastructure guidance plan' elaborated by the UIC. Something along these lines would certainly appear to be a basic need in the electrical field. In any case, however, the course of action cannot merely be left to the experts. It is indispensable that all undertakings be promoted and carried out by a high-ranking board bearing political responsibility.

Since 1978 there has been some progress. The 1979 UNIPEDE meeting in Warsaw discussed several aspects of all-European co-operation in the electricity field, but was restricted to technical matters. More interesting political aspects were brought up in an East–West workshop on prospects of co-operation in the field of energy sponsored by the Austrian government in 1979. The participants agreed on the general principle that any measure by a European state aimed at development or conservation of energy sources in such a way as to alleviate the global problem would be in the interest of all. Along these lines the ECE has taken up the task of preparing for the agenda of an all-European energy conference. After two ECE expert meetings in October 1979 and February 1980 the 'green light' is expected to be given by the Madrid CSCE meeting in November 1980.

21 Economic Co-operation as a Factor for the Development of European Security and Co-operation

MAX SCHMIDT

Today economic factors affecting peaceful coexistence between states with differing social systems are of growing importance. Advances made in science and technology help to push forward the development of international economic relations which mostly grow at a swifter pace than industrial output. There is an increasing trend towards the expansion of mutual economic contacts between various countries and regions.

Continuation of the process of political *détente* remains a chief trend in relations between socialist and capitalist countries in spite of the current complicated conditions on the international scene. Making *détente* irreversible continues to be the principal objective of the socialist countries. Politically influential forces in capitalist countries have expressed similar intentions. Given goodwill on both sides, it would be possible to make headway, particularly on the road to implementing the provisions of the Conference on Security and Co-operation in Europe and by way of more intensive efforts for gaining acceptance for the principles of peaceful coexistence in USSR–USA relations, with steps towards military *détente* being the heart of all efforts. In such a process the continuing competition between socialism and capitalism will become even more apparent in economics and economic relations and these sectors will in fact gain in importance.

The experiences — the negative ones from the period of the 'Cold War' as much as the positive ones from recent years — justify us in asserting that politics and the political climate are of prime importance for international economic co-operation, especially between states with differing social systems. This in turn includes the repercussions which durable economic links have on the stability of political relations. It has already become an axiom of political science that reduced political confrontation is conducive to economic co-operation. Conversely, the interests of the ruling forces connected with this economic co-operation bring a positive influence to bear on the process of *détente*.

The new type of political and state relations as a result of today's international balance of forces and the gradual implementation of the principles of peaceful coexistence increasingly determine the volume, content and character of economic relations between socialist and capitalist states.

(1) What is involved are relations between sovereign, equal and independent states taking due cognisance of the laws and the state, economic and social order existing in every country, without interference in their internal affairs and without discrimination against the interests of third countries.

(2) Economic relations should rest on a stable and long-term basis with consideration of the commercial conditions agreed upon between the governments and in keeping with the principles of mutual advantage and most-favoured-nation treatment and ruling out discrimination of whatever kind.

(3) In the final analysis, it is a question of bringing about an international system of economic relations allowing all parties, under the conditions of the social order prevailing in their countries, to develop the forces of production most effectively, making use not only of their own resources and potential, but to an increasing extent also of those offered by the international division of labour.

The economic relations developing between socialist states and capitalist industrialised countries under the conditions of political détente are above all characterised today by the following features:

(1) There is a considerable increase in trade between the members of the Council for Mutual Economic Assistance (CMEA) and the capitalist industrialised countries (turnovers rose from roughly 13 034 million roubles in 1970 to 44 339 million in 1976 at current prices). This increase by more than 240 per cent by far exceeds the growth of world trade as a whole. The positive trend also continued in 1978 in spite of many difficulties. The share of trade with

the West in the foreign trade of CMEA countries went up from 23.6 in 1970 to 31.1 per cent in 1976.

(2) There is a trend towards positive changes in the structure of trade between socialist and capitalist countries. As things stand today, about 25 per cent of Soviet machinery and equipment exports go to capitalist industrialised countries.

Economic conditions for an improvement of trade structures have developed strongly in the socialist countries. The mechanical engineering sector has become the lynchpin of economic integration of the CMEA countries and this ensures good opportunities for economic relations with other countries.

(3) New forms of co-operation are gaining acceptance on the basis of long-term agreements. These above all include co-operation, barter transactions, product-sharing arrangements as well as scientific and technological co-operation. The number of co-operation agreements in the EEC region has risen from 200 in 1970 to roughly 1500 now.

(4) Projects of the largest dimensions are today characteristic of co-operation between socialist and capitalist states. Some of them involve capital investment of between hundreds of millions and over a thousand million dollars. At the end of 1978, there existed some 100 barter agreements of this type.

(5) These and other commercial contracts are based on long-term intergovernmental agreements. It happens ever more frequently that treaties are concluded for terms of between five and ten, sometimes twenty or more years.

(6) An active and multifaceted mechanism of economic co-operation is developing. This applies, among other things, to the widening scope of activities on the part of joint government commissions for economic, industrial, scientific and technological co-operation.

(7) The CMEA countries' dynamic foreign trade relations with the capitalist industrialised countries are based on the sustained and planned growth of their economies within the framework of their socialist economic intergration. Their material resources double within a period of about fifteen years as a result of which they become more attractive as trading partners for the capitalist industrialised countries. The foreign economic policy of the CMEA countries is orientated towards an increasing use of possibilities and advantages inherent in all-embracing international co-operation on a long-term basis. It has been stated repeatedly and

proved in practice that this policy is not fortuitious or basically pragmatic, but designed for a long period.

(8) On balance, it is apparent that economic relations between socialist and capitalist industrialised countries constitute an extremely dynamic field of international economic life. Their importance is much greater than their former and current percentage share in world trade. A chief factor in giving substance to *détente* and a major element of security and co-operation, they contribute substantially to the fact that *détente* is proving itself as a viable, lasting and practically effective course in international relations.

Despite the positive trends in economic relations on the basis of objective political and economic processes in the world — above all the atmosphere of political *détente* and the specific interests of the two systems — opportunities for economic relations are by no means being fully utilised as yet.

(1) The aggravation of the political situation by anti-*détente* forces in the USA and some other NATO countries hampers economic co-operation, even if only temporarily and in certain sectors. Some elements in the main capitalist countries are making attempts — primarily harmful to these countries themselves — to misuse the economic sphere for political blackmail and interference in the internal affairs of the USSR and its socialist allies. Mention should be made here of the efforts on the part of the USA to reincarnate, practise or even expand embargoes from the period of the 'Cold War', to ban deliveries, etc. The primacy of politics is reaffirmed here, although in a negative way.

(2) To date there are but modest efforts on the part of capitalist countries and their governments to comply with the provisions contained in the second part of the Final Act of Helsinki and 'to reduce or progressively eliminate all kinds of obstacles to the development of trade' or to expand their mutual trade in goods and services and 'to ensure conditions favourable to such development'. Numerous capitalist industrial countries have, as trading partners of the CMEA countries, taken hardly any steps towards liberalisation during the past few years. This applies to customs tariffs, import quotas by way of quantities, EEC market regulations for agricultural products, credit arrangements and much more besides. In some instances additional difficulties have arisen.

(3) Among the obstacles in the way of more intensive economic contact between socialist and capitalist countries is also its current structure notwithstanding some positive beginnings. It is above all machinery and equipment exports by socialist to capitalist industrialised countries which were by no means in accordance with actual possibilities in 1977–8, although businessmen from capitalist countries have recently shown increasing interest in these items as the socialist countries step up their efforts to improve their export structure.

Although economic relations on a bilateral basis are predominant today, there are indications of the growth of multilateral relations also in economic co-operation between socialist and capitalist countries. This allows us to expect a major concentration of this material 'fabric' designed to strengthen the process of *détente* and thus substantially to increase the weight of economic relations as a level of peaceful coexistence.

(1) This especially holds for Europe. This continent tops the list among the regions of our world with regard to the development level obtained by the forces of production and the technological and economic level of the national economies. The greater part of the world's industrial output is produced on this continent. The annual growth rates of industrial output are higher in most countries here than in other regions. The volume of capital investment in both parts of Europe is also among the largest in the world. Europe has the most advanced communications and infrastructure in the world as well as possibilities of mutually supplementary raw material resources, scientific and technological potential and industrial structures. Overall, European trade can look back on great traditions and rely on a rich treasure of experience. In addition, there are other advantages arising from specific geographical conditions.

On the other hand, Europe still has — mostly for historical reasons — an excess of production complexes which exist parallel to one another and, consequently, are in a state of underdevelopment. Similarly, the discontinuation of many traditional intra-European economic relations in the period of the 'Cold War' as a result of the embargo policy pursued by the USA and other NATO states, has caused a great deal of damage.

In the long run, it is a question of arranging Europe's economy in an all-embracing and better balanced manner, above all as far as its individual branches are concerned, account being taken of the fact that differing social systems exist. Basically, socialist and capitalist countries have similar objective interests in this respect. The basis for constructive multilateral programmes is provided by the Final Act of Helsinki.

In the future this form of co-operation might play an important part in the settlement of problems carrying weight for the European continent. The European countries have so far had but little experience in carrying out multilateral projects. Serious efforts will have to be made here and this constitutes an active challenge for both sides. A great measure of responsibility for introducing multilateral activities in the European economic region rests on the two large integrated associations, the CMEA and the EEC. The lack of long-term contacts between them is quite obviously an abnormality hampering the further normalisation of the situation on the European continent and reducing the possibilities of joint multilateral measures.

The greater dimensions of economic co-operation provided for in the Final Act of Helsinki, however, call for regular and effective relations between the CMEA and the EEC. Here it should be borne in mind that on the one hand, integration within the two economic groupings will make further headway and, on the other hand, that the coexistence of the differing types of integration need not be an obstacle to developing businesslike relations and economic co-operation between the CMEA and the EEC and their members.

The following principles are particularly important for the normalisation of relations between these integrated groupings and their members:

(1) Recognition and application of general principles of co-operation between socialist and capitalist countries as well as between the CMEA and the EEC on the basis of the stipulations contained in the Final Act of the Helsinki Conference.

(2) Reduction and ultimate elimination of discrimination; application of the principle of most-favoured-nation treatment and pursuit of a customs and trade policy corresponding to the principles of European co-operation.

(3) Modification by both groupings of methods in the sphere of trade policy including the creation of a system of preferences with the aim of promoting mutually advantageous co-operation.

(4) Measures designed to expand and stimulate industrial, financial, scientific and technological co-operation between European socialist and capitalist countries.

(5) Use of practical possibilities available for united efforts by the members of the two groupings in settling all-European problems in the field of energy, the extractive industry, transport and telecommunications, scientific research, environmental protection, including concrete projects of all-European co-operation.

One of the most important steps in the sphere of co-operation could be the introduction by both parties on the basis of full most-favoured-nation treatment of all the relevant measures with a view to promoting the expansion of trade between their members based on the principles of non-discrimination and mutual advantage and the joint solution of other problems in the field of economic relations.

(2) Other specific avenues of multilateral economic co-operation exist in the spheres of environmental protection, the development of transport and in dealing with questions concerning the power industry.

In the energy sector, the co-ordination or unification of the electrical power and gas pipeline systems on the European continent, the creation of new international systems for the transport of fuel, the joint development of large fuel and power complexes, the opening up of the new energy resources and joint research in this field as well as measures designed to save energy would bring universal economic benefit and, at the same time, enhance political *détente*. Such problems could be dealt with at an all-European congress on energy issues.

In the field of environmental protection, it is a question of preventing transcontinental air pollution, joint actions to protect oceans and rivers, preparing special measures for eliminating the harmful consequences of the large-scale application of mineral fertilisers and carrying out joint research regarding the development of no-waste technologies and recycling techniques. Some achievement, in that context, has resulted from an EEC-sponsored Conference on Protection of the Environment.

Involved in transport are development projects for all-European main traffic arteries, above all the railways, motor roads and waterways, the construction of an all-European network of navigable waterways and the development of express traffic systems with a high capacity. A congress dealing with the development of traffic and transport systems might draw up certain co-operation projects, especially for the improvement of main European arteries in road, rail, navigation and combined traffic (including the simplification and acceleration of transit traffic) and adopt all-European conventions on transport.

In keeping with the Final Act of Helsinki, other special programmes of co-operation between socialist and capitalist countries might be drawn up. These could determine the basic trends of economic co-operation in Europe for decades. A long-term approach of this nature is in accordance with both the economic and political interests of all parties concerned. It would allow for a higher level of economic efficiency and strengthen the material foundation of security and lasting peaceful development on the European continent.

(3) Another promising field of economic co-operation with wide-ranging aspects — also with regard to world politics — is trilateral economic co-operation. This new sphere in the overall process of the international division of labour has been developing since the early 1970s. For the time being it is playing a relatively small role within the framework of economic contacts between partners from the socialist and capitalist world systems, but could be expanded to a far-reaching extent. The interests of all partners involved could be satisfied by trilateral co-operation. More particularly it allows for the use of the economic, scientific and technological experience gathered by socialist states and capitalist industrial countries in bringing about social progress in developing countries. This sector of co-operation contains factors which are particularly conducive to *détente* in many respects.

The motives of the socialist countries for their increasing emphasis on trilateral co-operation are of an economic and political nature. It is, in the first place, a matter of utilising to a greater extent the advantages resulting from the international division of labour. Another weighty motive is the fact that the material foundations of the policy of peaceful coexistence are strengthened by economic relations with the non-socialist economic sphere. Added to this should be the striving of the socialist countries for a refashioning of international economic relations on a democratic basis and their increased influence on the structure of the world market.

The intentions of the Western industrial countries are also politically and economically motivated, albeit on different premises. In the first place, they are attempting to use the friendly relations of a number of developing countries with the socialist community for the furtherance of their own interests. In the second place, capitalist trading partners are coupling these activities in the economic sphere with political attempts to counteract their waning influence in various countries or to regain positions already lost or to build up new ones in these regions. And in the third place, interests in markets and supplies of raw materials are decisive.

The developing countries for their part can intensify their relations with the community of socialist states further along the lines of solidarity and co-operation. This gives them an opportunity on the political plane increasingly to diminish the influence of neo-colonialist circles on their political and economic affairs and to make a more effective stand for a new economic world order. They receive effective support for their development schemes on the basis of trilateral co-operation.

The benefits arising for all participants are clear for everybody to see — provided the principle of mutual advantage is not violated. Tri-lateral industrial co-operation brings forth economic and social effects of dimensions which cannot be expected from any other form of co-operation. This is made possible by the pooling of the participating countries' or firms' economic and technological potential in the construction of large projects such as are often carried out in developing countries in opening up or processing raw materials and erecting complete industrial enterprises which, at the same time, involve immense costs and services for purposes of urbanisation and the development of the infrastructure. The technological and scientific services supplied by the partners coupled with the best possible conditions of production and supply of plant, building operations, licences and know-how, can mostly be applied at far greater economic benefit for all parties concerned than is the case with bilateral forms of co-operation.

There is no doubt that this not only depends on the interests of a given firm or country, but also on the climate prevailing in political relations. Close co-operation on a trilateral basis calls for a great measure of political stability in the relations between the countries involved and, over and above that, also between other states. For this reason the continued depending of the process of political *détente* is an indispensable condition for the all-round development of this extremely promising sector of co-operation, whose development, in turn, can result in positive repercussions on the stability of political relations.

Multilateral economic co-operation, so clearly defined and stressed in the Final Act of Helsinki as an important factor of the process of *détente*, can open up new prospects, not only for Europe. It can be developed into a significant factor in contributing to 'the restructuring of international economic relations on a just and democratic basis and the establishment of a new international economic order' which allow for a stepped-up elimination of economic backwardness in the developing countries and ensure the dynamic progress of all nations and mankind as a whole.

It is, of course, essential to be mindful in all spheres of the special character of economic relations between socialist states and capitalist industrial countries, as these are links between states with differing social conditions. The relevant chapter of the Final Act of the Conference on Security and Co-operation in Europe takes account of this fact fully and completely, as we all know. The Final Act states that participating states will develop co-operation in the field of the economy, science, technology and environmental protection being 'aware of the diversity of their economic and social systems' and 'reaffirming their will to intensify such co-operation between one another, irrespective of their systems'.

Appendix A

Report on 29 Pugwash Symposium Held in Zakopane, Poland 1978 on 'Security and Co-operation in Europe: Problems and Prospects after Belgrade'

INTRODUCTION

The 29th Pugwash Symposium was held in Zakopane, Poland, 12–15 April 1978. Thirty-two participants from fourteen countries attended, as guests of the Polish Academy of Sciences.

Both subjects on the agenda of the Symposium — Security and Co-operation in Europe — were first examined together in view of the close interconnection between them. Drawing fully upon the series of papers that had been submitted to the Symposium participants sought to identify those aspects which merited special attention in the light of the outcome of the Belgrade meeting, an assessment of which was reviewed by the participants. Thereafter, consideration of the two themes was pursued in two separate working groups.

A. POLITICAL AND MILITARY *DÉTENTE*

The Group discussed a range of problems relating to political and military *détente* and their close interrelation and complementarity as well as prospects for their further development. Difficulties and obstacles were analysed and some new ideas to overcome them suggested. Special attention was given to disarmament problems.

It was agreed that progress towards limitation of the arms race is very far from being satisfactory and the development of new weapon systems goes on more quickly than negotiations on curbing them. This relates first of all to the qualitative aspect of the arms race, which if unrestricted greatly increases the possibility of nuclear war. This is of prime concern to Europe, where the concentration of modern armaments is greatest. The problem of stopping the arms race and concluding concrete disarmament agreements is the most urgent and vital problem facing mankind.
1. The following main factors obstructing progress towards disarmament were particularly emphasised:

1.1. Relatively low level of mutual trust between states and existing misperceptions of the other side's intention in Europe and on a global basis;
1.2. Reliance on military forces as the main element safeguarding the security of states;
1.3. The dynamic nature of weapons developments.

2. While general and complete disarmament remains the ultimate objective the following measures might be undertaken now to pave the way for further development of military *détente*, especially in Europe:

2.1. Everything possible should be done to strengthen mutual trust between nations, as the growth of confidence is the main prerequisite for further progress in arms limitation. This process might be initiated by freezing the present level of armaments and armed forces both in quantity and quality in anticipation of rapid progress in the Vienna MFR negotiations. This might be done by unilateral declarations by states concerned. Step by step the real infrastructure of mutual confidence should be built up, to eliminate the ground for suspicions and misperceptions. The mass media could and should contribute substantially to this.
2.2. The growing gap between the increasing speed of technological development and slow progress in arms limitations requires new kinds of political initiative. A complete ban on new weapon systems would cut at the root of the arms race; public

understanding and awareness of the role of new weapons and their implications for disarmament would be a step in the right direction. In this context the possibility of deployment of the neutron bomb in Europe has been strongly opposed as working contrary to military *détente*. The decision not now to produce this weapon was appreciated and should thus provide an opportunity for new progress towards arms control and disarmament in Europe. There are other weapons in the pipe-line on both sides whose non-deployment would further improve such prospects.

3. The possibility of nuclear weapon-free zones in the various regions of the world including Central Europe should be urgently reconsidered. In particular *a proposal* was made for the *Reduction of Nuclear Arms in Europe*. This was in effect an updated version of a suggestion brought up at an earlier Pugwash Symposium and subsequently discussed several times at symposia and conferences. This proposal, which requires for its successful implementation an atmosphere of developing *détente*, is intended to stimulate and complement a substantial and simultaneous reduction of conventional armed forces and armaments and to reinforce the Vienna negotiations. The essential elements in the proposal are as follows:

(a) The denuclearisation of Europe from the eastern border of France to the western border of the Soviet Union.

(b) The limitation of United Kingdom and French nuclear weapons to the national nuclear weapons now deployed.

(c) Soviet MRBMs and IRBMs which are located so as to be capable of striking Europe should be limited to a number equal to the total of British and French weapons deployed.

(d) The implementation and terms of the Nuclear Non-Proliferation Treaty should be reinforced and the Partial Nuclear Test Ban Treaty be upgraded to an effective Comprehensive Test Ban Treaty and help to prevent any further spread of nuclear arms in Europe. It was emphasised that any development towards the acquisition of independent nuclear weapon capability by any European states not now possessing it would make the situation in Europe much more dangerous than it is now.

The proposal could lead to substantial disarmament and an improved political situation in Europe.

It should also be understood that many particular items which have been ignored or overlooked here will become of importance during possible actual negotiations. These include the disposition of nuclear-capable naval forces and other similar questions. But it is hoped such further details could be readily solved if the negotiations are in the spirit and scope of the items set out above.

It was felt that this radical approach may have a better chance of working than the traditional piecemeal attempts to ensure precise balance in every field each time a small disarmament proposal is made. Bold actions seemed to be the only practical way out of the present impasse.

4. It was strongly recommended that further study in Pugwash Working Groups or Symposia should be made of a number of ideas designed to create greater confidence between the countries of the two main political and military groupings of states. These included the following:

4.1. Establishment of a direct line of communication ('hot-line') between the WTO and NATO headquarters.

4.2. To avoid misinterpretation of each other's intentions the USA and the USSR should establish a system of regular meetings between experts for the exchange of information concerning unexplained major construction projects.

4.3. The drafting of a code of conduct concerning the provision of military assistance and arms sales to foreign countries and the terms on which military support to such countries might be internationally tolerated, on the basis of information and explanation provided to the UN.

5. The importance of using the opportunity provided by the forthcoming Special Session of the UN General Assembly for major new initiatives leading to a comprehensive programme of disarmament was stressed. In this connection the informing and education of public opinion on the issues involved is a vital task for the mass media.

B. TOPICAL PROBLEMS RELATING TO ALL-EUROPEAN CO-OPERATION

While it was recognised that, particularly at the present juncture, advances of major significance in all-European co-operation are increasingly linked to progress in political and military *détente*, it was strongly felt that meanwhile efforts at the unilateral, bilateral and multilateral levels should continue with renewed vigour to carry forward existing types, forms and methods of co-operation. Also new initiatives should be launched in specific fields which hold out promise of fruitful results and seek to overcome existing obstacles and difficulties. Even what seem to be 'small steps' can, when taken in their aggregate, appreciably strengthen all-European economic and related co-operation and exert a wholesome influence on other facets of global *détente*.

The assessment and proposals for action by Governments and the scientific community which are briefly set out below are deliberately focused only on those subject areas which in the view of the participants are of particular relevance after Belgrade and on which the Symposium felt competent to give a collective opinion.

1. Ongoing Co-operative Programmes and Policies

1.1. Policies to increase the volume, to widen the range and to diversify the pattern of East–West trade should be supported. The development potential and inherent dynamism of this trade flow remains considerable.

1.2. Industrial co-operation should be further developed with the aim of advancing the maximum coverage of possible links, and of proceeding, wherever feasible, to higher forms such as coproduction, involving joint investment, marketing and research.

1.3. Work already started in Europe on projects of common interest in the fields of energy resources, exploitation of materials and transport and communications (such as the Trans-European North-South Motorway and the recent Austrian-Polish agreement on Electric Power Exchanges) appears promising. Efforts directed towards identifying further projects of this kind should therefore be accelerated and be combined with the necessary studies of suitable institutional mechanisms and methods of financing.

1.4. As regards technological co-operation, greater emphasis should be placed on technologies designed to reduce waste of natural resources.

1.5. The information-base of all European co-operation should be further strengthened. In this connection the attention of the scientific community is drawn to the work undertaken in the UN Economic Commission for Europe (ECE) on the Overall

Economic Perspective for the ECE Region up to 1990, intended to provide Governments with overall views on the economic development of the region in the context of the world economy, and to aid them to identify long-term economic problems of common interest.

1.6. In the light of the results of Belgrade, progress in the work underway in the ECE on the holding in the near future of a high-level meeting on environment and the preparation of similar conferences or meetings on energy and transport is of exceptional importance. It is therefore the earnest hope of the Symposium that positive decisions on the matters will be taken at the current plenary session of the ECE. Only carefully prepared high-level meetings in these major fields of region-wide concern can ensure that the necessary action is taken at the national and international levels by the participating States, signatories of the Final Act.

2. Relations between the European Economic Community (EEC) and the Council for Mutual Economic Assistance (CMEA).

The Final Act envisages that European co-operation on a region-wide basis should be combined with co-operation at a sub-regional level. This implies the need for normalising and developing official relations between EEC and CMEA both in terms of direct contacts between the two bodies and of clarifying the trading relationships of their respective member countries. It was felt at the Symposium that in the forthcoming EEC-CMEA negotiations a multiplane model of relations should be worked out which would take account of both the requirements of EEC's trade policy rules and of the institutional characteristics of Eastern economic integration and trading systems.

3. Economic Co-operation in Europe and the New International Economic Order.

Economic co-operation in Europe must be geared to, and dovetailed with, action going forward at the global level to establish a New International Economic Order (NIEO). Peace and security in the region are vital preconditions for peace and security of the developing countries. All-European economic co-operation must go hand in hand with efforts of the CSCE Governments to narrow the income and welfare gap between developed and developing nations and thus remove the tensions which it engenders. Experience shows that a mere extrapolation of present trends in technology and economic growth cannot lead to this goal, and even less so a simple transfer of these methods to developing nations. Drastic changes will prove unavoidable, but despite these expected changes and different concepts of how to achieve them in order to restructure world economic relations, common action of CSCE countries in relation to third world countries should be encouraged: for instance, tripartite industrial co-operation, involving enterprises from Eastern, Western and developing countries; provisions to ensure that East–West economic links are combined with appropriate policies of trade with and assistance to Third World countries; participation in international schemes for an integrated international commodity policy; and collective efforts to work towards the enunciation of an agreed global development strategy to give effect to NIEO. In the areas of technological and scientific co-operation the CSCE countries should work also on problems of concern to the developing countries, related in particular to their need for indigenous Science and Technology capability. The forthcoming UN Conference on Science and Technology for Development could be a useful forum to consider this matter in greater detail.

The close link between Disarmament and Development was reiterated. Military *détente* and disarmament could liberate and mobilise enormous resources not otherwise available, for speeding the closing of the income and welfare gap between the developed countries and the third world.

4. Multilateral Meetings within the Framework of the Follow-up of the CSCE on Particular Subjects which it was Decided to Convene at Belgrade:

4.1. *Meeting of experts to prepare a 'Scientific Forum'* (Bonn, July 1978).

It was felt that the Scientific Forum should become a recurrent consultation between leading personalities in science having as its main task to give continuing guidance on major scientific problems of an interrelated character and international concern, including problems of the countries of the third world. More particularly, focus should be on issues which can be expected to arise in the future, and on ways and means of improving channels of communications; encouraging direct contacts and co-ordination of research activities; increasing the number of scientific exchanges in balanced fashion; and promoting collective and joint research, wherever feasible. Appropriate liaison arrangements should be made with ECE, UNESCO and other appropriate international bodies.

The Scientific Forum might, in particular, wish to foster studies on the feasibility of a number of desirable collaborative undertakings involving large investments of funds and manpower normally beyond the resources of any one country, such as:

(a) High energy facility of greater than 1000 GeV (1 million million electron volts) for fundamental research in particle physics.

(b) Centres for joint research on fusion, solar and other non-conventional sources of energy. (Suggested locations in both Eastern and Western Europe.)

(c) Joint research in molecular biology, especially genetic engineering, in already existing institutions (e.g. European Molecular Biology Laboratory at Heidelberg) and in new ones, if indicated.

(d) A large complex of health research institutes in co-operation with WHO for both clinical and laboratory, fundamental and applied research in such fields as cancer, cardiovascular disease, chemical toxicology (environmental pollutants and medicants), biomedical instrumentation. (Suggested location in Eastern Europe.)

(e) The Forum should also stimulate the establishment of centres of joint research in 'brain-intensive' and internationally integrated fields such as theoretical physics, chemistry, and mathematics, as a means to provide ample and expanding opportunities for the exchange of high-level scientific personnel.

In the field of the social and behavioural sciences consideration might be given to the convening of a group to consider possibilities of promoting studies in depth of processes of interaction and co-operation between CSCE countries, especially those having different economic, social and political systems, by scholars drawn from the different countries of the region, and analysing common approaches to promoting collaborative links and overcoming tensions and difficulties.

5. Meeting of Experts to Consider Procedures for the Peaceful Settlement of Disputes (Montreux, October 1978)

The hope was expressed that the experts will give due emphasis to the elaboration not only of legal procedures but also to devising appropriate machinery for negotiation and consultation aimed at removing difficulties and misunderstandings as they arise so as to prevent the eruption of major disputes.

6. *Meeting of Experts on Co-operation in the Mediterranean (La Valetta, February 1979)*

This meeting was welcomed as a concrete example of giving effect to the provision in the Final Act to take into account the interests of the developing countries throughout the world, including those among the participating States. This meeting could also serve as a concrete manifestation of the need to extend positive developments in Europe to other regions of the world.

7. *Other Measures which Should be Taken After Belgrade to Strengthen* détente *and Co-operation*

There is still need for more regular contacts and consultations at different levels to improve the political climate and to provide a firm political framework for *détente* and co-operation. Governments should therefore proceed in systematic fashion to a series of bilateral consultations on the follow-up process in the light of the outcome of Belgrade and bearing in mind the many constructive proposals in the field of co-operation tabled at that meeting. Such a purposeful strengthening of bilateral relations would help to prepare the ground for the meeting to be held in Madrid in 1980 and thus strengthen *détente.* To facilitate contacts and communications at the bilateral level with this end in view it would be helpful that focal points for matters relating to the follow-up of the CSCE be established, as necessary, in the Ministries for Foreign Affairs of all participating States.

The question of human rights was discussed in the context of the whole Declaration on Principles of the Final Act. It was agreed at the Symposium that efforts for the achievement of peace, security and co-operation through *détente* will assist in the consolidation and extension of such rights for all peoples, not only in Europe but throughout the world.

Among other measures which were discussed under this heading was a suggestion that consideration might be given to the holding of brief meetings of Heads of States or Governments of the signatories of the Final Act. Such meetings might be convened for instance mid-way between two follow-up meetings. They would last no longer than, say, 2–3 days and be held *in camera.* The summit meetings would not be expected to adopt decisions but should provide an opportunity to receive reports from the Heads of State or Government presented in a manner found suitable by them on the implementation of the Final Act in their countries; and thereafter to offer facilities for contacts, discussions and consultations among themselves of an informal nature.

Appendix B

Report on 33 Pugwash Symposium Held in Helsinki, Finland, 1979 on 'Impact of Current Political Developments and Arms Control Efforts of European Security

SALT

The importance of the SALT negotiations for European security was widely recognised. The expected signature of SALT II was particularly in the minds of participants, as were the prospects for ratification.

It was noted that an important part of the emerging SALT II agreement will be the joint Statement of Principles that will set the stage for the next round of negotiations. The maintenance of strategic stability will clearly be a principal goal. In this context concern was expressed about the possibility of technological innovation that may lead to the reality or even appearance of destabilisation.

Much attenton was paid to those technologies that have led to the development of more accurate missiles. Some participants suggested that in SALT III the phasing-out of land-based missile systems should be considered. There was, however, no consensus on that question. A difficulty is the asymmetry between the strategic force structures of the Soviet

Union and the United States. It was also pointed out by several participants that the degree of ICBM vulnerability should not be exaggerated. Severe disincentives to a first-strike attack remain. Others
stressed that perception of a serious threat to the survivability of the
ICBM-forces in itself is an important factor: the perception might be
politically utilisable by those who favour initiation of new weapons programmes to secure land-based missile survivability, but it was also
pointed out that if land-based missiles should be de-emphasised, meaures
to enhance the invulnerability of strategic nuclear submarines should
have high priority.

The view was expressed that because of the threat perception, a promising approach in future SALT talks might be to try to control the first-
strike mission. It was doubted, however, by some of the participants,
whether it would be possible to control accuracy improvements in such a
way that the possible restrictions could be adequately verified.

GREY-AREA SYSTEMS

Grey-area systems reflect incompatibilities between rapid technological
change and the formal criteria of existing arms control negotiations.
They comprise a wide range of multipurpose and multimission systems
that can be used both in an offensive and defensive mode, that is for
theatre tactical and theatre strategic roles with both nuclear and conventional warheads (dual-capable systems). No agreement could be reached
among the participants on a precise definition of the grey area.

Special concern about the implications of present and future grey-area
systems is warranted for the following reasons:

(a) SALT in the view of some West Europeans neutralises the strategic
    capabilities, and magnifies the significance of the disparities in the
    theatre nuclear regime.
(b) It was stated that the SALT process has rechannelled weapons
    modernisation to areas not covered by the negotiations. Mod-
    ernisation of theatre nuclear forces (TNF) has been and probably
    will be part of the domestic political price to make SALT
    agreements acceptable.

The assessment of TNF capabilities is based exclusively on Western
sources. Some participants referred to the hypothetical nature of these
figures while others stressed the need for the publication of detailed data

on the systems concerned. Various participants pointed to the overall negative political impact of the deployment of new long-range TNF in Europe and on the overall prospects for *détente* if arms control efforts should fail.

Participants agreed that the grey-area systems should be dealt with in an arms control framework, but expressed different suggestions as to how this should be done. The following alternatives were discussed: SALT III, a separate forum for theatre arms limitation talks (TALT), the Vienna talks, and other high-level discussions between the US and the USSR. Some participants argued that several grey-area systems could be dealt with at SALT III. It was suggested that the inclusion of these systems in SALT III may dramatise existing disparities and therefore provide legitimacy for a limited levelling up. The various views advanced included: a comprehensive approach to the whole substrategic balance in a separate forum (TALT) which might be preferable; unilateral self-restraint by the major countries concerned, e.g. public statements indicating that one country would not deploy more than a certain number of grey-area systems; the SS-20 should become the primary candidate for unilateral self-restraint; a return to the idea of disengagement. Concrete steps in military *détente* could open up potential for political and functional co-operation in various fields (e.g. economic, cultural) to be implemented on their own merits.

It was suggested that Pugwash should set up a working group on theatre nuclear systems and on questions of regional security in Europe.

NORDIC SECURITY

This was discussed with special emphasis on nuclear-free zone (NFZ) possibilities. The growing strategic importance of the Northern areas was seen to be due to a number of factors:

(a) the growth of naval potentials, especially submarines and SLBMs;
(b) surveillance and early warning systems;
(c) new technological developments that make use of the Arctic possible in military as well as in economic respects.

These developments have an impact on the security calculations of the Nordic countries. Different approaches to increasing security were proposed which included a Nordic NFZ and confidence-building measures in the Baltic.

The special features of the Northern 'security equation' were considered, especially the nuclear option of Norway and Denmark and the strategic weight of the Kola peninsula for the Soviet Union.

At least three different approaches to the Nordic NFZ were presented:

1. Individual countries could declare themselves nuclear-free, for example as suggested in the Draft Treaty presented by Pugwash in the Special Session on Disarmament in 1978.
2. A second possibility forwarded by some participants was a joint Nordic initiative in the form of a multilateral agreement or commitment to maintain and strengthen the existing non-nuclear weapon status of the Nordic area.
3. Some participants advocated a wider zonal agreement involving Scandinavian countries and also other states. One participant argued that this approach should include the withdrawal of nuclear weapons geographically close to the zone, notably those with limited delivery ranges making them generally suitable for attacking targets within the zone.

IMPACT OF DEVELOPMENTS OUTSIDE EUROPE

Consideration was also given to some of the ways in which developments in the rest of the world are now affecting European security and steps towards arms control and disarmament.

The oil crisis of 1973 and the general debate on 'limits to growth' have alerted not only governments but public opinion to the ultimately finite nature of the world's resources. The roles of industrialised nations in different parts of the world, their relationships with each other and with less developed countries, are now influenced by the growing competition for resources — energy supply, food and mineral raw materials.

Events in Iran have recently highlighted this aspect and there is concern about the future stability of other countries with oil and other resources. The situation in Southern Africa is proving particularly important in this respect because Western European countries are heavily dependent upon imported mineral raw materials. The United States and Japan are also affected. They are concerned that political developments may deprive them of access to supplies of materials such as vanadium, chrome, platinum and manganese and also facilitate interference with their lines of communication to and from the major oil production areas.

Some participants felt that this was a factor which might seriously affect attitudes to arms control and disarmament, even SALT III.

The African peoples of the region must be involved in any approach to these problems and their desire for political independence taken fully into account, as well as the development of a new world economic order. The prevention of conflict arising from competition for scarce resources requires a comprehensive and rational approach respecting the interests of both producers and consumers. The development of understandings and conventions with regard to this and the role of foreign intervention is necessary. The definitions of legitimate and illegitimate actions already evolved within the UN are not enough in themselves for confidence-building purposes. Similar problems are apparent in the Middle East. In spite of an attempted co-ordination amongst NATO and EEC countries of policies towards the oil-producing countries, there is a tendency for the fragmentation of relationships with the region. This cuts across the East–West basis for relationships within Europe and raises the question as to whether SALT and other negotiations may need in future to be on a multilateral basis. This would, however, make formal agreements or treaties even more difficult to achieve.

The role of China in the Far East also reflects in a different way back upon US–USSR relations and on East–West relations in Europe. While the prospects of a major conflict there may be relatively remote, and Soviet commitment to arms control and disarmament measures not affected, exploitation by NATO countries of a Chinese connection could well prove counter-productive for *détente* in Europe.

In general the importance of US–USSR negotiations and the significance of the strictly European aspects of European security was re-emphasised. Competition and rivalry in one form or other in areas outside Europe will, however, be in no one's interest: even tacit agreements about the limits and objectives of intervention in non-European areas would go some way towards alleviating apprehensions. In this connection, however, it was suggested by some participants that confidence-building measures relating to notification of movements of naval squadrons outside territorial waters may be particularly valuable. These would need monitoring by some form of UN peace-keeping force.

CONFIDENCE-BUILDING MEASURES (CBM)

Two aspects of CBMs were discussed, the first pertaining to military movements and the second to cultural, economic and scientific co-operation.

Prior notification of military exercises is useful in avoiding misinterpretation of their possible aggressive intent, particularly with respect to large-scale manoeuvres. Also attention was called to the poor impression made on the public when specific enemy targets are designated with particular weapons accordingly deployed.

Many participants considered as even more important CBMs associated with the need for increasing East–West co-operation in the cultural, economic and scientific spheres. The group noted and endorsed the measures for this purpose advanced at the Pugwash Symposium held in Zakopane in April 1978. The hope was expressed that this dimension be given special attention at the meeting on the Helsinki Final Act to be held in Madrid in 1980.

VIENNA MUTUAL BALANCED FORCE REDUCTION (MBFR) NEGOTIATIONS

The group noted with great regret the continued lack of progress in the MBFR talks. Some optimism was expressed that following the signing of SALT II progress could be expected in the Vienna talks.

ENERGY NEEDS, NATURAL RESOURCES

The impacts of energy needs and limited natural resources by various countries have great potential for increasing tension and precipitating conflicts. Since this problem is a highly complex one requiring careful study and analysis, the group recommended that consideration be given for holding a Pugwash symposium or workshop on the subject.

W. F. Gutteridge
J. K. Miettinen

Index

235